PC Basics

Get a Great Start

Notices

PC Basics Get a Great Start
is published by
Gateway, Inc.
14303 Gateway Place
Poway, CA 92064

Version 1.0

ISBN: 1-57729-288-X

DATE: 10-14-02

Printed in the United States of America

Distributed in the United States by Gateway, Inc.

Welcome

From the introduction of Your PC in Chapter 1 through troubleshooting in Chapter 10, *PC Basics Get a Great Start* provides you with what you need to know to discover the online world with your PC. This product is designed to accommodate your learning style, and to make learning easy, interesting, and fun. You can stick to just the bare essentials or learn in greater depth by practicing key skills and applying your new knowledge. Our goal is to show you how technology can enhance your life, provide some fun, and open up new opportunities.

More Than a Book

PC Basics is more than a book; it is a blended learning system that also includes interactive CD-ROM and Internet presentations and activities. These tools all work together to provide a truly unique learning experience. The book presents technical information in visual, practical, and understandable ways. The CD-ROM extends the book by providing audio, video, and animated visuals of important concepts. Continue learning online by logging on to www.LearnwithGateway.com. The enrollment key provided with this book gives you access to additional content and interactive exercises, as well as reference links, Internet resources, and Frequently Asked Questions (FAQs) with answers. This Web site allows us to keep you updated on rapidly changing information and new software releases.

Classroom Learning

In addition, a hands-on training course is offered. Additional fees may apply. Our classes are ideal solutions for people who want to become knowledgeable and get up and running in just three hours. They provide the opportunity to learn from one of our experienced and friendly instructors and practice important skills with other students. Call 888-852-4821 for enrollment information. One of our representatives will assist you in selecting a time and location that is convenient for you. If applicable, please have your Gateway customer ID and order number ready when you call. Please refer to your Gateway paperwork for this information.

Gateway ™

Learning map for

PC Basics
Get a Great Start

This map shows how the elements of Gateway's learning system work for you. The best of an easy to understand, highly visual book, the Internet and CD-ROM are all brought together to give you a unique and truly enjoyable learning experience. Notice how the interactive CD-ROM and Internet activities extend and complement the chapters in the book. Icons in the book will direct you to each element at the proper time.

Control Panel: Folder Options

Customizing Your PC

Intorduction to Control Panel

start Menu: Customizing

CHAPTER

Working in a Networked Environment

SEVEN

Control Panel: Accessibility Options

Desktop Options

Taskbar Options

CHAPTER

Using a CD Burner

SIX

Computer Organization

File and Folder Tasks

Folder Views

CHAPTER

Organizing Your Computer

FOUR

Files: Opening With Programs

CHAPTER

Working With Objects

FIVE

Files and Folders: Finding

Objects: Manipulating

CHAPTER

Exploring Windows XP

THREE

Dialog Boxes

Wizards

CHAPTER

Your PC Inside and Out

ONE

Multimedia Capabilities

Internet Terminology

CHAPTER

Introducing Windows XP

TWO

Fast User Switching

Start Menu Features

Taskbar Features

User Accounts

Windows XP: Logging On

On Your CD Rom

 On the World Wide Web

Firewall Basics

Network Components

Network Uses

Offline Files

CHAPTER

Customizing Windows XP

EIGHT

Firewall Settings

Folders: Sharing

Network Permissions: Granting

Add Printer Wizard

Printer Tasks

Printing Documents

Caring for Your Computer

Disk Cleanup

File Backup

CHAPTER

Caring for Your Computer

NINE

Anti-Virus Software

Defragmenting Hard Drives

Help and Support Features

Remote Assistance: Features

CHAPTER

Trouble-Shooting Your PC

TEN

Remote Assistance: Requesting

Trouble-shooting Problems

You can also take a Gateway class, and this is an ideal way to continue to expand your learning. Gateway instructors are dedicated to working with each individual and answering all your questions. You will be able to talk with other learners, practice important skills, and get off to a quick start. Additional fees may apply. Call 888-852-4821 to enroll. **See you in class!**

Contents

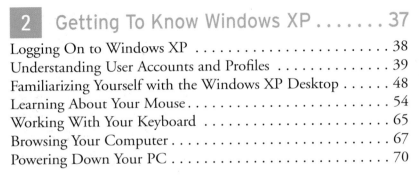

Contents

Contents

How to Use This Book

As you read the chapters in this book, you'll find pictures, figures, and diagrams to help reinforce key ideas and concepts. You'll also find numerous pictures, or icons, that serve as cues to flag important information or provide directions. Here is a guide to help you understand the icons you'll encounter in this book:

 A Note identifies a relatively important piece of information that will make things easier or faster for you to accomplish on your PC. Most notes are worth reading, if only for the time and effort they can save you.

 A Warning gives notice that an action on your PC can have serious consequences and could lead to loss of work, delays, or other problems. Our goal is not to scare you, but to steer you clear of potential sources of trouble.

 The CD-ROM flags additional materials including exercises and animations that you will find on the CD-ROM included with this book. Because some materials work better on your PC than in print, we've included many activities and exercises. These help you become more familiar with your system while practicing important skills.

 Because PC information and online resources are so dynamic, some material related to this book, including Web-based training, resides on the www.LearnwithGateway.com Web site. This allows us to keep that information fresh and up to date.

 The *Survive & Thrive* series includes several books on topics from digital music to the Internet. Where other titles can be useful in improving and expanding your learning, we use the Book icon to draw those titles to your attention.

 Gateway offers a hands-on training course on many of the topics covered in this book. Additional fees may apply. Call 888-852-4821 for enrollment information. If applicable, please have your customer ID and order number ready when you call.

You'll find sidebar information sprinkled throughout the chapters, as follows:

> ### More About . . .
>
> The More About . . . information is supplementary, and is provided so you can learn more about making technology work for you. Feel free to skip this material during your first pass through the book, but please return to it later.

Introducing the Computer

Welcome to the world of personal computers! A *personal computer* (often called a *PC*) is a device that, put simply, processes information. It can educate, entertain, and help you perform personal and business activities. A PC can be used to type letters, send messages, interact with other people, listen to music, play games, learn new skills, and much, much more.

Some people view PCs as mysterious boxes with a bunch of equipment and cables attached. This book aims to dispel the mystery surrounding computers and help you get the most out of your PC. To that end, this chapter examines how computers evolved and the numerous uses for computers through the ages. Then, you'll explore some of your PC's key elements, such as its tower, processor, memory, and storage device.

Exploring the History of Personal Computers

A PC (see Figure 1-1) is just one type of computer. In fact, computers come in all shapes and sizes. A computer can be so large that it fills a room, or so small it could get lost in a desk drawer. Computers are all around you, even though they're not always obvious—they're built into automated teller machines (ATMs), microwave ovens, children's toys, and even the digital radio in your car.

Although you can purchase a PC from a local store, over the phone, or online almost as easily as making airline reservations, you might not realize how much technology and history are behind the PC you use today.

Figure 1-1 A typical modern personal computer.

In its most basic form, a *computer* is a device that manipulates numbers, or *computes*. The earliest known computing device was an abacus, as shown in Figure 1-2. Although the abacus is not an actual "computer," it made complex arithmetic easier to understand and apply.

In 1642, Blaise Pascal took computing devices to the next level when he invented a numerical wheel calculator. Once mechanical devices provided a means to manipulate numbers, the rush to make the best "computer" was on! Early computers were basically calculators, used mainly to handle arithmetic. The least expensive calculator you can find today is far more powerful and much smaller than any of these early computers (see Figure 1-3).

Figure 1-2 An abacus was one of the original computing devices.

Figure 1-3 Early models of common computer components. (US Army Photos. Courtesy of Michael John Muus.)

By the early to mid-1900s, computers were evolving from mechanical to mostly electronic in nature, and used primarily in solving mathematical problems and processing financial data. By the 1970s, most of the common components of modern PCs were in use, such as printers, tape backups, disk storage, and memory. Over the years, such devices have become more advanced and barely resemble their original forms.

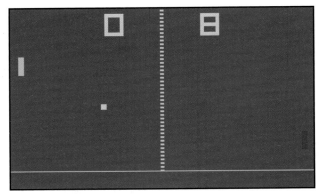

Figure 1-4 PONG for the PC (Copyright 2002 David Winter http://www.pong-story.com/).

In fact, the 1970s were a big decade for computers, as their uses began to expand dramatically. Basic word processing made its debut—though the first word-processing programs allowed you to erase words and letters while typing, but could do little else. Other innovations and uses for computers included the first video games, such as PONG® (see Figure 1-4) and Breakout®, the first mouse, and the first color monitor, to name just a few.

Even the Internet got its start in the 1970s. The U.S. Department of Defense, several major universities, and several research facilities developed the first network. This network linked sites in California, Utah, and Massachusetts. This network enabled computers from multiple, distant locations to communicate with each other and to exchange data quickly and securely. In 1991, commercial use of the Internet began. From its humble beginnings as a pure research project, the Internet has become the fastest growing communication medium today.

Figure 1-5 Early-model PCs from Hewlett-Packard and Sun.

By the 1980s, computers had started to become common household items. Several companies produced PCs designed for home, office, or school use. In fact, you might recall a few of these early systems, such as Commodore®, Apple®, Texas Instruments, Tandy®, and Radio Shack (see Figure 1-5). These systems offered elementary word-processing and spreadsheet programs, basic educational software, and games.

To learn more about Internet terms, select the web segment *Internet Terminology* in the PC Basics course.

In 1981, there were only about two million computers in use. By 1982, however, the total had jumped to more than five million. And by 1992, that number had swelled to 65 million (Figure 1-6). Today, more than 200 million computers are in use in the United States alone!

Figure 1-6 The rapid rate of expanding computer usage.

Figure 1-7 A notebook computer is small and transportable.

A major reason for the proliferation of computers over the past 30 years is the fact that, thanks to advances in chip technology and miniaturization, computers have gotten faster and smaller. Some computers are so small you can carry them with you wherever you go (notebook computers), as shown in Figure 1-7. The rate at which computers develop continues to soar. In fact, computing technology has advanced more in the last five years than it did in the previous 25. If cars had developed as quickly as computers, they would fly, need refueling only every 10,000 miles, and cost only $500!

Today, computers play a part in nearly every aspect of our lives. There are many obvious uses of computers today:

✦ Word processing

✦ Communicating with e-mail, instant messaging programs, newsgroups, and chat rooms

✦ Surfing the Web and shopping online

✦ Playing music from compact discs (CDs) and MP3s, and recording music from digital instruments

✦ Transferring files over networks or the Internet

✦ Playing virtual-reality games with people across the globe

You see, a computer isn't just a box with a monitor on your desk; computers are built into many electronic devices (see Figure 1-8). Many modern conveniences couldn't exist without computers. It's hard to predict what forms computers will take in the future.

Figure 1-8 Computers are everywhere you look!

It's hard to predict what forms computers will take in the future. Technological advances can come at any time and you can assume, that computers will most likely continue to get faster, smaller, and cheaper.

Understanding Common PC Components

Now that you've been introduced to the modern computer, let's review some standard computer terms and basic PC components. Becoming familiar with them will help you to get the most out of this book and your PC.

Hardware and Software

The two main classifications of a PC are *hardware* and *software*. All physical objects attached to a PC (things you can touch), including the monitor, keyboard, mouse, and printer, are considered hardware. Many types of hardware devices are available for PCs; a complete list is too long to include here. We do, however, discuss many common PC devices later in this chapter. Generally speaking, hardware devices can sometimes be called *hardware*, *devices*, or *components*.

Hardware is further divided into two groups by function: *input* and *output*. Input hardware is any object that is used to enter information (text, sound, or images) into a PC. Examples of input hardware include keyboards, mice, scanners, digital cameras, and microphones, as shown in Figure 1-9.

Figure 1-9 Common input devices.

Output hardware is any object that conveys something from inside the PC to the outside world. Examples of output hardware include monitors, speakers, printers, and MP3 players, as shown in Figure 1-10.

Figure 1-10 Common output devices.

Some devices are considered to be both input and output devices, including storage devices such as hard drives, floppy drives, Zip drives, and CD-RW or DVD-R drives. Devices that send and receive data, such as network interface cards (NICs) and modems, are input/output devices as well.

Software is a general term for "computer programs." Written in one of any number of computer languages, software tells the computer how to perform tasks. Common types of software include the following:

 To discover more about about the capabilities of computers select the web segment: *Multimedia Capabilities* in the PC Basics course.

Operating systems. An *operating system (OS)* is software installed on a PC that controls the way computer hardware and software interact. In other words, an operating system creates an environment in which software can operate on a PC. Examples of Microsoft® operating systems include Windows® 98, Windows Me, Windows 2000, and Windows XP® (see Figure 1-11). Other companies produce other operating systems, such as Sun Solaris®, Apple MacOS, and Red Hat Linux®, among many others.

Programs. The terms *program*, *application*, and *software* are typically used to describe the tools, utilities, or games that run on your PC. Examples of such programs include Microsoft Word (a word processor), Microsoft Excel (a spreadsheet program), WinZip® (a file-compression tool), Adobe® Acrobat® (a document viewer), Typing Tutor® (a typing trainer), and Hearts (a card game).

Figure 1-11 The standard desktop view of Windows XP, a common operating system.

Device drivers. A *device driver* is a special type of software that allows a specific hardware object to communicate with your PC. Without a device driver, hardware devices won't work with a PC. For example, the operating system requires a print driver to tell the computer how to interact with any printer. Most hardware vendors make driver installation easy—it usually requires no more effort than inserting a CD into your PC's CD-ROM drive and clicking an icon on a pop-up menu.

System Unit

The *system unit*, also referred to as a *case* or *tower*, is the box that that surrounds and protects the internal components of a PC (see Figure 1-12). The primary components include:

+ A motherboard

+ A central processing unit (CPU)

+ Memory cards

+ Storage devices

+ A power supply

Figure 1-12 A typical system unit, from the front, side, and back.

 You may encounter references to a system unit as "the CPU" (an abbreviation for *central processing unit*). This is technically incorrect, however, because the term *CPU* identifies only the main processor chip on a PC's motherboard—not the whole system unit.

Motherboard

The *motherboard*, sometimes called a *mainboard*, is the foundation of a modern PC. As shown in Figure 1-13, it features numerous *sockets* or *ports* that enable it to connect all devices in a PC, such as the CPU, memory cards, and storage devices. Each motherboard is typically designed for a specific type of CPU and memory card.

Figure 1-13 A typical motherboard.

> ## More About . . . Motherboards
>
> Every motherboard is different; each is designed to work with only a few specific CPUs and memory cards. Some motherboards support several types of memory, whereas most support only one type. Some motherboards can accommodate two or four CPUs, but most support only one. A motherboard that supports Intel CPUs does not support AMD CPUs, because each type of CPU uses different connectors. When you purchase a motherboard, CPU, or memory upgrade, make sure all such components are compatible.

CPU

The *central processing unit (CPU)* is the core component in a PC (see Figure 1-14). Sometimes referred to as the "brain" of the computer, the CPU interprets and carries out instructions, performs all computations, and controls the devices connected to the PC. There are a variety of CPUs available on the market. A well-known company is Intel®, which produces the Pentium® and Celeron® processors. Another company is AMD®, which produces the Athlon and Duron processors. In most cases, CPUs from Intel or AMD can be used with Microsoft operating systems.

Figure 1-14 A CPU not connected to the motherboard.

A CPU's speed is measured in hertz. Most CPUs today run at *gigahertz (GHz)* speeds, while some older systems are measured in *megahertz (MHz)*. MHz indicates how many million calculations a CPU can perform every second, while GHz indicates how many billion calculations a CPU can perform every second. Although Windows XP will run on a PC with a CPU working at a speed of 233 MHz, Microsoft recommends that your PC use a CPU that is 300 MHz or faster to achieve acceptable performance.

More About . . . CPUs

When you shop for a PC, it's important to consider the CPU speed. Most PCs on the market today include CPUs that operate at speeds of 1 GHz or faster—sometimes 2 GHz or more! Of course, the PCs with the newest, fastest CPUs tend to be more expensive than their slightly older, slightly slower predecessors. Buying one or two generations or speed levels behind whatever CPU is currently fastest can usually save you money. Besides, very few programs are designed to take full advantage of the highest speeds and advanced technologies built into the most cutting-edge CPUs. Ordinary home-user tasks such as word processing, surfing the Internet, listening to audio files, and even editing home movies rarely tax even 1 GHz CPUs.

Memory Cards

Your PC uses *memory cards*, also called *memory sticks* (see Figure 1-15), to store *random access memory*, more commonly called *RAM*. RAM temporarily stores data, software, and the operating system while the PC is operating.

Figure 1-15 A memory card.

 Data is stored in RAM until you assign it a permanent file name and storage location. For example, if you type a letter in WordPad on Windows XP and then turn off the power, everything you typed will be lost. But if you save your letter to a file on a storage device before you turn off the power, you can open that file to regain access to your letter after you turn the PC back on.

RAM is a very important part of a PC; in most cases, the more RAM a PC has, the better and faster it performs, and the more tasks it can handle at the same time. So, how much RAM is enough? Windows XP Home and Professional both require at least 64 MB, but Microsoft recommends 128 MB or more. In our experience, 256 MB is usually plenty for most activities in which a home user will engage.

> ### More About . . . RAM
>
> You can add RAM to a PC by inserting memory cards into the motherboard. There are many memory types and numerous memory features available. The user manual for your motherboard should indicate clearly what type of RAM it supports. In that user manual you may see some of the following names for memory components: SIMM, DIMM, SDRAM, DDR, and RDRAM. Other memory features listed in a user manual may include error checking (ECC), parity or non-parity, PC100, PC133, PC800, and PC2100. The specifics of what each of these acronyms and feature names mean are very technical. In most cases, you need to know only the type and features your PC requires.

Storage Devices

The information you enter in your PC needs to be stored somewhere; that's where storage devices come in. There are several types of storage devices available for PCs. The most common storage devices are:

- ✦ Hard drive

- ✦ Floppy drive

- ✦ CD drive

- ✦ DVD drive

 Floppy drives, CD-ROM drives, and DVD-ROM drives are all examples of *removable storage.* That is, each uses readable and writable media that can be removed from the drive itself. (The term media refers to the individual items such as a floppy disk, compact disc, and so on that you can insert into or remove from a removable storage device.) Other removable storage devices include tape-backup drives and Zip/Jaz drives.

The storage capacity of these devices is measured in bytes. A *byte* is a collection of eight *binary digits* or *bits,* where each bit must either be a 1 or a 0. Each byte can represent a single character, number, or symbol. A *kilobyte* (KB) is 1,024 bytes and equals about one printed page of double-spaced text. A *megabyte* (MB) is 1,024 kilobytes, or just over one million bytes, and equals about one normal-sized paperback book. A *gigabyte* (GB) is 1,024 megabytes, or just over one billion bytes, and equals about six full sets of encyclopedias (see Figure 1-16). Table 1-1 compares the byte capacities of common storage devices.

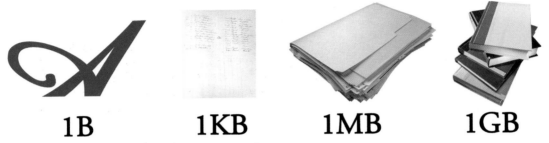

1B　　**1KB**　　**1MB**　　**1GB**

Figure 1-16 The relationships of storage capacity.

Table 1-1 Common storage devices.

STORAGE DEVICE	DISK CAPACITY	USES
Hard drive and data files	Varies, 20 GB to 140 GB or more	Store operating system, programs
Floppy drive	1.44 MB	Store small numbers of (small) files
CD-ROM drive	600 to 700 MB	Distribute software, back up personal data
DVD-ROM drive	4.7 to 7 GB	Distribute movies, back up personal data

Hard Drive

A *hard drive,* as shown in Figure 1-17, is the most common PC storage device. It's typically located inside the system unit. The hard disk stores both the instructions and data the computer needs to run. Most hard drives offer capacities in the gigabyte range. Today's PCs typically feature large hard drives to enable users to store multimedia content in the form of MP3s, videos, and photos. These types of files require more hard drive space than simple word-processing documents or spreadsheets; hence, extra capacity is essential.

Figure 1-17 A hard drive.

In general, a hard drive offers faster access to data than does any other storage device except RAM. But, unlike RAM, hard drive storage is permanent. Anything stored on a hard drive remains there until it's deleted.

More About . . . Hard Drives

Hard drive space is precious—especially when you run short of room! Fortunately, you can easily upgrade your PC's storage by adding another drive to your machine. (Most PCs support at least two and as many as four hard drives. The first hard drive in a system is typically assigned drive letter C: by default. If another hard drive is present in a PC, it is assigned a subsequent letter.)

Unless your PC supports only one hard drive, adding a second drive is preferable to replacing the existing one; that's because when you replace a hard drive, you must reinstall the operating system and other software and restore all your personal data. (If you must replace an existing drive, consider hiring a professional to migrate your software and data files for you. It could save you time and unnecessary heartache.)

Floppy Drive

A modern *floppy drive* reads information on and writes information to 3.5-inch *diskettes* or *floppy disks* (see Figure 1-18), a common type of removable storage medium. A typical floppy disk holds up to 1.44 MB of data. Floppies can back up small amounts of data and may be used to transfer files between two PCs. Floppy disk drives are typically assigned the drive letter A:, however, it can be the drive letter B:.

Figure 1-18 3 1/2-inch floppy disks.

CD Drives

There are three types of CD drives:

+ CD-ROM

+ CD-RW

+ CD-R

Figure 1-19 A typical CD.

A *CD-ROM* drive reads information on CD-ROMs (or CDs, for short). A CD-ROM, as shown in Figure 1-19, can hold between 650 and 700 MB of data, or about 600 times as much as a single floppy disk. The "ROM" in "CD-ROM" stands for "read-only memory," meaning that unlike a floppy disk, which can be read and written to, a CD-ROM can only be read by your PC.

CD-R and *CD-RW drives,* on the other hand, enable you to write data to CDs, a process called *burning*. To do this, however, you must use a special type of CD:

CD-R. A *CD-R* is a writable CD that can be written to only once. Once burned, a CD-R becomes a CD-ROM. You can burn a CD-R using either a CD-R drive or a CD-RW drive.

CD-RW. A *CD-RW* is a CD that you can write to many times. (The "RW" stands for "rewritable.") You can only burn a CD-RW using a CD-RW drive. Figure 1-20 shows a CD-RW drive.

Figure 1-20 A CD-RW drive not installed in the system unit.

More About . . . CDs

Using CDs to store data, music, and photos is very popular—so much so, in fact, that Windows XP includes built-in support for burning CD-Rs and CD-RWs. If your PC has a CD-R or CD-RW drive, you can burn your own CDs without any other components or software.[1]

---

[1]We encourage you to comply with all applicable laws, including music licensing.

DVD Drives

A *DVD* is a type of media that looks like a CD. Unlike CDs, however, which max out at between 650 and 700 MB of data, DVDs can hold as much as 7 GB of data—enough for a full-length movie!

In order to read DVDs, your PC requires a special drive, called a *DVD drive*. Also available are DVD-R/RAM drives, which enable anyone with a PC to burn their own DVDs (provided special DVD-burning software is installed on their machine). With a DVD-R/RAM drive, you can write to a DVD-R once, or to a DVD-RAM multiple times. Most DVD drives can also read CDs, as well.

Power Supply

The *power supply* provides electricity to most installed components, such as the motherboard, hard drive, CD/DVD drives, and so on. The PC's main power cable plugs into the power supply on the back of the system unit case. The connection port for the power cable is often located near a fan, which helps cool the power supply so it can function efficiently.

Identifying Connection Types

Peripherals, also called *add-on devices* and/or *external devices*, are hardware devices that connect to a PC. Some peripherals are required, such as a keyboard, mouse, and monitor. Others are optional, such as a printer, digital camera, scanner, speaker, modem, and network interface card (also called NICs). To do its job, each peripheral must somehow connect to the PC itself.

Internal and external devices use a variety of connections to *link* to a system unit. Each connection invariably involves some kind of cable that uses one or more specific type of connector (sometimes, in fact, you'll find different types of connectors on each end of a cable). A basic understanding of connection types and connectors on your PC is helpful, because there's a good chance you'll want to add a peripheral at some point.

Before we discuss common PC peripherals in more detail, let's examine common connections and related connectors that you'll find both inside and outside your system unit.

Internal Connections

If the inside of your system unit is a mystery, this section will help you understand the connection types you see there. It will also help you to make intelligent decisions when upgrading components, such as the memory.

Most internal connections are found directly on the motherboard, which is the fundamental component of any system unit. Figure 1-21 shows a typical motherboard; notice its various slots and connection points. Table 1-2 shows the male and female versions of each connection type available on most motherboards.

Here are specifics for each of the connection types listed in Table 1-2:

Figure 1-21 A typical motherboard.

PCI slots   AGP port

Figure 1-22 PCI slots and an AGP port.

✦ **PCI (Peripheral Component Interconnect).** The PCI slots are the most obvious connection points on the motherboard, as shown in Figure 1-22. Some motherboards have as few as two PCI slots, whereas others have as many as six.

✦ **AGP (Accelerated Graphics Port).** Another type of connection on the motherboard is the AGP port, which connects high-speed video cards. In most cases, an AGP port is brown in color, and is located next to the PCI slots. Most motherboards have only one AGP port.

Table 1-2 The common external male and female connection types.

PORT	COMMON USES
PCI	Sound cards, modems, NICs, and video cards
AGP	High-speed video cards
ATA/IDE hard drives	Hard drives (two per port on a cable), CD and DVD drives
IDE floppy	Floppy drives (two per port on a cable)

More About . . . Video Cards

Video cards provide the output you see on your monitor. Most new video cards include their own CPUs and memory to manage the increased display requirements for modern applications or games.

Although Windows XP can operate with only 4 MB of video card on-board memory, many applications and most games demand far more memory. For example, many new 3-D games require at least 32 MB of video memory to display complex graphics smoothly and manipulate advanced game environments in real time. For this reason, new video cards typically include 32 or 64 MB of on-board memory. The more memory on a video card, the richer and crisper images appear on a monitor.

✦ **ATA (Advanced Technology Attachment).** An ATA connection enables connections for Integrated Drive Electronics (IDE) hard drives (discussed shortly) and CD and DVD drives. An ATA ribbon cable connects one or two IDE drives to each ATA connection port. Most newer motherboards include two ATA connection ports (see Figure 1-23) for as many as four IDE drives.

ATA connection ports

Figure 1-23 ATA connection ports on a motherboard.

You'll also find another ATA connection on most motherboards; it's a bit shorter than the previously described ports. This is the floppy-connection port, as shown in Figure 1-23. A floppy ribbon cable connects one or two floppy drives. Most modern PCs have only a single 3½-inch floppy drive connected to this port.

More About . . . IDE

Most PCs include built-in support for IDE hard drives. Each IDE port on a motherboard can connect to one or two hard drives, and most motherboards include two IDE ports. When two drives connect to a single IDE port, one is set as a slave and the other as the master drive. Master and slave are simply designations that allow the motherboard to know with which drive it is communicating.

The IDE drive itself may be set to act as a master or a slave using a control built onto the drive itself. Instructions for applying these settings are sometimes printed directly on a hard drive's case, but the details are most likely covered in a hard drive's manual or the manufacturer's Web site.

In addition to the connection types listed in Table 1-2, your computer may utilize other types of connections:

+ **Serial.** Most PCs built today have two of the smaller DB9-pin serial ports; whereas, older systems typically have one DB9 and one DB25 connector (see Figure 1-24). Both types of serial ports on the system unit are male, and require a female cable to connect to external devices. In most cases, only a single device can be connected to each serial port.

PS/2
USB
VGA
Parallel
Serial

Microphone
and Speaker

Figure 1-24 The collection of external ports on the back of a system unit.

More About . . . Serial Ports

If you use external serial devices, you are bound to run into difficulty at some point in connecting them to your system. That's because serial ports on the back of your PC are always male, but the serial ports on devices can be either male or female. In addition to having different genders, there are two sizes for serial connectors: DB9 and DB25. To accommodate all possible combinations when connecting your serial devices, you may need to obtain the following:

+ A serial cable with a male DB9 connector at each end.

+ A serial cable with one male DB9 and one female DB9 connector.

+ A serial connector converter that has a female DB9 on one side and a male DB25 on the other.

+ A serial connector converter that has a male DB9 on one side and a female DB25 on the other.

✦ **Parallel.** The parallel port (also called a *DB25 port*) on the system unit is always female (see Figure 1-25). In most cases, only a single external device can be connected to a parallel port.

 Both parallel and the larger serial ports use the same DB25 connector type. However, serial and parallel ports are quite different types of connection interfaces. The parallel port on the system unit case is always female, and the two serial ports on the system unit case are always male.

✦ **SVGA/VGA (Super VGA/Video Graphics Array).** Most modern video cards and monitors support SVGA, which is an enhanced version of VGA capable of improved display resolution and color depth. The SVGA/VGA port is the same size and shape as the small serial port, but has 15 pins instead of 9 (see Figure 1-25) and is female on the system unit.

✦ **PS/2.** Two female PS/2 ports are found on most desktop PCs (see Figure 1-25). One is reserved for the mouse, and the other for the keyboard. Most notebooks, on the other hand, have only a single PS/2 port, which can be used to attach either an external mouse or

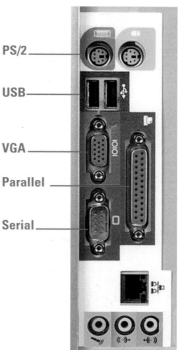

Figure 1-25 Serial, parallel, VGA, USB, and PS/2 ports.

✦ **USB (Universal Serial Bus).** USB connections (see Figure 1-26) allow faster response and take advantage of Windows XP's Plug and Play feature, which allows you to simply plug a peripheral into the USB port and use it immediately. The operating system automatically installs drivers for the peripheral (you may be prompted for the driver disk), and you'll rarely need to restart your PC. USB is available in two versions: 1.1 and 2.0. The 2.0 version of USB offers throughput speeds that are even greater than FireWire..

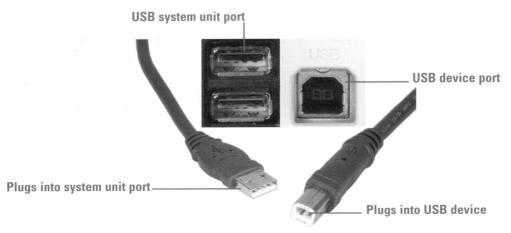

Figure 1-26 The ends of a USB cable and the USB ports on a system unit and a USB device.

The wide range of USB devices available includes keyboards, mouse devices, printers, hard drives, CD and DVD drives, digital cameras, scanners, PDAs, and tape-backup units. Some USB devices are powered, meaning they include external power supplies that must plug into a power strip or surge protector. Others, such as keyboards and mouse devices, are unpowered, meaning they draw power through the USB connection itself.

More About . . . USB

Most new PCs have at least two USB ports. Some PCs also have built-in USB ports on the front. If you find yourself in need of additional USB ports, you need a USB hub, a device that transforms a single USB port into 2, 4, 8, or 16 ports. In all, USB ports can be used to interconnect as many as 127 devices.

If multiple devices that draw power from the USB port are connected to a single USB port on the system unit via a USB hub, those devices may not receive sufficient power to operate properly (as a rule, no more than three unpowered USB devices should be connected to a single USB port on the system unit). To resolve this issue, a powered USB hub can be used to boost the power available to USB devices through the USB connection.

✦ **IEEE 1394.** IEEE 1394, also commonly referred to as FireWire (see Figure 1-27), offers fast throughput (much faster than USB 1.1) and can support as many as 127 devices (the same as USB). FireWire is actually a trademark of Apple Computer and is part of the IEEE 1394 standard. PCs with built-in FireWire support usually have two ports in the back and at least one in the front.

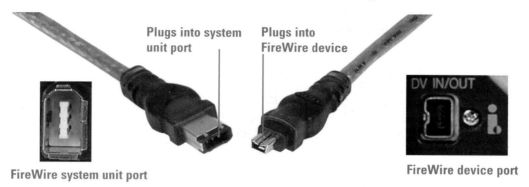

Plugs into system unit port   **Plugs into FireWire device**

FireWire system unit port   **FireWire device port**

Figure 1-27 FireWire system unit port, cable ends, and device connector port.

More About . . . FireWire

FireWire is similar to USB in several ways:

✦ Unpowered FireWire devices draw power from the connection.

✦ Powered FireWire devices have their own separate power supplies.

✦ The number of unpowered FireWire devices on a single port should be limited to three or fewer.

✦ **PC Card.** This connection type, once known as *Personal Computer Memory Card International Association (PCMCIA),* was renamed PC Card because it was used for more than memory cards. PC Card slots hold PC Cards. Although PC Cards are used mainly on notebooks, PC Card adapters are available for desktop PCs, which means you can use the same peripherals or interfaces with both desktop and notebook PCs.

Understanding Input Devices

Input devices are tools you use to get information from the world into your PC. You won't believe how many input devices have been developed for the PC; some of the most common include a mouse, keyboard, scanner, and digital camera.

Keyboards

A *keyboard* (see Figure 1-28) is probably the most familiar input device for a PC. You use the keyboard to enter numbers, letters, symbols, and even control commands into your PC. From the keyboard, you can control programs and input data. A keyboard is typically connected to a PC through a PS/2 or USB connection.

Figure 1-28 A typical keyboard.

More About . . . Keyboards

If you suffer from carpal-tunnel syndrome or other similar maladies, then working with a traditional keyboard may exacerbate your symptoms. Fortunately, several manufacturers offer ergonomic or natural keyboards, designed to help you straighten your shoulders, relax your arms, and maintain a more natural hand and wrist posture while you work.

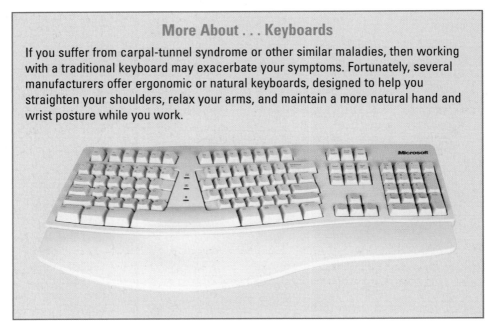

The Mouse

A *mouse* (see Figure 1-29) is a small device that you use to move the mouse pointer on the screen. This handheld device is essential to working with *graphical user interfaces (GUIs)* and games. A GUI uses graphics, windows, and icons instead of just text to allow the PC user to interact with the PC. You use the buttons on a mouse to select options, buttons, or commands when the mouse pointer hovers over them. A mouse is typically connected to the PC through a serial, PS/2, or USB connection.

Figure 1-29 An optical mouse.

More About . . . Mouse Devices

There are several alternatives to the common mouse shown in Figure 1-29, including trackballs, cordless mouse devices, touchpads, graphical tablets, and mouse sticks.

Scanners

A *scanner* is a device that converts just about any image—from slides or photos to transparencies, graphics, or even text—into digital form. A scanner (shown in Figure 1-30) usually includes software that can then be used to capture, print, or transfer the image. Some scanners also provide fax and copy functions at the touch of a button. After you scan an image and save it to a file, you can do many things with it. For example, you can e-mail it to friends or make it your desktop wallpaper. A scanner is typically connected to a PC through a USB or FireWire connection.

Figure 1-30 A typical scanner.

 Some high-end scanners include a feature called Optical Character Recognition (OCR) allowing a scanned text image to be converted into an object that a word-processing application

Digital Cameras

Digital cameras photograph still or, in some cases, video digital images that can be fed directly into your PC. Unlike regular cameras, digital cameras (see Figure 1-31) don't use film; instead, they store images on memory cards or rewritable optical disks. A digital image is just like any other image in your PC. You can edit, print, view, or send them to others via e-mail, or even post them to Web sites. A digital camera is typically connected to a PC through a USB or FireWire connection..

Figure 1-31 A typical digital camera.

Working with Output Devices

An *output device* is any hardware component that produces something you can touch, see, or hear. There are too many output devices to name them all, but some of the most common include monitors, printers, speakers, and MP3 players.

Monitors

A *monitor*, which looks a lot like a television screen, displays visual output for a PC (see Figure 1-32). With a monitor, you can see your documents, view pictures, watch movies,

and interact with your PC's operating system (you'll learn more about performing such actions later). Monitors come in a wide range of sizes, from 15 to 21 inches (this measurement reflects the length of the diagonal from one corner to the other); the larger the display area, the more detail you can see on the screen. Typically, monitors connect to a PC through a VGA connection on a video card (you should note that a high-end monitor requires a high-end video card to produce acceptable images on your screen).

Figure 1-32 A flat panel monitor.

There are two major types of PC monitors available today:

+ **Tube monitors.** A *tube monitor* looks like a television set—heavy, large and boxy. The size and weight of a tube monitor comes from its core component: a glass cathode ray tube (CRT).

+ **Flat panel monitors.** *Flat panel monitors* are narrow in profile in comparison with tube monitors, and provide crisp, clean images that are more vibrant and brilliant than some tube monitors. For this reason, flat panel monitors are usually more expensive than a tube monitor of the same size.

The improved display of flat panel monitors stems from its flat, pixel-based display (not a projection onto a curved surface, as with a CRT). The *size* of both tube and flat panel monitors is a measurement of the diagonal distance from one corner across the screen to the opposite corner. The viewable area is typically less on a tube monitor versus a flat panel.

Although the term "monitor" can apply to a tube or a flat panel monitor, this term occurs more often when discussing tube monitors. When flat panel monitors are mentioned, they are often called "flat screens or flat panel" rather than "monitors." The term "LCD monitor" is also common, but is technically incorrect. Most new flat panel monitors use a type of technology that differs from LCD (Liquid Crystal Display).

More About . . . Monitors

A monitor's quality is usually rated in the density of its display and its refresh rate. A monitor's *density* is rated in dot pitch in millimeters (mm) and indicates how closely the points of color are packed together. *Dot pitch* is the distance between points of color on a monitor screen. The better the monitor's display, the lower its dot-pitch rating. A rating of 0.22 is fairly good. A monitor's *refresh rate* is how often the displayed image is re-drawn. In tube monitors, refresh rate is rated in hertz (Hz) (re-draws per second), where a larger number indicates better quality. A refresh rate of 85 Hz is fairly good. A flat panel monitor's refresh rate, on the other hand, is rated in response time in milliseconds (ms), where a smaller number indicates better quality. A response time of 30 ms is fairly good.

Printers

A *printer* is a device that prints text or graphical images from your computer on paper (see Figure 1-33). Printers can produce black or color output. Most printers use standard paper, but some can print on transparency film, slide film, drafting paper, and photo paper, as well as labels and envelopes. A printer is typically connected to a PC through a parallel or USB connection.

Figure 1-33 An inkjet printer.

There are two main types of printers:

✦ **Inkjet.** *Inkjet printers* produce output by spraying microscopic drops of ink onto the paper as it passes through the printer. Most inkjet printers can print both color and black images, but sometimes the ink can smear or bleed. Inkjets are fairly inexpensive, but they print slowly in comparison with laser printers.

✦ **Laser.** *Laser printers* produce output by using a system of lasers to adhere and bond a powdered toner onto paper. Laser printers produce detailed high-quality images, and laser printer output rarely smears. Some laser printers can print color images, but most produce only black text on white paper, or grayscale images. Laser printers are usually more than twice the price of a comparable inkjet printer, but they produce much more detailed output at a much faster rate.

 In addition to inkjet and laser printers, there are also many types of specialty printers on the market, such as label printers, photo printers, plotters, and slide printers. These printers handle unique output media that a typical inkjet or laser printer is sometimes unable to handle efficiently, if at all.

More About . . . Printers

When purchasing a printer, it's important to shop around and compare features. The challenge is, every printer company describes a printer's capabilities using different terminology and ranking methods. To make a meaningful comparison, find a computer store with multiple printers on display so you can print on each one. Without side-by-side comparison of the same document from multiple devices, you can't tell which printer actually produces higher-quality output.

Also, realize that the most-expensive printer is not always the best printer. Printers often offer features or capabilities that home users don't need or want. Many such features, such as an extra large-capacity auto-feed paper tray or a sorting attachment, dramatically increase prices. Look for models that provide the features you need, without too many unwanted features.

Speakers

Speakers produce audio output from a PC (see Figure 1-34). Through speakers or a set of headphones, you can hear operating-system sounds, music, sound effects from games,

 or the soundtracks of DVDs. Speakers are typically connected to a PC's sound card using one or more ⅛-inch stereo jack(s), the same type of connector at the end of the headphones you use on your portable radio or CD player.

Figure 1-34 Common speakers.

MP3 Players

An *MP3 player* (see Figure 1-35) is a portable device that plays digitally recorded music. MP3 players have either a large amount of memory or a hard drive on which digital music is stored. Once you transfer music from a PC to the player, you can use the player anywhere to listen to your favorite tunes. MP3 players may typically be attached to a PC using a serial, USB, or FireWire connection (the faster the connection, the quicker it will be to download music to your player from your PC).

Figure 1-35 An MP3 player.

Discovering Communication Devices

Some types of hardware, such as modems and NICs, allow two or more PCs to communicate. These are called communication devices. The communication devices described in this section connect to expansion cards installed inside the system unit, or to an external serial, USB, FireWire, PC Card, or network interface card (NIC) connections.

Modems

A *modem* is a device that allows a PC to communicate with other PCs. A voice modem uses a standard phone line. A modem can be an expansion card installed inside the system unit (see Figure 1-36) or an external device connected to a PC via a serial cable. Modems offer maximum throughput of 56 Kbps.

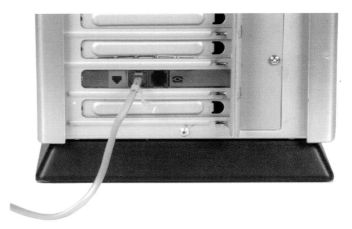

Figure 1-36 A expansion-card modem with connected phone cord.

More About . . . Communication Speeds

Just as storage devices are rated with KB, MB, and GB, the speed at which a communication device sends and receives data has ratings too. These ratings are called *throughput*, which refers to how much data can be sent or received by a device within a specific amount of time.

There are three common measurement terms used to describe throughput: *Kbps*, *Mbps*, and *Gbps*. The "bps" part of these terms stands for "bits per second." (Remember that a bit is a single binary digit of a 1 or a 0.) Kbps is Kilobits per second, or 1,024 bps. Mbps is Megabits per second, or 1,024 Kbps. Gbps is Gigabits per second, or 1,024 Mbps.

Notice that throughput uses a lowercase b in its speed ratings, while hard-drive capacity uses an uppercase B. The lowercase b stands for *bits*, while the uppercase B stands for *bytes*. There are 8 bits in a byte, so a 1 MB file transmitted over a 1 Mbps connection would take about 8 seconds to complete.

Cable Modems

A *cable modem* (see Figure 1-37) is used to connect to a high-speed broadband Internet service. Many cable-television companies offer this type of service. Cable Internet service typically offers up to 2 Mbps for downloads and 300 Kbps for uploading data. Cable Internet service is a shared medium, however, which means that if many people in your neighborhood use their cable modem connections at the same time, everyone's connection runs slower. Cable modems are typically external devices that connect to a PC through a NIC.

Figure 1-37 A cable modem.

DSL Modems

DSL (digital subscriber line) modems (see Figure 1-38) use a new feature of digital telephone service to provide high-speed Internet access. DSL requires that the telephone

company deploy specific hardware in your area; in addition, your house must be located within a specific distance from the switching station where DSL access is made available to local subscribers.

Figure 1-38 A DSL modem.

A DSL connection uses your phone line, but allows you to place and receive calls while also connected to the Internet. DSL connections typically offer 384 Kbps to 1.5 Mbps download and 128 Kbps upload throughput. The real benefit of DSL is that it's a dedicated medium. In other words, the presence of other DSL users in your neighborhood won't affect your upload and download speeds. DSL modems are either expansion cards installed inside the system unit or external devices connected to a NIC.

NICs

A PC connects to a network using a *NIC*, short for *network interface card* (see Figure 1-39). A network allows multiple PCs to share files, printers, data, and even Internet connections. A NIC permits a PC to attach to a network, through which you can connect to the Internet as well. A PCI NIC is an internal expansion card that gets installed inside the system unit case onto the motherboard by attaching to a PCI slot. A PC Card NIC is an expansion card about the size of a credit card that slips into a PC Card slot on the side of a notebook PC.

Figure 1-39 A PCI NIC and a PC Card NIC.

Reviewing Power Devices

Your PC needs electricity to operate, but providing electricity introduces certain risks. The electricity that powers our homes and offices is not as reliable and consistent as we might like. The electric company, other houses in the neighborhood, and appliances within your own home can cause minor fluctuations in the flow of electricity—for example, you've probably seen your lights dim when your air conditioner or refrigerator turns on.

At least three peripheral devices—surge protectors, UPSs, and static guards—can prevent electricity from damaging your PC system.

Surge Protectors

A *surge protector* (see Figure 1-40) is both a power-outlet multiplier and an electric-spike protector. An absolute must for any electronic device, especially a PC, a surge protector includes a fuse or built-in circuit breaker that disconnects power if a spike occurs. This protects your system from electric-spike damage, but the sudden loss of power might cause you to lose unsaved data.

Figure 1-40 A surge protector.

 Be sure to select a surge protector that has a guarantee and warranty.

UPSs

A *UPS (uninterruptible power supply)* is a battery and power conditioner for your PC (see Figure 1-41). A UPS connects between the wall outlet and your PC. It conditions electricity so your PC is fed only clean, consistent power. If the electricity fails, a UPS can continue to

Figure 1-41 An uninterruptible power supply.

supply a PC with power from the battery. The length of time a UPS can provide battery power depends on its battery size and the amount of power that the attached devices draw. In most cases, a UPS provides at least 10 minutes of emergency power. This provides ample time to perform a clean "shutdown" on a running system before the power is exhausted.

A UPS should be purchased for any system that must remain operative even during a power failure, or if you don't want to risk having your power instantly terminated by a surge protector. Be sure to purchase a UPS that supports your PC for at least 10 minutes.

Anti-Static Devices

Anti-static devices (see Figure 1-42) channel static electricity from your body to a safe ground. These devices can be wristbands, ankle bands, or desktop mats, and typically connect to the ground screw in a power outlet. They work only when you touch the static guard before touching any PC

Figure 1-42 An anti-static device.

equipment. In many cases, true protection persists only if you remain in contact with the static guard throughout the entire time you are touching the PC. If you often shock yourself on doorknobs or other people, this peripheral is a must for you!

Unfortunately, even a minor power spike can damage a PC. Under some circumstances—such as when you might open your system unit and handle internal PC components or the motherboard—the sensitive electronics within a PC may not withstand even a small spark of static electricity.

TO KEEP ON LEARNING . . .

Go online to **www.LearnwithGateway.com** and log on to select:

+ *Internet Terminology in the PC Basics Course*
+ *Multimedia Capabilities in the PC Basics Course*
+ *Internet Links and Resources*
+ *FAQs*

With Gateway and the *Survive & Thrive* series, refer to *Communicate and Connect to the Internet* for more information on:

+ *Using the Internet*
+ *Networks and NICs*

Refer to *Create and Share Digital Photos* for more information on:

+ *Digital cameras*

Refer to *Use Your PC to Explore Digital Music* for more information on:

+ *Digital music*
+ *Working with audio on your PC*

Gateway offers hands-on training courses that cover many of the topics in this chapter. Additional fees may apply. Call **888-852-4821** to enroll. Please have your customer ID and order number ready when you call.

Getting to Know Windows XP

Logging On to Windows XP

Every time you power up your computer to use Windows XP, you must *log on*—that is, select a user account and provide a password, if one is required. If there's only one user account on your PC, and the account requires no password, then you are logged on to the system with that one user account automatically.

If, however, your PC supports multiple user accounts and is a *stand-alone machine* (that is, not part of a network), then Windows XP displays its default logon screen when the PC is

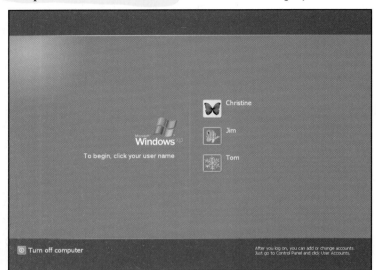

powered on. This default screen, shown in Figure 2-1, is called the "Windows Welcome screen," and lists all defined user accounts in alphabetical order. To log on using an account, simply click its name in the list. If a password has been defined for that account, you will be asked to provide it. After you log on, you are presented with your desktop.

Figure 2-1: The Windows Welcome screen.

If your PC is part of a network, instead of seeing the Windows Welcome screen, you'll see the Welcome to Windows screen in Figure 2-2. This screen instructs you to press the

CTRL+ALT+DELETE key combination in order to produce a standard Windows networking logon prompt, called the Log On to Windows dialog box (see Figure 2-3). Type your account name in the User name text box, and if you've defined a password for your account, type it in the Password text box.

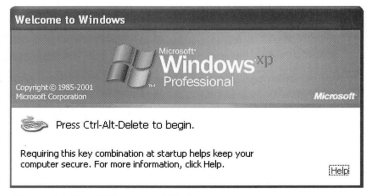

Figure 2-2: The Welcome to Windows screen.

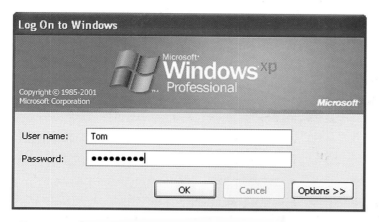

Figure 2-3: The Log On to Windows dialog box.

 To learn more about logging on, elect the Web segment *Windows XP: Logging On* in the PC Basics course.

Understanding User Accounts and User Profiles

As you work with your PC, which includes creating and saving documents and installing new software, your desktop will change. For example, additional icons may be added to the desktop and start menu. In addition, you'll discover other ways to customize your desktop as your computer knowledge grows—for example, by applying different color schemes and background images to your desktop.

If more than one person uses your PC, however, it can be difficult to maintain your desktop the way you like it. You might like your icons to be neatly aligned on a plain background, while others prefer their own system of ordered chaos.

User accounts enable Windows XP to identify individual collections of personal data. This personal data is gathered in a *user profile,* which includes the settings that define how your desktop looks, sounds, and operates. At first, all user profiles are the same. But as you use your PC and change its look and feel, your user profile becomes unique. Because every user account has a unique user profile, each user can customize his or her desktop and PC environment without affecting other users.

It is recommended that each person who uses a PC have his or her own user account.

A user profile includes information about the following items or settings:

- ✦ Desktop icons
- ✦ Internet Explorer favorites
- ✦ Color settings
- ✦ Outlook Express e-mail settings
- ✦ Sound schemes
- ✦ The location of the user's personal files
- ✦ The start menu

More About . . . User Profiles

Customizing your user profile can include changing the colors that Windows uses, altering the sounds Windows plays, picking new wallpaper, manipulating icons on your desktop and start menu, changing the taskbar's placement and look, and much more.

In addition to enabling every person who uses your PC to customize the Windows XP work environment to suit his or her taste, user accounts can also add an important layer of security to your machine, enabling you to keep others from accessing your personal data. This is especially true if you require users to enter *passwords* in order to access their accounts. Once a password has been defined for an account, users must enter that password in order to access the account. Unless the correct password is provided by the user, the account remains inaccessible.

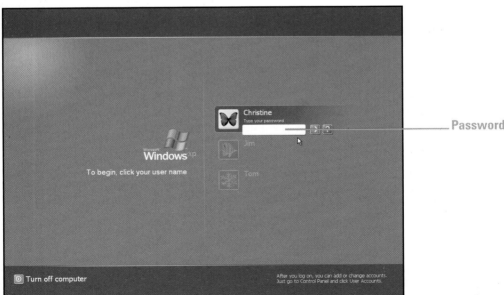

Password text box

Windows XP supports two kinds of user accounts: Computer administrator and Limited. With a *computer administrator user account,* you can perform all the following activities:

✦ Create, manage, and delete user accounts

✦ Change configurations for all users on the PC

✦ Install programs

✦ Access all files on the PC

Using a *limited user account* (i.e. logging on with a limited user account), on the other hand, you can perform the following set of activities:

✦ Change or delete the limited user account's password

✦ Change the accounts picture, theme, and desktop settings

✦ Access any files the account creates

✦ Access files in the Shared Documents folder

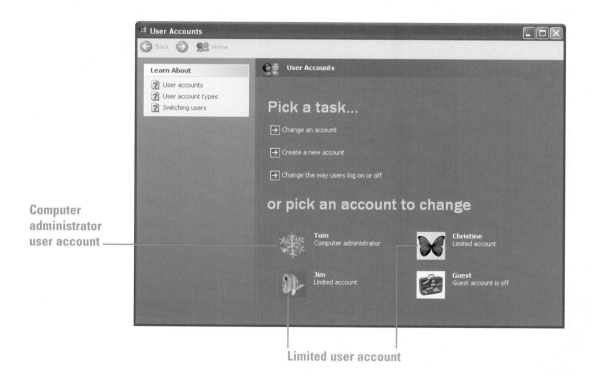

Computer administrator user account

Limited user account

It's a good practice to assign only one person to manage a PC using a computer administrator user account. That person, however, should also have a separate limited user account for regular PC access, and use the computer administrator user account only when it's needed to manage the PC.

Creating User Accounts

To create limited user accounts for all the people who use your PC (including yourself), make sure you're logged on as the computer administrator. If you're using the account you created after Windows XP initial setup process, then you're set to go. Then, do the following:

1. Click the start button, click Control Panel, and then click User Accounts.
2. The User Accounts window opens. Click Create a new account.
3. The Name the new account screen appears. In the Type a name for the new account text field, enter a user name for the account. It can be anything you like, as long as it contains fewer than 20 characters. Click Next.

 Internally, Windows uses a security ID—a long, complex number—to identify the account. Externally, however, the account is identified by its user name, which is far easier to remember. As long as you can remember the account's user name, Windows knows who you are.

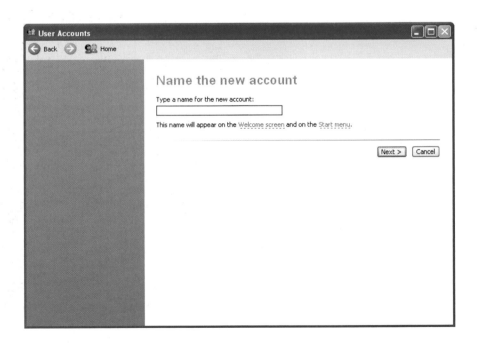

④ The Pick an account type screen appears. Click the Limited user account option.

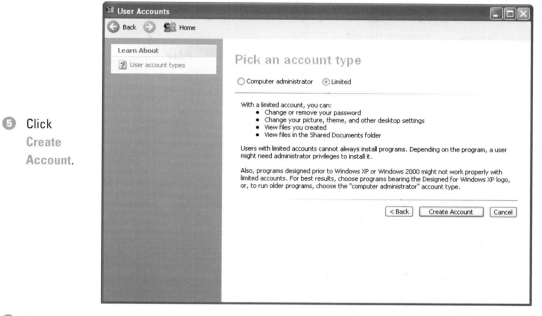

⑤ Click Create Account.

⑥ As shown in Figure 2-4, the new user account appears at the bottom of the User Accounts window. To create additional limited user accounts, repeat steps 2 through 5.

Debbie _____

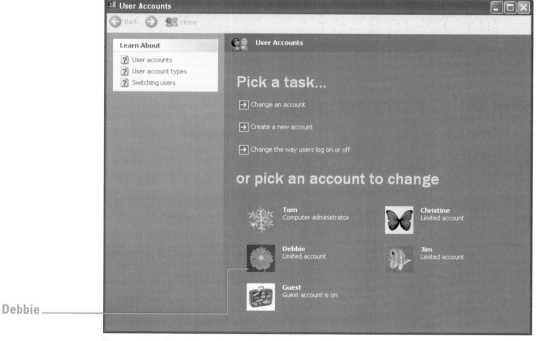

Figure 2-4 The User Accounts window with user accounts.

To create additional computer administrator user accounts, follow the procedure for creating limited user accounts, but select Computer administrator instead of Limited in step 4.

 To see how to setup a user account, select the Web segment *User Accounts* in the PC Basics course.

Managing User Accounts

After you've created a user account, you can change its user name, define a password, or manage any number of other aspects of the account from within the User Accounts window. To start, simply click the account you want to change. As shown in Figure 2-5, this opens a What do you want to change about x's account? window, where *x* is the account's user name.

Depending on what type of account you're managing, the What do you want to change about x's account? contains various options:

✦ Change the name. Click this option, type a new name for the account, and then click Change Name.

✦ Create a password. Click this option, type the desired password once, type the same password again, type a word or phrase to use as a password hint, and then click Create Password.

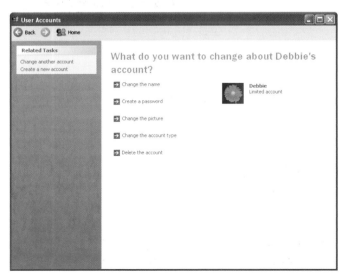

Figure 2-5 The What do you want to change about Debbie's account? screen.

After you've defined a password for a user account, you must supply that password when you log on. If you forget your password, click the question mark in the blue box to see a password hint. Be sure your password hint is not the password itself, and that it is not too specific. It should be a clue to jog your memory, not a way to share your password with others. Also, a new command, Remove the password, appears on the What do you want to change about this account? screen. Use this command to remove a password from the user account.

+ Change the picture. Click this option, click one of the alternate picture icons, and then click Change Picture.

+ Change the account type. Click this option, select either Computer Administrator or Limited, and then click Change Account Type.

+ Delete the account. Click this option, click Keep Files or Delete Files, and then click Delete Account.

To delete a user account you must be logged on as a computer administration. If you delete a user account, you'll lose all the e-mail, Internet favorites, and configuration settings associated with that account. You can, however, save the data files and the contents of the user account's desktop to a folder on your desktop (i.e. the currently logged on computer administrator account) by clicking the Keep Files button. The resulting folder on your desktop takes the name of the deleted user account. Clicking Delete Files, on the other hand, removes everything associated with that user account from the PC.

+ Set up my account to use a .NET passport. A .NET passport account is an account with Microsoft that manages access to numerous Internet sites.

Switching Accounts

When you've finished using your user account, or when another user wants to use your PC, there are two ways to switch accounts:

+ Log off

+ Use Windows XP's Fast User Switching feature

Logging Off

The *logoff* process closes your user account and returns you to the logon screen, enabling the next user to log on. It prevents others from easy access to your personal data.

To log off, do the following:

① Click the start button, and then click Log Off (see Figure 2-6).

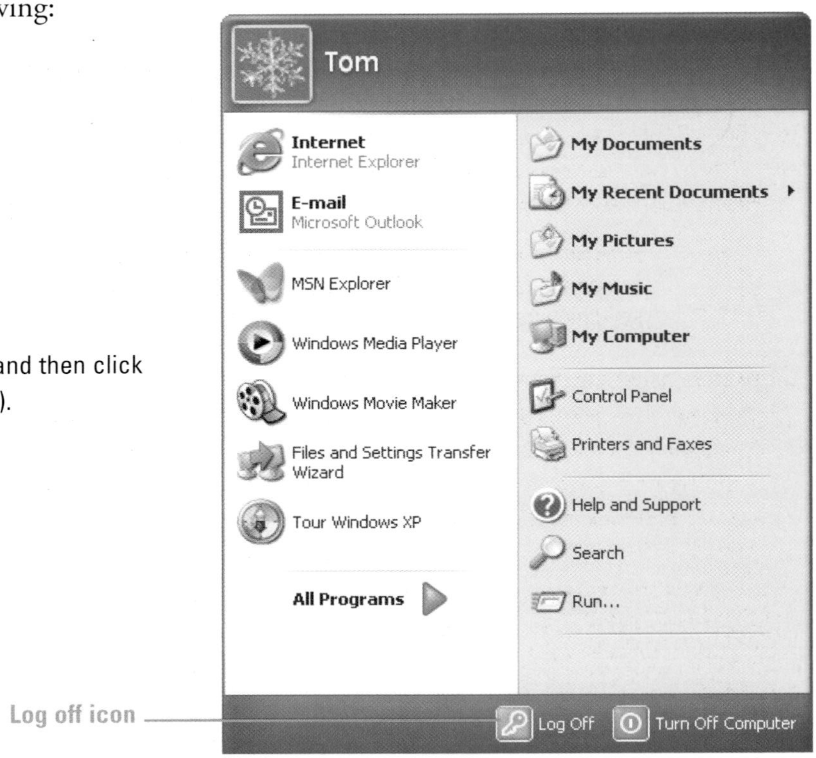

Log off icon ——

Figure 2-6 The Log Off icon on the start menu.

② The Log Off Windows dialog box opens, as shown in Figure 2-7. Click the Log Off button to log off your user account and return to the logon screen.

Figure 2-7 The Log Off Windows dialog box.

Fast User Switching

Suppose you're balancing the family's electronic checkbook on your PC, but your daughter needs to quickly look something up on the Internet in order to complete her homework. Using Windows XP's Fast User Switching feature, your daughter can log on without requiring you to log off first. You can leave all your programs open, switch users, let her find the information for her homework, and then switch back to your desktop—without losing any of your work!

 Even though Fast User Switching will allow you to return to your desktop after someone else uses the PC, it is always a good idea to save your work before switching users. If the other user crashes the PC, you will lose your data.

To switch users via Fast User Switching, do the following:

1. Click the start menu, and then click Log Off. (If you logged off in the previous exercise, you will need to log on.)
2. The Log Off Windows dialog box opens. Click the Switch User button.
3. The Windows Welcome screen appears. As shown in Figure 2-8, a line below your user account lists the number of programs still running. To log on to another user account, click its icon in the Windows Welcome screen, and enter the accounts password if one is required.

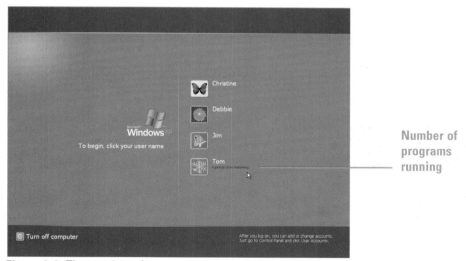

Figure 2-8 The number of programs running listed under a user account.

When the other user finishes using her user account, she can log out. This displays the Windows Welcome screen; simply click your user account to reopen your desktop. You'll find everything running just the way you left it.

Although your desktop is hidden when another user logs on using Fast User Switching, your open programs continue to run. For example, if you are in the process of downloading a file and you use Fast User Switching to switch user accounts, that activity will continue even though your desktop is hidden.

 Select the segment *Fast User Switching* in the PC Basics course.

Familiarizing Yourself with the Windows XP Desktop

The first thing you see after logging on to Windows XP is Windows XP's computing environment, known as the *desktop*. The desktop is so named because you use it in much the same way as you use the desk in your home or office: as a place to keep and access objects on which you are working. Just as you might have a clock, folders, documents, and work-related tools on your physical desk, you can find the same sorts of computer tools on your Windows desktop. Figure 2-9 shows the desktop with its default background, called *Gateway Box*. There are many other desktop backgrounds to choose from, and you can even supply your own! Refer to Chapter 7, "Customizing Windows XP," for more information on changing and customizing the desktop.

Figure 2-9 The Gateway desktop.

If your computer has a new installation of Windows XP (as opposed to an upgrade from a previous version of Windows), the first thing you notice is the clean, uncluttered look. In fact, the only things on your desktop are the Recycle Bin icon and the taskbar, which includes the start button and notification area.

 If you upgraded your computer to Windows XP from an older operating system, however, you will see the icons that were previously on your desktop.

The Recycle Bin

The *Recycle Bin* icon represents a temporary storage location for recently deleted files (see Figure 2-10). You use the Recycle Bin like the wastebasket beside your desk. If you throw away a paper document and decide later you should keep it, you can always pull it out

 of the wastebasket—until you empty your trash, that is. Likewise, if you delete a file, you can recover it from the Recycle Bin until you tell Windows to empty it. The Recycle Bin is the only icon on the desktop by default, and is located in the lower-right corner. For complete information on using the Recycle Bin, see Chapter 5.

Figure 2-10
The Recycle Bin.

The Taskbar and Start button

The *taskbar* (see Figure 2-11), located along the bottom edge of your screen, helps you keep track of all the programs and documents open on your computer. When you start a program or open a window, a button representing that program or window appears in the taskbar. These buttons, called *taskbar buttons*, make it easy to switch between open windows or programs; you simply click the button for a program or window in the taskbar to switch to it.

An important feature of the taskbar is the *start button,* which you click to open the *start menu.* From the start menu, you can start programs, find documents, configure your computer, and much more. Both the start menu and taskbar are customizable; you'll learn how to do that in Chapter 7.

Figure 2-11 The taskbar and start button.

Windows XP's start menu and taskbar look and behave differently from the ones in earlier versions of Windows. For example, the start menu keeps track of the programs you run most often, and displays those to you first. Also, the taskbar groups multiple documents that are open in the same application under one button; this keeps your taskbar neat and easy to read.

Another useful feature of the taskbar is the *notification area*, located on the far right side (see Figure 2-12). This area displays small icons that represent programs that are running, but that do not appear on your desktop, such as anti-virus software. The notification area also conveys information about various system conditions, such as when your notebook computer is running on battery power, when an update is available for your operating system from Microsoft, when you have received an e-mail message, and so on.

Figure 2-12 The notification area of the taskbar.

 After seven days of inactivity, icons in the notification area become hidden. When any icons are hidden, a white arrow in a blue circle appears on the left edge of the notification area. Click the arrow to reveal these hidden icons; click the arrow again to hide them.

The system clock appears to the right of the notification area, and displays the current time. Depending on your screen resolution and the way you customize your taskbar, the day and the date may also appear. If you don't see the day and date, move your mouse pointer over the clock and leave it there for about two seconds. A ToolTip appears that names the day of the week, the month, the date, and the year. If that information is incorrect, follow these steps to adjust it:

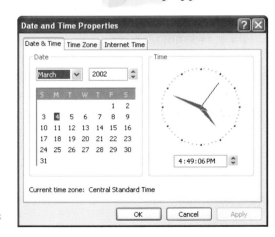

1 Double-click the current time in the notification area. The Date and Time Properties dialog box opens.
2 On the Date & Time tab, verify the correct date, month, year, time, and time zone and make any changes as necessary.
3 If you have made changes, click Apply.
4 Click OK. The Date and Time Properties dialog box closes and you are returned to the Windows XP desktop.

 Select the segment *Taskbar Features* in the PC Basics course..

If you don't want Windows XP to hide inactive items in the notification area, you can override that default behavior. Simply follow these steps:

1. Right-click a blank area in the notification area and then click Properties in the shortcut menu that appears. (If your taskbar is set to Auto-hide, simply move your mouse pointer to the area of the desktop where it's hiding, and it pops up.) The Taskbar and Start Menu Properties dialog box opens.

2. The bottom half of this dialog box contains options to customize the notification area. Click the Hide inactive icons check box to clear the check mark. This means inactive icons will no longer be hidden, and will therefore appear whether active or inactive.

3. If you click OK, you will apply your changes. For purposes of this book, click Cancel. The dialog box closes and you are returned to the Windows XP desktop.

Start Menu

Although it doesn't look like much—it's just a little green button on the taskbar with a four-color pane to the left and the word "start" to the right—the start button hides most of the Windows desktop controls. Click your mouse on the start button and presto! there's the start menu, as shown in Figure 2-13. From here, you can get to just about any Windows program or access key collections of Windows resources.

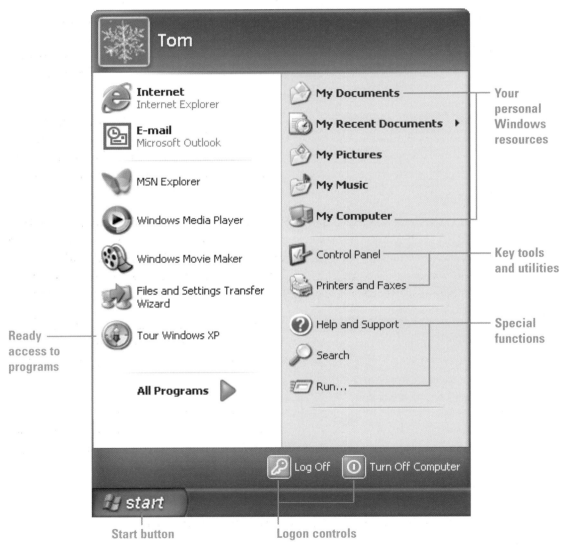

Figure 2-13 The start menu.

The labels on this figure cover much of what Windows XP can do:

- **Ready access to programs:** The left side of the start menu contains two lists of programs separated by a thin horizontal line. Above this line are programs that will always appear in that menu; below that line are the programs you've used most recently. Click entries in either list to start those programs quickly and easily.

- **Your personal Windows resources:** The top portion of the right side of the start menu includes pointers to your personal Windows resources. These include the contents of the My Documents folder (where many Windows applications save files by default), My Recent Documents (pointers to documents you've accessed recently), and My Computer (a view of your PC's files and storage devices). If you're on a network, you'll also see My Network Places (a list of network resources you've visited recently, with pointers to general network resources should you need them).

- **Key tools and utilities:** The middle portion of the right side of the start menu includes two key Windows tools and utilities. Control Panel provides access to most of Windows XP's controls and management tools. Printers and Faxes allows you to inspect any printer or fax you can use, and manages any files you might be trying to print or fax.

- **Special functions:** These include Help and Support, Search, and Run. Help and Support provides access to Internet-based information and assistance. The Search utility allows you to look for things on your PC, your network, or even on the Internet. The Run command lets you tell Windows to run a program or execute a single command, without having to open a command window.

- **Logon controls:** The Log Off and Turn Off Computer buttons permit you to log off from a user account, or to shut down or restart Windows. Turn Off is covered in more detail in the "Powering Down Your PC" section later in this chapter.

As you can probably tell, there's a lot going on behind the start menu. It's something you can't help but get to know well as you become more familiar with Windows XP. That also explains why we discuss it in more detail elsewhere in this book, most notably in Chapter 7.

 Select the segment *Start Menu Features* in the PC Basics course.

Learning About Your Mouse

Most mouse devices have two buttons, the *primary* and *secondary buttons,* with a small *wheel button* nestled between them. By default, the primary button is the one on the left, and the secondary button is the one on the right.

Moving Your Mouse Pointer

Using your mouse involves two basic actions: moving the mouse to correctly position your *mouse pointer* (a small, white, left-pointing arrow that appears somewhere on your screen) over an object, button, menu, or other screen item; and clicking either the primary or secondary button on your mouse in order to perform some sort of action. Before you can move your mouse to position the mouse pointer, however, you should learn the proper hand placement for controlling your mouse device. Gently place your pointer finger on the primary mouse button and your middle finger on the secondary mouse button. Figure 2-14 shows the correct hand placement.

Figure 2-14 Proper hand placement for controlling the common mouse.

For Lefties Only . . .

If you're left-handed, you may find that moving your mouse to the left-hand side of the keyboard is more comfortable. That way, you can use your left hand to maneuver the mouse. If you do, it's a good idea to reverse the mouse buttons, so that the right button becomes the primary button and the left button becomes the secondary button.

To change the orientation of the mouse from right-handed to left-handed, perform the following steps:

① Click start, and then click Control Panel.

② The Control Panel opens. Click Printers and Other Hardware.

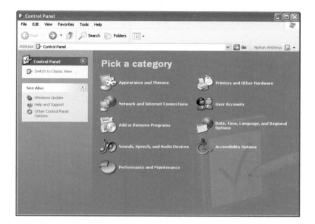

③ The Printers and Other Hardware screen appears. Click Mouse.

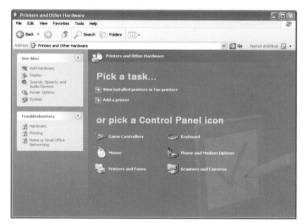

④ The Mouse Properties dialog box opens. Select the Switch primary and secondary buttons check box.

⑤ Click OK.

⑥ Click the Close button in the Printers and Other Hardware screen.

Once you've placed your hand on the mouse, simply slide the mouse across your mouse pad. The mouse pointer on the screen moves in the same direction as the mouse in your hand. If you hit the edge of your mouse pad or the extent of your reach, simply pick up the mouse, set it in the center of your mouse pad, and continue moving. As you become more experienced with the mouse, you'll find that you lift it often to reposition your hand for more comfortable operation.

The shape of the mouse pointer may change depending on what type of screen element it's resting on or, if you've clicked one of the mouse buttons, what action you've instructed your PC to perform. As shown in the following table, you might see any of the following *pointer images*

POINTER	DESCRIPTION
	An arrow is used to select objects.
	An I-beam (shaped like a capital "I") is used when editing documents to place the pointer where the next letters will be inserted, modified, or deleted. This is called the *insertion point*.
	A thin arrow with two heads or a set of crosshairs indicates that an object can be moved or resized.
	An hourglass indicates that some action is underway.
	An arrow with an hourglass indicates that although the PC is busy performing some task, you can continue to select objects and initiate other tasks.
	A pointing finger indicates the presence of a *hyperlink* on an Internet document or Web page. You can click a hyperlink to open a file or go to another page.

More About . . . Pointer Images

If you're not thrilled with the pointer images Windows uses by default, you can change them by selecting a different *pointer scheme.* For example, one pointer scheme uses pointer images that look like dinosaurs! You select an alternative pointer scheme using Control Panel.

Clicking

The most common mouse action is the *click.* To click, you position the pointer over an object on your screen. Then, without twitching the mouse, press and release the primary mouse button. When you click an object, it becomes highlighted; this indicates that the object is *selected.*

To get the hang of clicking, try the following:

1 Move the mouse pointer so it rests over the Recycle Bin icon on your desktop. After a moment, a ToolTip appears, informing you that the Recycle Bin contains files and folders you have deleted.

> **More About . . . ToolTips**
>
> If you're not certain what a particular object on your screen does, try resting your mouse pointer on it for a second or two. A ToolTip may appear, providing basic information about the object.

2 Click once on the Recycle Bin icon. Notice that the icon itself and the name under the icon become highlighted, as shown in Figure 2-15. This indicates that the object is selected. Any action you instigate using the mouse or keyboard will affect the selected object.

Figure 2-15 The Recycle Bin icon after it has been clicked.

3 Click anywhere on the desktop, but not on the Recycle Bin icon or the taskbar. (The *taskbar* is the long bar at the bottom of your screen.) Notice that the Recycle Bin icon is no longer highlighted, indicating that it is no longer selected.

④ Click the **start** button. The start menu appears, as shown in Figure 2-16.

Figure 2-16 The start menu.

⑤ Click anywhere on the desktop, and the start menu disappears.

Double-Clicking

Some objects require you to *double-click* the primary mouse button in order to initiate an activity. This action is similar to clicking, except you click the button twice, quickly, without moving the mouse.

 Beginners often unintentionally twitch the mouse between clicks. This puts the pointer in a different place for each click, which the computer interprets as two single-clicks. If the mouse pointer moves on the screen before or while you click, you might perform some action or issue some command you didn't intend.

To practice double-clicking, try the following:

① Double-click the **Recycle Bin** icon on the desktop. The Recycle Bin window opens.

② Click the **Close** button (the X in the upper-right corner) in the Recycle Bin window. The Recycle Bin window closes.

Dragging

Dragging, also called *clicking and dragging,* is a technique that enables you to move text, graphics, files, and objects of any kind on your screen. Simply position your mouse pointer on the object to be moved, press and hold down the primary mouse button, and slide the mouse. Depending on what type of object you're dragging, either the object will move across the screen or the mouse pointer will change into an arrow with a box below it to indicate an object in motion. When the object reaches its destination, release the primary mouse button to place, or *drop,* the object in that location.

 Dragging also enables you to resize windows, extend selections, and more.

Work through the following steps to practice dragging objects:

1. Position the mouse pointer over the Recycle Bin icon.
2. Press and hold down the primary mouse button.
3. Move the mouse. Notice that the Recycle Bin icon moves with the mouse pointer.
4. Position the Recycle Bin icon in the upper-right corner of the desktop, as shown in Figure 2-17.
5. Release the mouse button.
6. Repeat steps 1 through 5 to return the Recycle Bin icon to its original location.

Figure 2-17 Moving an object using click and drag.

Use your ability to move objects with care. You can safely move any document or file you create, such as a word-processing document or a photo. You can even move objects around within a document, such as repositioning a picture in a greeting card. Moving system and software files from their original folders, however, can cause problems because the system may not know how to find them once they've been moved. As with real estate, location is crucial for these files!

If you try to move a desktop icon and it does not move, the Auto Arrange feature is probably enabled. Auto Arrange automatically arranges all desktop icons in columns and rows starting at the upper-left corner of the screen. To disable this feature so you can move objects around the desktop, right-click over an empty area on the desktop. In the shortcut menu that appears, select Arrange Icons By, and then click Auto Arrange. If the Auto Arrange check box is selected, the feature was enabled. Clear the check box to disable the feature.

Selecting Objects

You know that you can select an object on your screen by clicking it. But what if you want to perform the same action on multiple objects, such as moving several icons from one part of your desktop to another? Rather than dragging each icon to the new location one-by-one, you can select all the icons you want to move and drag them to the destination, all at the same time.

To select multiple objects, place the mouse pointer near the set of objects you want to select. Then, press and hold down the primary mouse button and drag the mouse pointer across the objects to be selected. A shaded box appears, with one corner located where you first clicked the mouse button and the opposite corner located at your current mouse-pointer position. As you enclose objects within this box, they become highlighted, indicating that they have been selected (see Figure 2-18). When all the necessary objects are selected, release the primary mouse button, and perform the desired action using your mouse or keyboard.

Figure 2-18 A click-and-drag selection action performed within Windows Explorer.

Let's practice selecting multiple objects:

1 Click start, and then click My Computer.

2 The My Computer window opens. Place your pointer to the left of the bottom row of icons.

3 Press and hold down the primary mouse button.

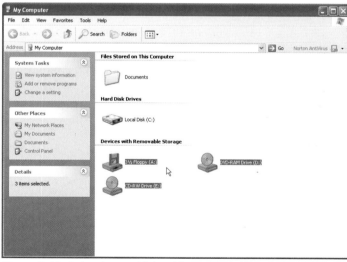

Figure 2-19 Selecting multiple objects with click and drag.

4 Move the mouse pointer toward the upper-left portion of the window. Notice how objects become selected as you drag the selection box over them, as shown in Figure 2-19.

5. When you've selected a few of the objects, release the mouse button.
6. Once objects are selected, you can perform an action, such as opening, copying, or exploring all selected objects at once. At this time, however, refrain from performing any of these actions. Instead, close the My Computer window by clicking the Close button.

Right-Clicking

Although the secondary mouse button is used less frequently than the primary button, it has several interesting tricks up its sleeve. If you click the secondary button once (this is called *right-clicking*), a shortcut menu appears. A *shortcut menu* is a menu that is context or content sensitive; that is, the object or objects under the mouse pointer determine the commands that appear in the menu. You can also use the secondary mouse button to drag selected objects to a new location and then select a command from a shortcut menu.

To get a handle on right-clicking, do the following:
1. Right-click an empty area of the desktop.
2. A shortcut menu appears. Click the primary mouse button anywhere else on the desktop.
3. The menu disappears. Click start, and then click My Computer.
4. The My Computer window opens. Double-click Local Disk C:.
5. The contents of drive C: are displayed. Right-click any file and hold down the mouse button.
6. Drag your pointer to an empty area in the window and release the button.
7. A shortcut menu appears, as shown in Figure 2-20. Notice the commands that appear in the shortcut menu.

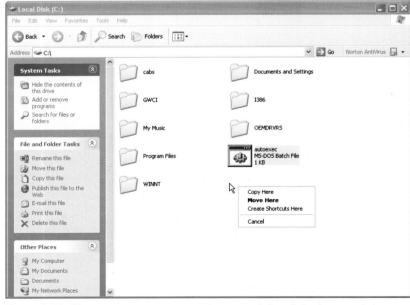

Figure 2-20 Shortcut menus appear when you right-click, drag, and drop.

⑧ At this time, do not select any of the commands. Instead, move your pointer to an empty area and click the primary mouse button. The shortcut menu closes, and action stops.

⑨ Click the **Close** button in the My Computer window to close it.

Using the Wheel Button

When a window isn't big enough to display the entire contents of a document or page, vertical and/or horizontal *scroll bars* appear (see Figure 2-21). These allow you to scroll up and down or left and right through the page or document so you can view all its contents. To use the scroll bars, you simply click on one of the arrows on either end of the scroll bar, or drag the *scroll box* (the small box that appears in the scroll bar) in the direction you want to scroll.

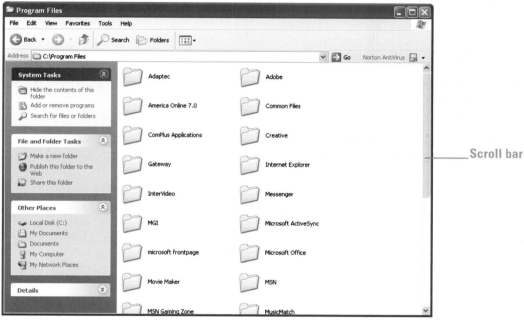

Scroll bar

Figure 2-21 A window with a scrollbar.

Alternatively, you can use the wheel button on your mouse to scroll through your document. This button is multi-functional—it can be either rotated or clicked. Typically, rotating the wheel allows you to scroll up and down through the text or graphics in a window to view all its contents. Pressing the wheel until it clicks, on the other hand, locks your mouse into scroll mode; in this mode, the mouse pointer changes to a two-headed arrow inside a circle, as shown in Figure 2-22. When in scroll mode, you can simply move your mouse to quickly scroll up and down in a window. (Click the wheel again to turn scroll mode off.)

Figure 2-22 The scroll-mode mouse pointer.

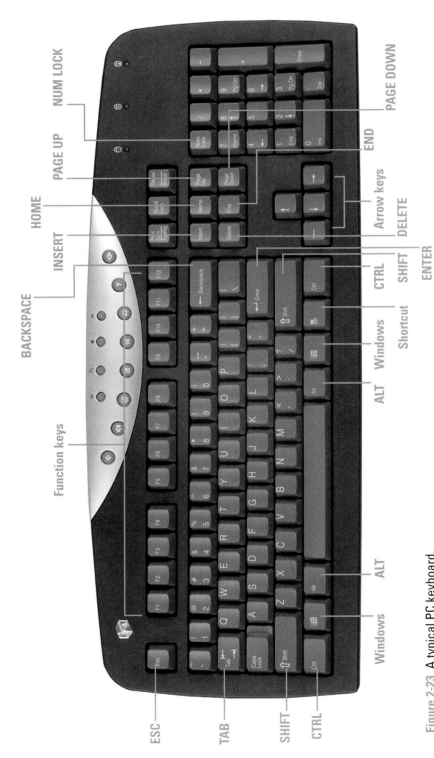

Figure 2-23 A typical PC keyboard.

Working with Your Keyboard

If you've ever used a typewriter, then your PC's keyboard should look somewhat familiar. As shown in Figure 2-23, computer keyboards, like typewriters, contain keys that enable you to input letters, numbers, and symbols. In fact, the layout of the letters, numbers, and symbols on your PC's keyboard mirrors that of typewriters of old.

You may notice, however, that your keyboard contains several keys not found on traditional typewriters. These additional keys, whose functions are described in Table 2-1, enable you to use your keyboard to issue commands and control many aspects of your PC's activity.

Table 2-1 Common keys and their uses.

KEY	USE
ALT and CTRL	The ALT and CTRL keys are sometimes used in combination with each other and the SHIFT key to send special commands to your PC.
SHIFT	Press the SHIFT key in combination with a letter key to enter uppercase letters.
Arrow keys	Press the arrow keys to move the insertion point within a document or move the selection highlight from one option or command to another within a menu or a dialog box.
Windows and Shortcut	Press the Windows key to open the start menu, or press the Shortcut key to open a shortcut menu based on the pointer's location.
ESC	Press the ESC key to exit the current menu, dialog box, or window. In some cases, it closes an program, but not always.
Function keys	The function keys are those keys marked F1, F2, and so on, through F12. The F1 key usually opens help information. Programs often assign special features or commands to function keys; to learn how a particular program uses these keys, read its documentation.
BACKSPACE	Press the BACKSPACE key to delete the character immediately to the left of the insertion point, to delete selected object(s), or to move backward in a wizard or dialog box.
ENTER	Press the ENTER key to start a new paragraph when working within a document. It can also be used to execute a selected command within a menu or dialog box.
INSERT	Press the INSERT key to toggle text-editing modes from overwrite to insert mode. The default setting is insert mode. In insert mode, keystrokes you type are added into a document, shifting the existing text to make room. In overwrite mode, for every key you press, a character to the right of the insertion point is deleted.

Key	Use
DELETE	Press the DELETE key to delete the character immediately to the right of the insertion point or to delete selected object(s).
HOME and END	Press the HOME key to move the insertion point to the beginning of the current line within a document, or CTRL+HOME to move the insertion point to the beginning of the document. Pressing the END key moves the insertion point to the end of the current line, while pressing CTRL+END moves the insertion point to the end of the document.
PAGE UP and PAGE DOWN	Press the PAGE UP and PAGE DOWN keys to scroll up or down within a document or window, one page at a time.
NUM LOCK	Many keyboards include a numeric keypad on the far right side; this keypad works like a standard accounting 10-key pad and is great for entering numeric data. To enable the numeric keypad and illuminate the Num Lock indicator light on the keyboard, press the NUM LOCK key. If the numeric keypad is already enabled, press the NUM LOCK key to disable it; when the keypad is disabled, you can use its keys as arrow keys as well as PAGE UP, PAGE DOWN, END, HOME, INSERT and DELETE keys.

There are many other features and functions for a keyboard, which typically rely on multi-key combinations discussed throughout this book to enter commands. Make yourself familiar with the layout and the keys available on your keyboard to help you get the most out of your PC.

More About . . . Keyboards

Some PCs come equipped with multifunction keyboards. Multifunction keyboards provide additional capabilities. Such added capabilities take the form of additional keys or buttons that speed access to programs or places you visit or use most often. With a push of a button, you can jump to the Internet, open e-mail, play a CD, open the Help system, or launch a word processor. Some keyboards offer CD and DVD controls so you can play, pause, stop, skip forward or back, or adjust the volume while listening to music or watching your favorite movies. Often you can program extra buttons to perform customized tasks or activities. Some keyboards incorporate track balls or touch pads, so you won't even need a separate mouse.

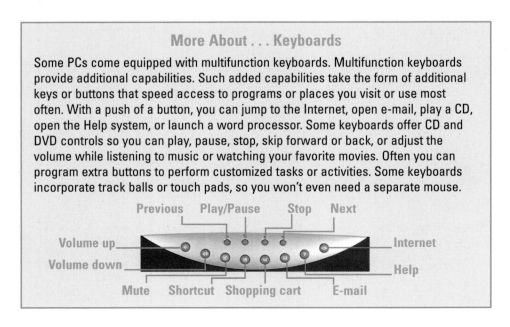

Browsing Your Computer

In general terms, the word *browse* means to look through casually, in search of something of interest. When you browse your computer, you are probably looking to see what is stored there, perhaps searching for a specific document or program.

Browsing in My Computer

To browse your computer using the My Computer window, perform the following:

1. Click the start button and click My Computer in the start menu. The My Computer window opens. You'll see a file folder for every account created on your computer and for each of your disk drives. You'll also see all the removable storage devices in your computer (a floppy drive, for example). On the left of the screen are several sections, giving you the ability to perform system tasks, browse other places, and get details on everything in the window.

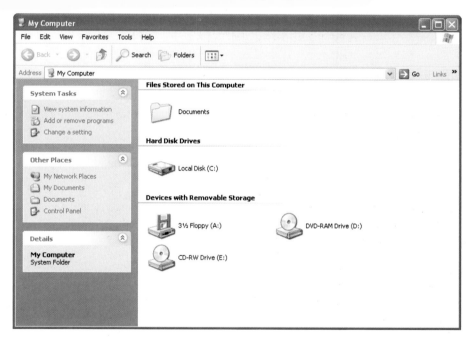

2. Click a drive letter. The details section displays how this drive is formatted, the amount of free space available on the drive, and the total size of the drive.

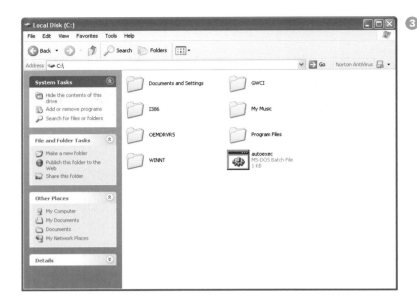

3 To view the contents of a drive, simply double-click it. The screen displays the folders and files stored on that drive. Notice, too, that the left side of the screen has changed, now listing File and Folder tasks.

4 Click a folder. The list in this section expands with more options, enabling you to rename, move, copy, or delete this folder.

 Files or folders that appear lighter in color, as if they are behind frosted glass, are used by the Windows XP operating system and should not be manually modified in any way!

⑤ Double-click a folder to see what is inside. Again, the File and Folder tasks section may change, depending on what is in the folder you choose.

⑥ To return to where you started, click the Back button in the button bar of this window. Each click of this button will take you back one step.

⑦ The graphics you are viewing (the bright yellow file folder and the picture of a hard disk) are called tiles. There are four other views, or ways to view the information displayed. Click the Views button (on the far right of the button bar) and experiment with all five.

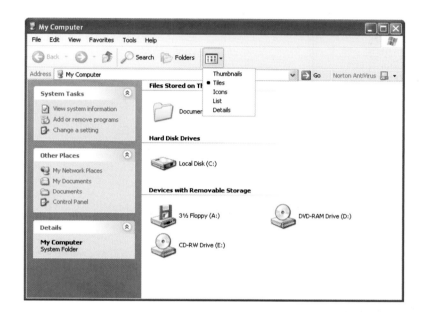

⑧ Click the Close button (the X in the upper-right corner) to close the My Computer window and return to the desktop.

Browsing with Explore

Another way to browse a computer is to *explore* it. To do so, click the start button, right-click My Computer, and then click Explore. The left pane in this screen looks different,

as shown in Figure 2-24. On the left side of the My Computer window you see a view of the desktop, organized as a collection of folders, storage devices, My Network Places, and the Recycle Bin. But the right pane is identical, listing Files Stored on this Computer (Shared Documents), Hard Disk Drives (with a drive icon and letter for each such drive installed on your PC), and Devices with Removable Storage (with a drive icon for each removable media drive on your PC, including floppy, DVD, CD, removable disk drives, and so on).

Figure 2-24 The My Computer window accessed using the Explore command.

Powering Down Your PC

When you're finished using your PC and want to turn it off, perform a shutdown. A *shutdown* is the process whereby Windows XP saves important data still resident in memory, closes the desktop and the operating system, and then powers off the PC. Shutdown is a graceful process designed to prevent damage to your PC and to avoid data loss.

 Never press the power button on your PC without performing a shutdown first; otherwise, any data stored in memory not yet saved to disk will be lost. Plus, hard drives and other devices can be damaged if they lose power while operating. The shutdown process informs all components and attached peripherals that the PC is about to be turned off, and instructs them to prepare for that event safely.

To shut down your PC, click the start button, and then click Turn Off Computer.

The Turn off computer dialog box opens, as shown in Figure 2-25.

Notice that there are several buttons in this dialog box:

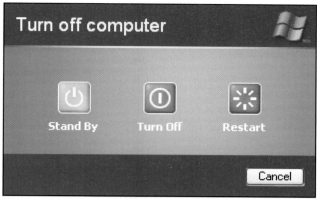

Figure 2-25 The Turn off computer dialog box.

+ **Turn Off.** Click this button to save important data, close the operating system, and power down the PC.

 Some PCs automatically turn off their own power, whereas others display a screen informing you that it's safe to turn off your power.

+ **Restart.** Click this button to restart the PC without losing power. This option is handy when you want to restart the system so it can load new drivers or use a new configuration setting.

+ **Stand By.** If standby is enabled, the left button is labeled "Stand By." Click the Stand By button to send the PC into standby mode. *Standby* saves your desktop and system state to memory, then puts the system into a low-power operating state without actually turning the PC off. The next time you press the power button or another key, you return to your desktop exactly as you left it.

+ **Hibernate.** If standby is not enabled, the left button is labeled "Hibernate." Click this button to send the PC into hibernate mode. *Hibernation* saves your desktop and system state to the hard drive, and then turns off the PC. The next time you power up your PC, you return to your desktop exactly as it was before.

 Press and hold the SHIFT key to change the Stand By button to Hibernate.

+ **Cancel.** Click this button to cancel the shutdown process and return to the desktop.

In addition to turning off your computer, you can also log off by clicking the start menu and clicking the Log Off button in the Log Off Windows dialog box. The logoff process closes your desktop and returns you to the logon screen. Logging off is especially useful if multiple people use your PC; doing so gives the next user quick access to the logon screen. Logging off also prevents others from easily accessing your personal data.

Emergency Shutdown

Performing a graceful shutdown is preferred over any other shutdown process—this allows the PC to save its data and turn itself off. That said, you may not always get the opportunity to perform a graceful shutdown. If your system hangs, freezes, or otherwise becomes unresponsive, your options for a graceful shutdown may be limited or non-existent.

In the event your system becomes frozen, the first thing you should do is press the CTRL+ALT+DEL key combination. This starts Windows Task Manager. In Windows Task Manager, click the Shut Down menu, and then select one of the shutdown options (Standby, Hibernate, Turn Off, Restart, Log Off, or Switch User), as shown in Figure 2-26.

If you are unable to open the Task Manager or access the Shut Down menu, wait about 10 minutes. In some cases, a frozen system returns to a functioning state if left alone for a while. As a last resort, press the power button on the system unit. You may have to hold the button in for several seconds before the power is cut off. After the power goes off, wait a few moments before turning the power back on to restart your PC. During the reboot, the PC may perform additional checks make sure the system is working properly.

Figure 2-26 The Shut Down menu in Windows Task Manager.

Go online to www.LearnwithGateway.com and log on to select:

✦ *Windows XP: Logging On* in the PC Basics course
✦ *User Account Setup* in the PC Basics course
✦ *Fast User Switching* in the PC Basics course
✦ *Taskbar Features* in the PC Basics course
✦ *Start Menu Features* in the PC Basics course
✦ *Internet Links and Resources*
✦ *FAQs*

Gateway offers hands-on training courses that cover many of the topics in this chapter. Additional fees may apply. Call 888-852-4821 to enroll. Please have your customer ID and order number ready when you call.

2

Working With Windows XP And Its Programs

A *program*, sometimes called an application, is a piece of software designed to work with your PC's operating system to perform one or more tasks and manage various types of information (text, numbers, images, etc.). For example, any time you read your e-mail, surf the Internet, play a computer game, or edit your digital photographs, you are using a program to complete that task.

Windows XP and many programs supported by Windows XP use a common set of tools including windows, dialog boxes, and wizards to display information and solicit input; each tool has its own unique components and controls. To get the most out of your PC, you'll need to learn how to use these tools, as well as how to start and exit programs and use multiple programs simultaneously.

Discovering the Programs on Your PC

Windows XP is more than an operating system; it also includes several useful programs. Windows XP includes the following programs by default (see Figure 3-1).

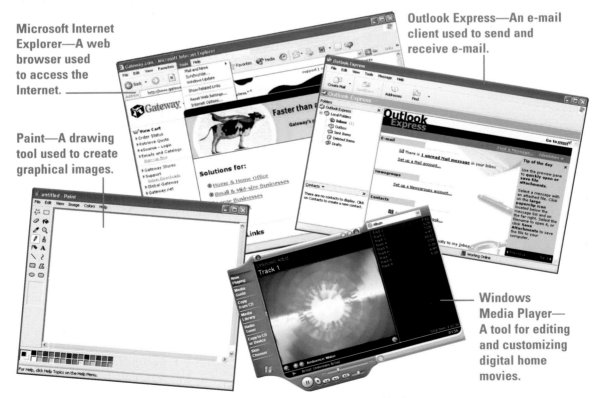

Microsoft Internet Explorer—A web browser used to access the Internet.

Outlook Express—An e-mail client used to send and receive e-mail.

Paint—A drawing tool used to create graphical images.

Windows Media Player—A tool for editing and customizing digital home movies.

Figure 3-1 Windows XP includes loads of built-in programs of many kinds.

Your Gateway PC includes several pre-installed *third-party programs*. A third-party program is any program that is not included in the operating system. This includes programs by Microsoft as well as other software companies. Some examples of third-party programs you may find pre-installed on your system include games, anti-virus software, Microsoft Office (a suite of productivity software), photo-editing tools, system-management utilities, and custom configuration tools. And of course, you can always purchase and install additional programs you may need on your PC.

 This book introduces you to the basics of launching and interacting with Windows-based programs. It does not explore all of the various programs that came pre-installed on your computer. Fortunately, most software includes documentation, which you can read to get up to speed.

To determine which programs are installed on your computer, click the start button, point to **All Programs**, and browse the entries in this menu.

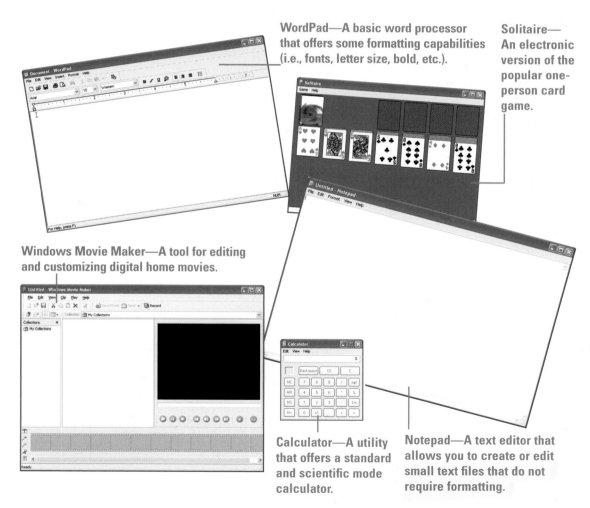

WordPad—A basic word processor that offers some formatting capabilities (i.e., fonts, letter size, bold, etc.).

Solitaire—An electronic version of the popular one-person card game.

Windows Movie Maker—A tool for editing and customizing digital home movies.

Calculator—A utility that offers a standard and scientific mode calculator.

Notepad—A text editor that allows you to create or edit small text files that do not require formatting.

Starting a Program

Before you can work with a program, you must first start it. To start a program, click its icon in the start menu. If the program is represented by an icon on the desktop, however, you can double-click the icon to start the program.

To get the hang of starting a program, let's start WordPad.

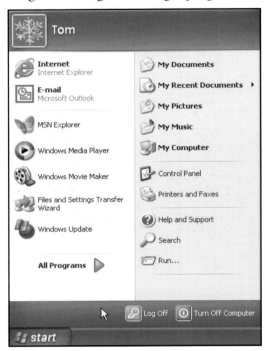

1 Click the **start** button. The start menu appears.

2 Position your mouse pointer over **All Programs** to view the first sublevel of the start menu.

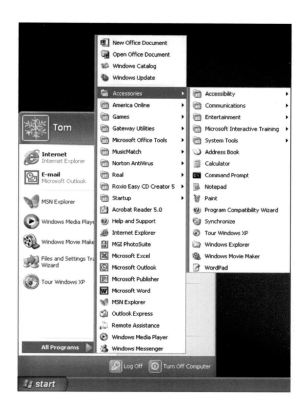

③ Position your mouse pointer over the **Accessories** folder. The Accessories sublevel of the start menu appears.

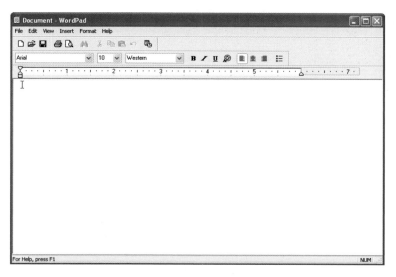

④ Click **WordPad**. The WordPad program starts, and the WordPad window opens.

Now that WordPad is open, let's explore some common elements and controls of Windows programs.

Discovering a Window

Windows XP gets its name from its use of windows to display programs, files, information, and system settings. A *window* is a rectangular area displayed on your desktop that contains numerous common elements, such as a workspace, toolbars, a menu bar, and other standard controls. Almost every Windows-based program uses a window as its primary interface.

Figure 3-2 shows the window of a common Windows XP program, namely WordPad. As you can see, a thin blue border defines the edges of the WordPad window, clearly separating it from the underlying desktop.

As shown in Figure 3-2, even the simplest window has many components.

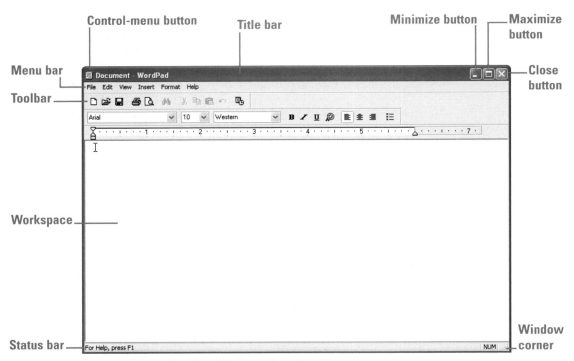

Figure 3-2 WordPad is a Windows-based program.

The Title Bar

Every window has a *title bar*, which displays the name of the program. When the window contains an open file, the title bar also displays that file's name. (The default name of new, unsaved documents is usually "Document.") In most cases, the name of the file appears first, and the name of the program appears second. The title bar shown in Figure 3-3 displays a file name of "Document" and the program name "WordPad."

Figure 3-3 WordPad's title bar.

The title bar also includes the Minimize, Maximize/Restore Down, and Close buttons, as well as the control-menu button; all these are discussed in the sections that follow.

Moving Windows

Because Windows XP allows you to work with multiple windows, as discussed later in this chapter, at some point, you'll need to move an open window on your desktop. It could be to reveal the contents of another window or to access something on the desktop. To move a window, position the mouse pointer on the window's title bar, press and hold the mouse's primary button (avoid clicking title-bar buttons or the top edge of the window—you might issue some other command or perform a different action than intended), and drag the window to the desired location. When you release the mouse button, the window becomes set in its new position.

To practice moving a window, perform these steps:

1. Position the mouse pointer on a window's title bar.
2. Press and hold down the primary mouse button.
3. Move the mouse around to move the window.
4. Once the window is in the desired spot, release the mouse button.

The Minimize Button

Notice the three buttons on the right end of the title bar. The first of these buttons is the Minimize button. Click this button to minimize, or hide, the program window, thus

Minimize button

freeing up space on your desktop, without shutting down the program. When you minimize a window, the program remains open and running, but occupies no space on the desktop.

You might minimize a window in the following situations. You're finished working in a window for the time being, but may need to view it later. Instead of closing it, you can simply hide it. Or maybe you need to view the desktop or another window located behind the one that's currently open.

Notice that when a window is minimized, its taskbar button appears to be raised. To restore a minimized window to its previous size, simply click its taskbar button. Once the window is again displayed in the foreground, its taskbar button appears pushed in.

To learn how to use the Minimize button, work through the following steps:

1. If WordPad is not already running, start it. (Click the **start** button, point to **All Programs**, point to **Accessories**, and then click **WordPad**.) The WordPad window opens.
2. Click the **Minimize** button on the WordPad title bar. The WordPad window disappears, and the WordPad taskbar button appears raised.
3. Click the **WordPad** taskbar button. The WordPad window reappears, and the WordPad taskbar button appears pressed.

WordPad taskbar button

The Maximize/Restore Down Button

Maximize button

If the window covers only a portion of the desktop, you can maximize it to completely fill the screen. To maximize a window, click the Maximize button, located immediately to the right of the Minimize button.

Why maximize? You want the largest workspace possible—for example, if you are working on a long document and want to be able to see as much of it as possible at once. Or you want to hide other windows or the desktop itself.

 As a shortcut, double-click any blank area of the title bar to maximize its window.

When a window is maximized, the Restore Down button restores the maximized window to its original size.

Restore Down button

You might restore a window for various reasons. You may want to return a window to its original size. You can reduce the size of the window to view more than one window at a time. If you want to move a window, it needs to be restored. Maximized windows cannot be moved. See the "Moving Windows" sidebar that appeared earlier in this chapter.

Let's practice using the Maximize/Restore Down button.

1 If WordPad is not already running, start it. (Click the **start** button, point to **All Programs**, point to **Accessories**, and then click **WordPad**.) The WordPad window opens.

2 Click the **Maximize** button on the WordPad title bar. The WordPad window expands to fill the screen.

3 Click the **Restore Down** button on the WordPad title bar. The WordPad window returns to its pre-maximized size.

Close button

The Close Button

Click the Close button, the button on the far right of the title bar, to close the program window and thus exit the program. If the program window contains a document that you have not yet saved, most programs will prompt you to save it before exiting.

You might need to close a window in numerous instances. For instance, you're finished using the window and want to exit the program, or the program is causing your system to run slower than normal.

Let's practice using the Close button. Do the following:

1 If WordPad is not already running, start it. (Click the **start** button, point to **All Programs**, point to **Accessories**, and then click **WordPad**.) The WordPad window opens.

2 Click the **Close** button on the WordPad title bar. The WordPad program stops running, the WordPad window closes, and the WordPad taskbar button disappears.

The Control-Menu Button

On the far-left side of the title bar is the control-menu button. As shown in Figure 3-4, you can click this button to open a menu of window commands, called the *control menu*.

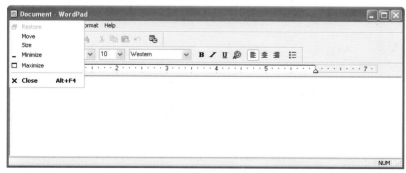

Figure 3-4 WordPad's control menu.

You can also access the control menu by right-clicking a program's taskbar button.

In most programs, the control menu contains six commands, as shown in Table 3-1.

Table 3-1 Control-menu commands.

COMMAND	DESCRIPTION
Restore	Selecting this command is the same as clicking the Restore Down button on the title bar.
Move	Select this command to move the current window around on the desktop. For more information about moving windows, refer to the section "The Title Bar" earlier in this chapter.
Size	Select this command to resize the window. You'll learn about resizing windows in the section "The Window Corner" later in this chapter.
Minimize	Selecting this command is the same as clicking the Minimize button on the taskbar.
Maximize	Selecting this command is the same as clicking the Maximize button on the taskbar when the window is not maximized.
Close	Selecting this command is the same as clicking the Close button on the taskbar.

 As with all Windows menus, commands that appear "dimmed" cannot be selected. For example, in Figure 3-4, the Restore command is dimmed because the window is not maximized. If the window were maximized, then the Restore command would be available, and the Maximize command would not.

The Menu Bar

Most windows include a *menu bar*, which appears just below the title bar. The menu bar contains a list of words or names, called *menu names*.

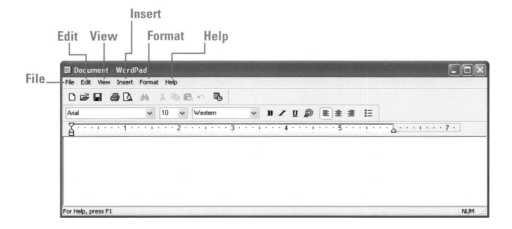

Click a menu name to reveal its program- or document-specific command menu (see Figure 3-5). Once the menu is open, move the mouse pointer to highlight the command you want; when the command is highlighted, click the primary mouse button to execute the command.

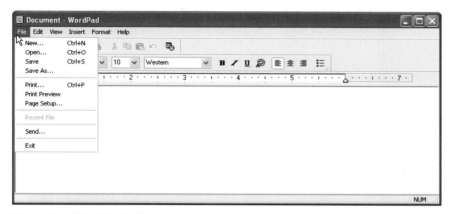

Figure 3-5 WordPad's File menu.

If you decide you don't want to execute a command, and instead want to close the open menu, do any of the following:

✦ Click the menu name a second time.

✦ Click anywhere in the program window or desktop outside of the menu area.

✦ Press the **ESC** key on your keyboard.

 If you click one menu name, but want to see the contents of another, reposition the mouse pointer over the second name. Doing so closes the first menu and opens the second.

Highlighting certain commands opens a submenu; when a submenu is present, an arrow appears beside the command. You select and execute submenu commands just as you do the commands on the main menus.

Toolbars

Many windows have *toolbars*, which appear below the menu bar but above the workspace. You click the buttons located on the toolbar to access common functions or perform common tasks. (In most windows, every toolbar button represents a command found in the menu bar.) Some toolbar buttons have commands or selections hidden within a drop-down list. Click the down arrow that appears right beside the toolbar button to access this list.

Toolbar buttons usually include a picture that represents the button's associated command. Even so, it is sometimes difficult to determine a button's function just by looking at it. To find out what command or function is associated with a particular button, position your mouse pointer over that button. After a moment, a ToolTip appears, explaining the button's

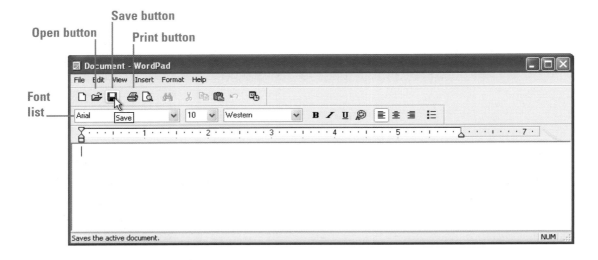

In addition to toolbar buttons, many toolbars feature drop-down combo boxes. For example, WordPad's toolbar contains drop-down combo boxes that enable you to set the font and point size of text in the WordPad document. To use a drop-down combo box, you can either type your selection in the text box or click the down-arrow to the right of the text box and click one of the options that appears. (You'll learn more about drop-down combo boxes in the section "Understanding Dialog Boxes" later in this chapter.)

 Some drop-down combo boxes contain lists that are so long they contain a scroll bar. Drag the scroll box up and down the scroll bar to locate the option you want.

The Status Bar

Many windows feature a status bar, typically located along the window's bottom edge. The status bar displays window-specific information and messages. In WordPad, for example, the status bar displays the messages "For Help, press F1" and "NUM," as shown in Figure 3-6. (The first message indicates how you can receive help with the program, and the second indicates that the NUM LOCK key is toggled on.) The status bar in Windows Explorer, on the other hand, displays details about selected items. For example, when a drive is selected, the status bar displays its total free space; when a file is selected, the status bar displays details such as the file's type and size and the date it was last modified.

Figure 3-6 WordPad's status bar.

 In some programs, the status bar displays information about a toolbar button when you position your mouse pointer over the button.

The Workspace

The *workspace* is the area between the toolbars and the status bar. In many windows, the workspace acts like a piece of paper. For example, in WordPad, the workspace is where the words you type appear. Likewise, in Paint, the workspace is where you "draw" and interact with your designs. In other programs, however, the workspace acts more like an interface. That is, you interact with the workspace by clicking buttons, choosing options from drop-down lists, and so on to complete a task. For example, the workspace in Calculator consists of the series of buttons you click to enter equations into the text box.

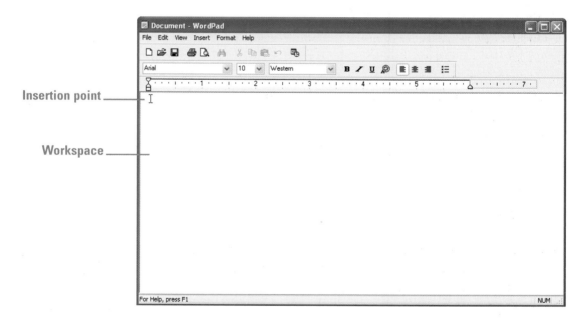

Insertion point

Workspace

The Window Corner

As you work with windows, you may encounter instances when you need your window to be larger or smaller. Of course, one way to resize your window is to click the Restore Down button in the title bar (refer to the section "The Maximize/Restore Down Button" earlier in this chapter). Alternatively, however, you can use the window corner for more precise control. Located in the lower-right corner of the program window, the window corner enables you to alter both the height and the width of the window at the same time.

To resize a window using the window corner, perform the following steps:

1. Position your mouse pointer over the window corner, making sure the tip of the pointer is just inside the window border. The mouse pointer changes to a diagonal two-headed arrow.

— The Sizing handle

2. Press and hold down the primary mouse button.
3. Drag your mouse slowly in any direction. Notice how the window size changes based on how you move the mouse.
4. Move the mouse so that the window is larger than it was before you started this exercise.
5. Release the mouse button.
6. Repeat steps 1 through 5, but this time move the mouse so that the window is smaller than it was before you started.
7. Release the mouse button.

All four corners of a window function just like the window corner. Simply position your mouse pointer over any corner, making sure the tip of the pointer is just inside the window border; the mouse pointer changes to a diagonal two-headed arrow. Then click and drag the mouse to resize the window.

 If you wish to resize the width but not the height of your window, position your mouse pointer on either side of the window border, click, and drag. Likewise, to resize the height only, place the pointer on the top or bottom window border, click, and drag.

Understanding Dialog Boxes

A *dialog box* is another item you'll frequently encounter. Dialog boxes appear when Windows XP needs more information to perform an operation or when it wants to confirm an operation. They often appear as a result of selecting certain menu commands. Dialog boxes let you tell the computer what you want it to do.

Although you may encounter any number of different dialog boxes while using your PC, all dialog boxes utilize pieces of a basic set of elements to gather information from you. For example, many dialog boxes use tabs (see Figure 3-7). A dialog box with tabs operates

like a dictionary with tabs; you select a tab to display its contents, just as you turn to a tabbed page in a dictionary to view words that begin with the letter on the tab. Some dialog boxes only use a single tab, whereas others may have many. Some dialog boxes, on the other hand, don't use tabs at all (see Figure 3-8).

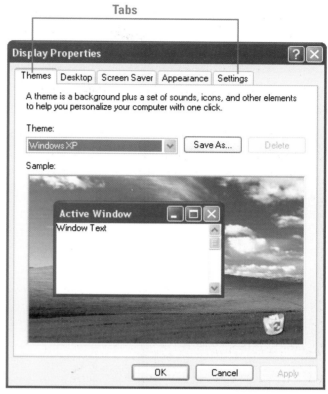

Figure 3-7 A dialog box with tabs.

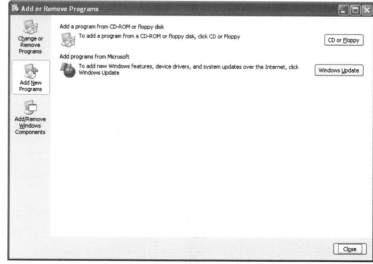

Figure 3-8 A dialog box without tabs.

Other elements commonly found in dialog boxes include:

◆ **Option buttons.** You use option buttons to select only one item from a list of options. If you attempt to select a second option button, the one selected first becomes deselected. To select an option button, simply click it; when an option button is selected, a dot appears inside it.

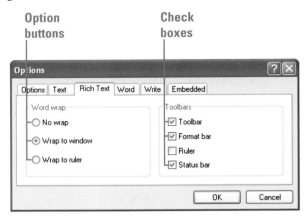

◆ **Check boxes.** Check boxes are used in lists of options in which more than one option can be selected, or when a single option can be turned on or off. To select a check box, click it; when a check box is selected, a small check mark appears inside it. To deselect a box, simply click it to remove the check mark.

◆ **Object-selection fields.** An object-selection field is an area that lists one or more options. In most cases, you can select only a single item at a time; the selected item is highlighted.

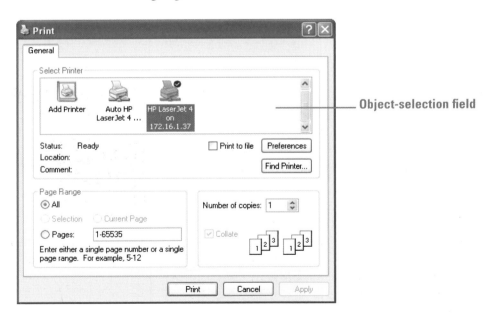

✦ **List boxes.** List boxes contain a list of options from which the user can select. Some list boxes contain lists that are so long they contain a scroll bar; drag the scroll box up and down the scroll bar to locate the option you

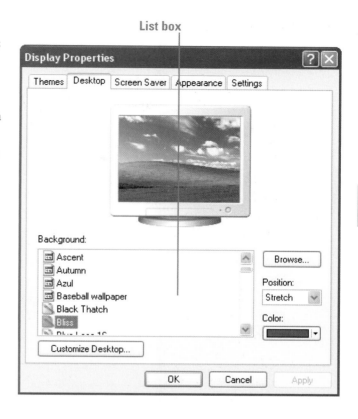

List box

✦ **Drop-down list boxes.** Drop-down list boxes work in the same way as regular list boxes, in that they contain a list of options from which the user can select. In order to view the list of options in a drop-down list, however, you must first click the drop-down arrow button that accompanies it. Some drop-down list boxes contain lists that are so long they contain a scroll bar; drag the scroll box up and down the scroll bar to locate the option you want.

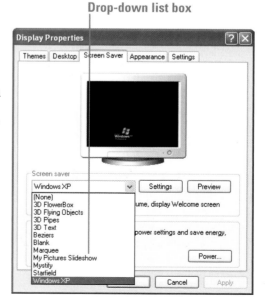

Drop-down list box

✦ **Text boxes.** A text box is a box in which you can enter data, such as a file name or a range of pages, using your keyboard. In some instances, an option button or a check box accompanies text boxes. In such cases, the text field is available for use only if the option button or check box is selected.

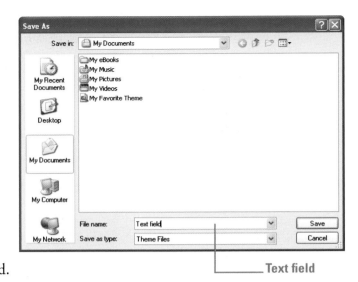

Text field

Combo box

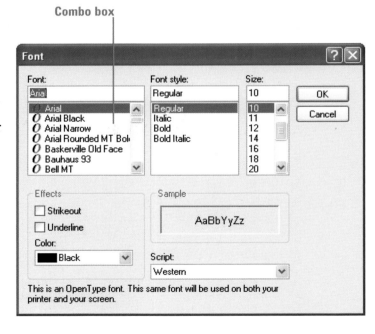

✦ **Combo boxes.** These elements enable you to either type your selection in the text box or select it from the accompanying list box (hence the name combo box).

✦ **Drop-down combo boxes.** With a drop-down combo box, you can either type your selection in the text box or select it from the accompanying drop-down list box.

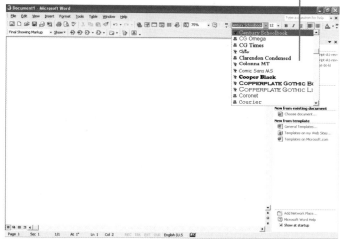

Drop-down combo box

✦ **Spin boxes.** You use a spin box to input a numerical value. For example, in WordPad's Print dialog box, you use a spin box to specify how many copies of your document should be printed. To use a spin box, click the up- or down-arrow button to increase or decrease the displayed number by 1. Alternatively, instead of using the spin box's arrow buttons, you can simply type the desired number in the spin box's field.

✦ **Buttons.** Buttons are common in dialog boxes. You click them to execute a command or apply whatever settings you've selected in the dialog box.

Common buttons include Close, Cancel, Apply, Print, Open, and Save; in most cases, the name or description on the button defines what that button does.

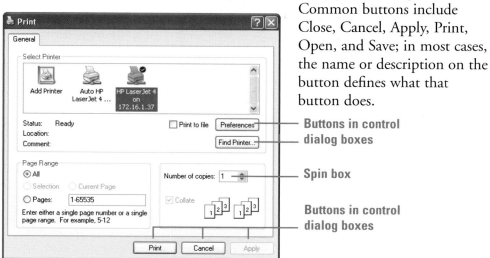

Buttons in control dialog boxes

Spin box

Buttons in control dialog boxes

Go online to **www.LearnwithGateway.com** and log on to select: *Dialog Boxes* in the PC Basics course.

Using Wizards

A *wizard* is similar to a dialog box, in that it presents you with a series of options from which you must choose. But unlike a dialog box, which presents you with all the available controls, options, and selections at once or on multiple tabbed screens, a wizard presents them to you one at a time, in a specific order.

Wizards appear most often—and not by magic—when you initiate a system-configuration change or some other complex activity. In fact, you already encountered a wizard when you stepped through the Windows XP setup process.

You navigate a wizard using the three buttons located at the bottom of the wizard screen:

✦ **Back.** The Back button isn't always present, but when it is, you can click it to return to the previous wizard screen in order to change your selections or settings.

✦ **Next.** Clicking the Next button advances the wizard to the next screen. In most cases, you must make a selection on the current wizard screen in order to activate the Next button.

✦ **Cancel.** Clicking Cancel stops the wizard and returns you to the previously active program or dialog box.

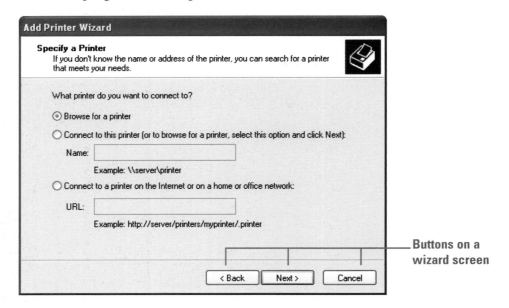

Buttons on a wizard screen

 Go online to **www.LearnwithGateway.com** and log on to select: *Wizards* in the PC Basics course.

Working with Multiple Programs

Windows XP enables you to run more than one program at a time, a feature you'll appreciate as you become more familiar with your PC and its various programs. For example, suppose you're typing a letter in WordPad and need some information from the Internet. With WordPad still open, you can quickly open Internet Explorer and find what you need. Or maybe someone sent you an e-mail message with information about a topic discussed in your letter. Again, with WordPad still open, you can start Outlook Express and find the message. Once you've found the information you want, you can switch back to WordPad and continue your letter where you left off.

 Windows XP can handle a large number of open programs at the same time, but just how many depends on how much memory your PC has. The more memory your PC has, the more programs you can run simultaneously.

Starting Multiple Programs

Whether your desktop is empty or already contains an open program window, you open a new program using the start menu or by double-clicking the program's desktop icon (if available). You do this to start the first program you want to open, the second program, the third program, and so on. To open several programs, do the following:

❶ Click the **start** button, and then click **Control Panel**. The Control Panel window opens.

❷ Click the **start** button, point to **All Programs**, point to **Accessories**, and then click **WordPad**. The WordPad window opens.

❸ Click the **start** button, point to **All Programs**, point to **Accessories**, and then click **Paint**. The Paint window opens.

❹ Click the **start** button, point to **All Programs**, point to **Games**, and then click **Solitaire**. The Solitaire window opens.

❺ Click the **start** button, point to **All Programs**, point to **Accessories**, and then click **Calculator**. The Calculator window opens. Figure 3-9 shows the Windows XP desktop with all these programs

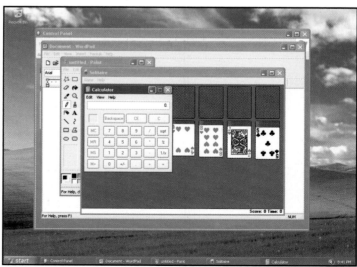

Figure 3-9 The Windows XP desktop with several windows open.

Switching Between Multiple Programs

When you have multiple programs running on your desktop, the ability to switch from one to another is crucial. With Windows XP, you can do this using a few different techniques:

- ✦ By clicking the desired program window's window
- ✦ By clicking the desired program window's taskbar button
- ✦ By pressing the **ALT+TAB** keyboard shortcut

 In Windows XP, the active program is the one whose window has a darker title bar; the title bars of inactive program windows are more subdued in color. In addition, the active program's taskbar button appears pressed in, while taskbar buttons of inactive programs appear raised.

Clicking the Program's Window

To switch to another program, you can simply click anywhere in the desired program's window. To switch programs using this method, do the following (these steps assume your desktop looks like the one shown in Figure 3-9):

1 Click any part of the **Solitaire** window. The Solitaire window becomes active, and appears in front of all other windows.

2 Click any part of the **Paint** window. The Paint window returns to the front.

Clicking the Program's Taskbar Button

If the program window you want to activate is completely obscured by other open windows on your desktop, thus preventing you from clicking it, you can click the program's taskbar button instead. A program's taskbar button includes the program's icon, followed by a file or document name, followed by the program name. If a program doesn't use files or documents, or if neither is open, only the program name appears. To practice switching programs using taskbar buttons, do the following (again, these steps assume your desktop looks like the one shown in Figure 3-9):

1 Click the **WordPad** taskbar button. The WordPad window becomes active and appears in front of all other windows.

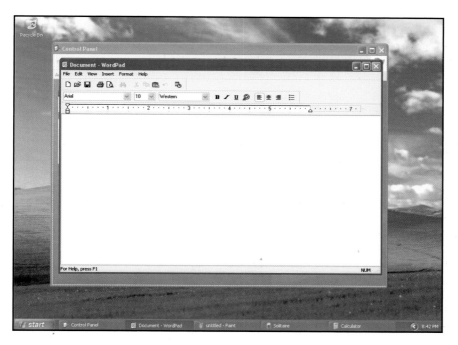

2 Click the **Paint** taskbar button. The Paint window returns to the front.

More About . . . Taskbar Buttons

There is no limit to the number of buttons the taskbar can hold. When numerous buttons are on display, however, they may be reduced in size (depending on your screen resolution) in order to fit on the taskbar. This usually means that less of the file and program name fits on the button. To view the entire file and program name for a taskbar button, position your mouse pointer over the button. After a few moments, a ToolTip appears, displaying whatever file- and program-name data is available.

If you have two or more windows open in a single program, and the taskbar holds six or more taskbar buttons, the taskbar collapses same-program windows into a single taskbar button, called a *multi-window taskbar button*. These types of buttons are indicated by the presence of a number between the icon and the program name. (This number also indicates how many windows are accessible from that button.) Multi-window taskbar buttons also feature an arrow pointing downward at their right edges (see Figure 3-10).

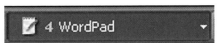

Figure 3-10 A multi-window taskbar button for WordPad.

Clicking the multi-window taskbar button opens a menu listing the names of all the files and documents currently open in the program; click an entry in the list to move its window to the fore. To get a handle on using a multi-window taskbar button, do the following (again, these steps assume your desktop looks like the one shown in Figure 3-9):

1 Click the **start** button, point to **All Programs**, point to **Accessories**, and then click **WordPad**. The WordPad window opens.

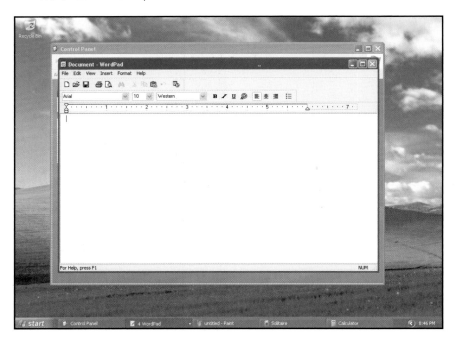

2 Repeat Step 1. Your desktop should now contain three separate program windows for WordPad, stacked on top of each other.

③ Click the **WordPad** taskbar button. A menu appears, displaying the names of the documents open in each WordPad window.

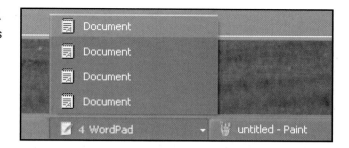

④ Click the top document in the menu. The corresponding WordPad window becomes active and appears in front of all other windows.

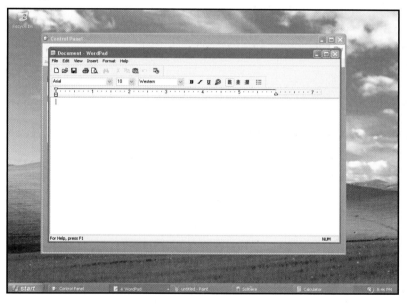

⑤ Close all open WordPad windows except one (click the **Close** button in the upper-right corner of each window).

Pressing the ALT+TAB Keyboard Shortcut

Another way to switch between open programs is to use the ALT+TAB keyboard shortcut. Here's how:

① Press and hold down the **ALT** key on your keyboard.

② With the **ALT** key still pressed, press the **TAB** key once. A dialog box appears, displaying an icon for each open window on your desktop. The active window's icon is at the far left of the dialog box, and the icon to its immediate right is selected.

③ With the **ALT** key still pressed, press the **TAB** key a second time. The next icon in the dialog box is selected.

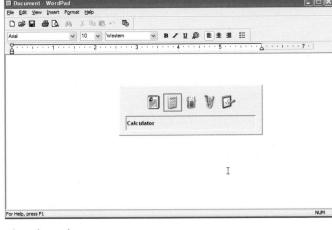

④ Continue pressing the TAB key until the window you want to activate is selected.

⑤ Release the ALT key. The window you selected is activated on the desktop.

Viewing Multiple Windows Simultaneously

If you are working with multiple windows at the same time, the ability to view them simultaneously can be quite helpful. For example, if you are writing an e-mail to a friend about a Web page, you could be viewing your Web browser at the same time you are composing your e-mail message.

To view multiple windows simultaneously, do the following:

① Right-click an empty area of the taskbar.

 If numerous icon buttons populate your taskbar, finding an empty area might get tricky. Usually, however, there's just enough space between the start button and the notification area to right-click.

② As shown in Figure 3-11, a shortcut menu containing numerous commands opens. Choose one of the following four commands:

> ✦ **Cascade Windows.** Selecting this command repositions all open windows into a cascade layout, and resizes all windows so they are the same dimensions (typically, about half the area of the screen). This

Figure 3-11 The taskbar shortcut menu.

layout enables you to easily switch between windows by clicking their displayed title bars or bottom-left corners. Notice that this command manipulates only those windows that have not been minimized.

✦ **Tile Windows Horizontally.** Clicking this command resizes and repositions all open windows so that they appear stacked on each other, stretched across the screen from left to right. This layout works well if you're juggling multiple document programs. For example, this makes it easier to view the content of one or two documents while you write a third. Notice that this command manipulates only those windows that have not been minimized.

✦ **Tile Windows Vertically.** Clicking this command resizes and repositions all open windows so that they appear side-by-side from the top of the screen to the bottom. Use this layout for the same reason you might choose to tile windows horizontally —it's up to you which view is easier to use. Notice that this command manipulates only those windows that have not been minimized.

 Although tiling can help you display multiple windows on your screen, the usefulness of tiling decreases as the number of open windows increases. Use these commands only if the resulting window layout improves your ability to interact with several program windows simultaneously.

✦ **Show the Desktop.** Selecting this command minimizes all open windows, enabling you to access a desktop icon or perform other desktop-related operations. To practice using these commands, do the following (these steps assume your desktop looks like the one shown in Figure 3-9):

① Click anywhere in the **Control Panel** window to activate it.

② Click the Control Panel window's **Minimize** button. The window is minimized.

③ Click anywhere in the **WordPad** window to activate it.

④ Click the WordPad window's **Minimize** button. The window is minimized.

⑤ Right-click an empty area of the taskbar.

⑥ Click the **Tile Windows Vertically** command. Your screen should look similar to the one shown in Figure 3-12. Notice that the minimized windows are not tiled.

Figure 3-12 Three windows tiled vertically.

7 After you issue a Tile command, a new command appears in the taskbar shortcut menu: Undo Tile. This command restores the open windows to their previous sizes and locations. To issue the Undo Tile command, right-click an empty area of the taskbar, and click **Undo Tile** in the shortcut menu.

8 Right-click an empty area of the taskbar, and click the **Tile Windows Horizontally** command in the shortcut menu. Your screen should look similar to the one shown in Figure 3-13.

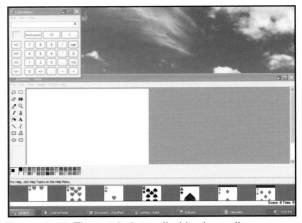

Figure 3-13 Three windows tiled horizontally.

 Notice that the Calculator window overlaps the Paint window in Figure 3-13. That's because some windows have a restriction for height, width, or both. When a tiling command is issued, Windows attempts to accommodate the request. But neither the tiling command nor manual resizing can override built in minimum display restrictions for program windows.

9 Right-click an empty area of the taskbar, and click the **Undo Tile** command in the shortcut menu.

10 Right-click an empty area of the taskbar, and click the **Cascade Windows** command. Your screen should look similar the one shown in Figure 3-14.

 Notice that the Calculator window is smaller than the other cascaded windows. That's because the Calculator window has built-in display restrictions that the Cascade command cannot override.

11 Just as with the Tile command, a new command appears in the taskbar shortcut menu after the Cascade command is issued: **Undo Cascade**. This command restores the open windows to their previous sizes and locations. To issue the Undo Cascade command, right-click an empty area of the taskbar, and click Undo Cascade in the shortcut menu.

12 Close all open windows by clicking the **Close** button in each window.

You should feel a little more comfortable working with windows, dialog boxes, wizards, and multiple windows. Keep in mind that practicing will help you fine-tune these skills.

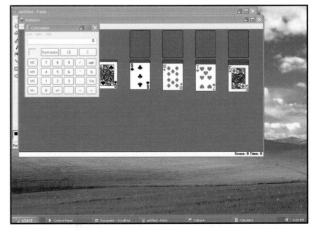

Figure 3-14 Three windows in a cascade formation.

To Keep on Learning . . .

 Go to the CD-ROM and select the segment:
- *Parts of a Window* to explore the use of various parts of a window

 Go online to **www.LearnwithGateway.com** to find out more about:
- *Dialog Boxes* in the PC Basics course
- *Wizards* in the PC Basics course
- *Internet Links and Resources*
- *FAQs*

 Gateway offers hands-on training courses that cover many of the topics in this chapter. Additional fees may apply. Call **888-852-4821** to enroll. Please have your customer ID and order number ready when you call.

3

Organizing Your Computer

This chapter is filled with information about how to use your PC's hard disk to organize and store your work. First, you'll learn how to create folders and subfolders in which to store your work. Next, you'll find out how to create, save, and update simple documents, or files, and how to use floppy disks to open and save files. Then, you'll learn how to associate files with specific applications. Finally, you wrap things up by learning about creating and managing logical *folder structures* within which you can organize files and subfolders.

Creating Folders and Subfolders

Chances are, you use a filing cabinet at work or at home to organize important papers and other items. Like a filing cabinet, your PC's hard disk enables you to "file" your important documents. You can do so in your My Documents folder, which acts like a drawer in a filing cabinet. You can even create and label your own set of folders within this "drawer"; this lets you organize the documents, or *files,* you create using your PC. You can even create *subfolders* and place them inside other folders. In an organized folder structure, you can locate your documents easily.

Follow these steps to create a folder and subfolder in My Documents:

1 Click the **start** button, and then click **My Documents**. The My Documents window opens.

 Go to the CD-ROM and select the segment: *Computer Organization*

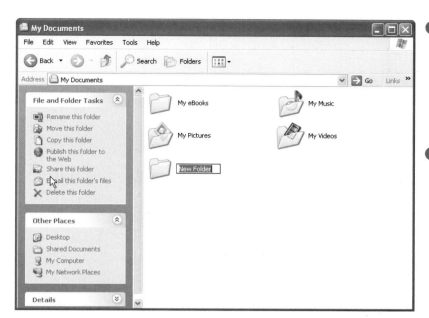

2 Under File and Folder Tasks, click **Make a new folder**. A new folder icon appears in the window, with the name "New Folder" selected.

3 Type **My First Folder**, and press **ENTER**. This replaces the name "New Folder" with "My First Folder."

4 Position your mouse pointer over the new folder. A ToolTip appears, telling you that the folder is empty.

5 Double-click **My First Folder**. The title of the window changes from "My Documents" to "My First Folder."

6 Under File and Folder Tasks, click **Make a new folder**. A new folder icon appears in the My First Folder window with the name "New Folder" selected.

7 Type **My First Subfolder**, and press **ENTER**. This replaces the name "New Folder" with "My First Subfolder."

8 Click the **Back** button twice to return to the My Documents window.

9 Place your mouse over My First Folder. The ToolTip now lists the subfolder you just created as the contents of this folder.

10 Click the **Close** button to close the My Documents window and return to the desktop.

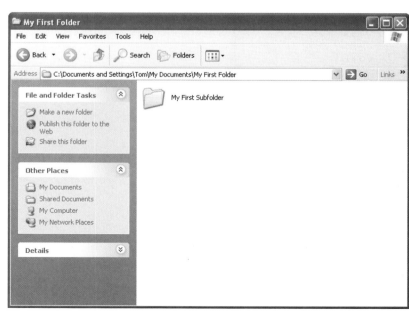

Creating and Saving Files

Your computer most likely arrived with several programs installed—that is, software designed to create specific types of files or accomplish specific tasks. Likewise, programs include various commands and ways to save the documents or data files they use. Saving a document or file permits you to store it on your hard disk, so you can access it again at another time.

Creating and Saving a File Using a Program

To create a simple file using a program (in this case, WordPad), do the following:

1 Click the **start** button, point to **All Programs**, point to **Accessories**, and click **WordPad**.

2 The WordPad program starts, displaying a window labeled "Document – WordPad".

3 The blinking vertical bar (called the insertion point) in the upper-left corner of the workspace indicates where text will appear when you start typing. Type **This is my first new document using Microsoft Windows XP and WordPad**. Notice that the insertion point moves across the page as you type.

4 Click **File** in the menu bar, and then click **Save**. Notice that the Save As dialog box opens (you'll learn about why this happens in the next section).

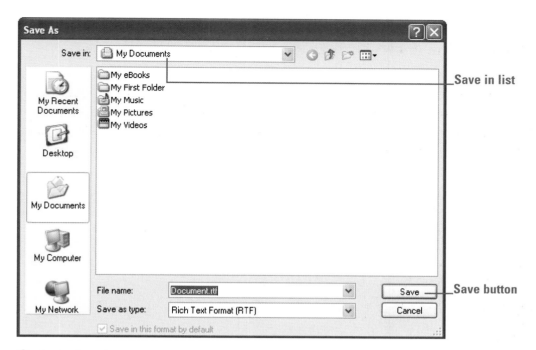

Save in list

Save button

4

⑤ In the **Save in** list, find the folder named "My First Folder" (remember, it's in My Documents). When you locate My First Folder, double-click it so it opens up. (The folder icon to the left changes from a closed folder to an open one.)

⑥ In the **File name** text box, double-click the default entry **Document** to highlight that name, and then type **My New File**. This is how you replace a default name for the file with the name you actually want to use.

⑦ Click the **Save** button to save the document, close the Save As dialog box, and return to the WordPad window. Notice that the name of the file, "My New File," now appears in the title bar at the top of the screen.

⑧ Click the **Close** button to close the WordPad window and return to the desktop.

The Save As and Save Commands

When you first create a document, it resides only in your PC's memory. This means if the power fails, you'd lose your document forever. If you've only typed a sentence or two it's no big deal, but for an hour's or a day's work, that's different. Thus, it is important that you save your document to a different location, such as your hard disk or a floppy disk. Consequently, the first time you save a file, the Save As dialog box appears automatically so you can tell the program where to save the file, and assign a file name and file type.

The basic Save command, by contrast, only works when you've already defined a file to associate with a document or data file. When you use the Save command, you're telling the program to store a new copy of that file's contents and replace the previous copy of that file with the one you're saving

Thus, whenever you're ready to save your work in a typical Windows program, you can choose one of two commands to save your changes:

✦ **Save as**: Saves an updated document into a new file. This preserves your latest changes in a new file, but also preserves the previous version under its original file name. Click the **File** menu and then click **Save As** to open the Save As dialog box. Here, you must select a location and provide a unique file name, just as you did when you saved your WordPad document in the preceding exercise.

✦ **Save**: Saves the updated document into an existing file. This stores your latest changes, and replaces the previous version of the document (it's gone). To save a document into the current file, click the **File** menu, then click **Save**, or simply click the **Save** button on the toolbar.

In the next section, we explore the Save As dialog box and describe all of its features.

Touring the Save As Dialog Box

In most Windows programs, the only way to access the Save As command is through the File menu except when saving a file for the first time. That is, you won't see a toolbar icon for Save As. Using this command to create a new version of an existing file requires some extra clicks on your part, but is worth using from time to time. Let's explore the components of the Save As dialog box (see Figure 4-1; described in Table 4-1) to better understand the Save As command.

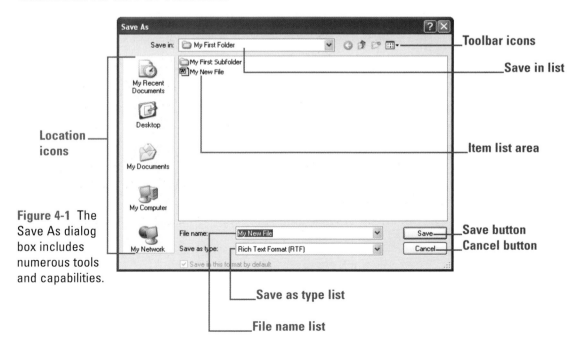

Figure 4-1 The Save As dialog box includes numerous tools and capabilities.

Table 4-1 Touring the Save As dialog box and its elements.

	ELEMENT EXPLANATION
Save in list	Click the down arrow to see a list of all top-level locations available for saving.
Toolbar icons	Back, Up One Level, New Folder, and List Properties buttons
Location icons	Select icons to set Save in location; includes My Recent Documents, Desktop, My Documents, My Computer, and My Network.
Item list area	Shows drives, files, folders, or other items inside whatever Save in location is selected.
File name list	Type a new file name for saving (list shows other available file names).
Save as type list	Pick from a list of file types for the document to be saved (provides a handy way to convert to alternate formats).
Save button	Click this button to save the file specified in the File name list of the type specified in the Save as type list.
Cancel button	Click this button to stop the save activity and close the Save As dialog box.

As a review of Table 4-1 indicates, Save As provides lots of ways to specify file locations. You can use the Save In list, the Location icons, and the first three toolbar icons to find and select a location. Use the Properties button on the toolbar to change the way items appear in the Item list. The other controls are self-evident, or explained in the table.

More About . . . Saving Files

When saving files, here are a few tips to keep in mind:

◆ All file names must be fewer than 255 characters long; limiting file names to 20 characters or fewer makes viewing in lists and sorting easier.

◆ Use any character on the keyboard in a file name, except the following: / \ : * ? " < > |

◆ Assign your files descriptive names so you can remember what they are without having to open them. This is particularly true when saving multiple versions of the same file.

4

Creating a File with the Shortcut Menu

Depending on the number of programs installed on a PC, sometimes navigating the All Programs menu can be cumbersome. Luckily, there's another way to start programs and create files—using the *shortcut menu* that appears when you right-click your desktop. Follow these steps to create a file using this method:

➊ Right-click a blank area of your desktop.

➋ A shortcut menu appears. Point to **New** to reveal the New submenu.

➌ Click **Text Document**. A new text document icon appears on the desktop with the name "New Text Document" selected.

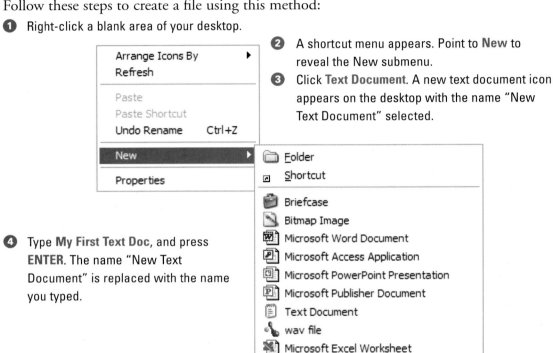

➍ Type **My First Text Doc**, and press **ENTER**. The name "New Text Document" is replaced with the name you typed.

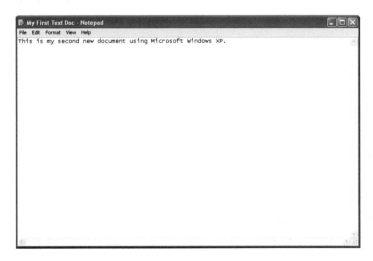

➎ Double-click the **My First Text Doc** icon on your desktop. The Notepad program starts and the My First Text Doc – Notepad window opens.

➏ Type **This is my second new document using Microsoft Windows XP**.

7 Click **File** in the menu bar, and then click **Save**. Because you have already named this document (My First Text Doc), and saved it to a location (the desktop), no Save As dialog box opens.

8 Click the **Close** button to close the Notepad window and return to the desktop.

Opening, Revising, and Saving Existing Files

Congratulations! You have created two files with two different programs, and saved these files in two different locations on the hard disk. Now it's time to learn more about opening existing files, revising their contents, and saving them when you're done with them.

Opening and Retrieving a File

In Windows XP, the act of opening a file often involves navigating within the folders, subfolders, and files in the file system. As you work your way through the various ways to open files, you'll see that in many cases part of what's involved is locating and pointing to a file, so you can instruct a program to do something with it. Keep this in mind as you read the sections that follow.

Opening a File Using a Program

Once you start a program, you can use its built-in file handling capabilities to open existing files that you want to work on. You can always use the program's built-in menus to do this, but in most cases, you can also click a toolbar icon to do the same thing. Here's an example using menus in WordPad (click **start**, then **All Programs**, then **Accessories**, then **WordPad** to open that program):

1 Click the **File** button in the menu bar. The File menu appears.

2 Click **Open** in the File menu. The Open dialog box opens.

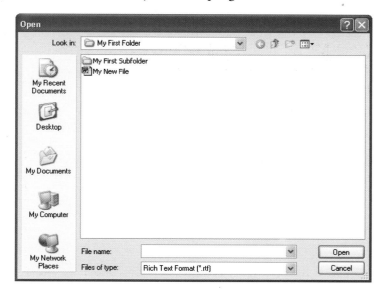

❸ This should open with My First Folder in the Look in list, because that's where you left off last time. If not, navigate through **My Documents** to **My First Folder**. This displays the contents of that folder in the item display area below the list.

❹ Select the **My New File** icon in the item display area, and then click the **Open** button. This opens your file in WordPad's workspace. You're ready to go to work!

❺ To prepare for the next exercise, close WordPad by clicking the **Close** button.

 To perform the same actions covered in the preceding steps using the toolbar Open button, simply skip steps 1 and 2, and click the **Open** button on the program's toolbar instead. Replacing two steps with one explains why this is a good approach.

That's how you open files when you're already running some particular program. If you're starting work in a program that's not already running, there's another way to get to work. It involves using the icon that represents the file you want to work on, and is explained in the next section.

 To see how files can be opened within programs, go to the Web segment *Files: Opening with Programs* in the Beyond PC Basics course.

Opening a File Using the File Icon

Opening the My First Text Doc file is easy, because you saved it to the desktop. Simply locate its icon on your desktop and double-click that icon to open the file inside NotePad. This same principle works for other files as long as you can find the icon for a file to double-click it. Also, Windows must recognize what program to use with the file (we talk about what that means later in this chapter in the section titled "Managing File Associations").

Here's how to open your text document by clicking its file icon:

❶ Close any open applications so you can see your desktop. Notice the My First Text Doc icon on your desktop.

❷ Double-click the **My First Text Doc** icon to open that document.

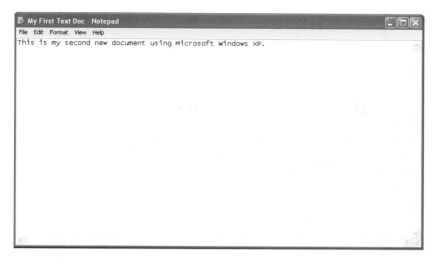

❸ The document opens in Notepad, ready for you to get to work. Note how easy and convenient it is to open a file from the desktop!

❹ Click the **Close** button to exit Notepad.

Revising and Saving a File

Once you've opened a file, getting to work requires only that you position the insertion point where you want to add new text. Otherwise, you'll use various commands within the program to make whatever other changes may be needed.

You should always remember to save your file (or files) as you get ready to exit any Windows program. But if you forget, many programs prompt you to save any changed file or files before they close, just to give you one last chance to retain your latest changes. Even so, we'd also like to recommend that you get in the habit of saving those files you work on regularly—at least every time you get up to walk away from your machine, if not more often. That way, if a power failure occurs or something else happens that causes your PC to turn off unexpectedly, you'll lose only as much work as you've done since the last time you saved that file. Think of it as a way of avoiding unnecessary repetition, if that helps!

Let's make an addition to revise My New File, so you can save that work. Here's how:

❶ Click **start** and click **WordPad** in the recently used program area on that menu to open WordPad.

❷ Click the **Open** button on WordPad's toolbar to produce the Open dialog box.

❸ Click **My New File**, then click **Open** to open the file.

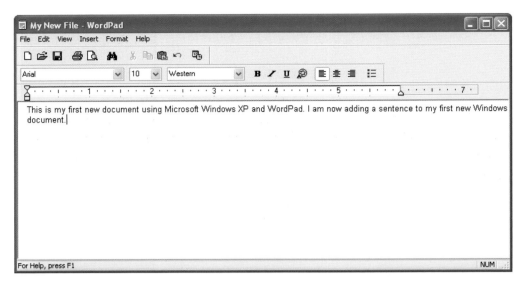

④ Position the insertion point at the end of the only sentence in My New File. This permits you to add new text at the end of the file.

⑤ Type **I am now adding a sentence to my first new Windows document.** The corresponding text appears in WordPad's workspace.

⑥ Click the **Save** icon (looks like a small floppy disk) in the WordPad toolbar to save your addition.

Save button

⑦ Click the **Close** button to close WordPad.

⑧ Click **start**, and then click **WordPad** in the recently used programs area on that menu. This re-opens WordPad.

⑨ Click the **Open** button on the toolbar; the Open dialog box appears. It displays the contents of My First Folder automatically.

⑩ Select **My New File**, and then click the **Open** button. The file opens, and it includes the old sentence from the previous version, followed by the new sentence from your last save operation.

⑪ Click the **Close** button to close WordPad.

Working with Floppy Disks

You may have the need to save files to a floppy disk for numerous reasons, such as sharing the data with others if you're not on a network or connected to the Internet. However, floppy disks can hold only about 1.44 MB of data. If the size of your files exceeds the space available on a floppy disk, you might have to use a CD (see Chapter 6 for information about recording data to CDs). In the sections that follow, we explain how to save and open files from a floppy disk.

Saving a File on a Floppy Disk

Floppy disks are handy; they're designed to allow you to store a small file or two. To practice saving a text document to a disk, follow these steps:

Push disk securely into floppy disk drive

1. Insert a blank formatted disk into the floppy disk drive in the front of your PC.

2. Click **start** and click **My Computer**. The My Computer window opens.

3. Under Devices with Removable Storage, double-click the **3½ Floppy (A:)** icon. The 3½ Floppy (A:) window opens; notice that there are no files or folders displayed in this window.

4. Click the **Minimize** button in the 3½ Floppy (A:) window to minimize the window.

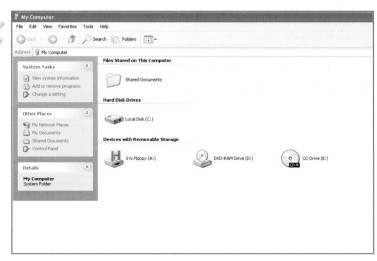

⑤ Locate the file you want to copy to the disk (in this example, the My First Text Doc file located on the desktop), right-click it, and click **Send to** in the shortcut menu that appears. Click the 3½ **Floppy (A:)** item in the resulting pop-up menu to save the file to the disk. (A Copying dialog box appears while the file is being copied, but it may come and go so quickly you won't see much.)

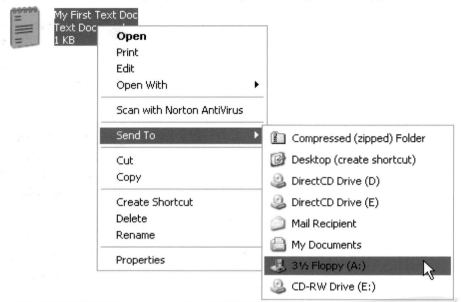

⑥ A copy of My First Text Doc is saved to the disk, and its icon appears in the 3½ Floppy (A:) window. Click the **Close** button to close the 3½ Floppy (A:) window.

 It's always a good idea to remove disks from the floppy disk drive immediately after use. If you leave a diskette in the floppy drive then restart your PC, it can interfere with operating system start-up.

Opening a File on a Floppy Disk

To open a file saved on a floppy disk and transfer it to your PC, first insert the disk into the floppy disk drive on your PC. Then, do the following:

① Click **start** and click **My Computer**. The My Computer window opens.

② Under Devices with Removable Storage, double-click the 3½ **Floppy (A:)** icon. The 3½ Floppy (A:) window opens. Notice that this window contains one or more icons representing files—in this case, the My First Text Doc file that you saved to disk in the preceding section.

 Be sure to scan all files from outside sources (disk from a friend or company, CD, e-mail attachment, or the Internet) for viruses before opening or running any of the files. Chapter 8 includes information about Chapter 9 includes information about Norton AntiVirus®, software to help protect your PC from viruses.

3 Double-click the My First Text Doc icon in the window; this opens the file in Notepad.

4 Click the **Close** button to close the Notepad window.

5 Click the **Close** button to close the 3½ Floppy (A:) window.

6 Remove the disk from the floppy disk drive of your PC.

In the next section, we explore this topic as we explain the concept and operation of file associations in Windows.

Managing File Associations

By now, you've probably noticed that nearly all Windows files have associated types. For example, type names appear in the Save as type list box in a Save As dialog box. In file names, file types are expressed as *file name extensions,* which are groups of three or more characters that appear to the right of the rightmost period in a file name. Windows uses this information to decide which programs to use with particular files.

By default, Windows XP hides these characters when it shows you icons for files and other objects. You can see them if you alter your folder options in My Computer or Windows Explorer, and instruct the software to show you that information. Here's how:

1 Click **start** and click **My Documents**. This lists that folder's contents.

2 Double-click **My First Folder**. This lists its contents, including My New File.

3 Click **Tools** and click **Folder Options** in the Tools menu. The Folder Options window opens.

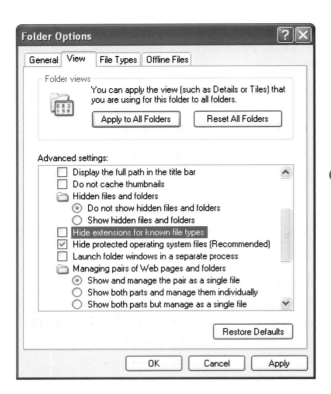

④ Click the **View** tab to look at its contents, and then clear the **Hide extensions for known file types** check box. Click **OK** to close the Folder Options dialog box.

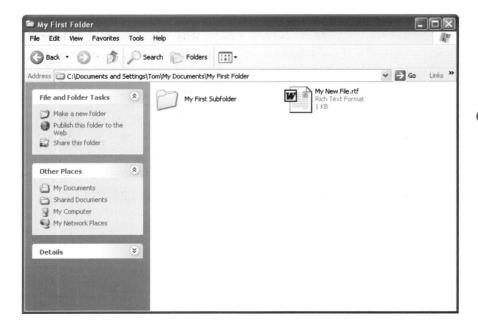

⑤ You should now see My New File.rtf as the file name in the My First Folder listing.

⑥ Click **Tools**, click **Folder Options**, click the **View** tab, and then click the **Restore Defaults** button to return to the original settings. Click **OK** to close the dialog box.

⑦ Click the **Close** button to close the My First Folder window.

Windows XP associates the file extension .rtf with WordPad and Microsoft Word as well. On machines where both programs are installed, double-clicking a file with an .rtf extension opens Word, not WordPad, because it is a preferred file association.

In the sections that follow, we explain how files and folders work in the Windows XP environment, and how you can create and organize your own folders to help you find files when you need them.

Working with Files and Folders

When you start working with multiple programs or creating lots of individual files, a single folder really can't provide sufficient organization to help you keep track of your many separate interests and activities—and the files that go with them. Nor does it make sense to mix up your collection of music lyric files with your monthly checkbook statements. That's why creating your own collection of folders is so important.

Organized Files Need Folder Structures

Getting your PC organized means understanding what kinds of programs you use, what kinds of files you work with, and what kinds of activities you conduct. All of these elements can help guide how you organize folders on your hard drive. This organization should build from a relatively small set of primary activities at the highest level (those folders that contain the most subfolders) to an increasingly large set of individual, specific activities within the primary folders as the number of levels goes up.

Let's walk through an example to illustrate this concept. Nearly every person or family must deal with financial matters to handle the demands of everyday life. It's predictable that many PCs could include a Finances folder, as shown in Figure 4-2, that appears at the top level of Local Disk (C:). Within the Finances folder, you'd organize various aspects of your financial life. Let's assume that this set of folders makes sense for our hypothetical personal or family PC.

Figure 4-2: Finances folder.

In this sample illustration, it's pretty clear that Tom and Christine have their finances well in hand. They've got categories for all kinds of forward-looking money, including College Fund (for their childrens' college funds), Investments, Savings, Retirement, and even Vacation Fund. In addition, they've got the everyday basics covered, including a household Budget folder, Checkbooks, Credit Cards, Loans, and Taxes. What's important to note is that they've set up a collection of folders (with files inside them) that mirrors the various activities and individual people or items that must be tracked separately.

For example, that explains why the contents of the Loans folder include a 98-Explorer folder (for Christine's car) and a 99-Focus folder (for Tom's car).

Once you have a sizable collection of files and folders to manage, as our Finances example shows, you must get comfortable navigating within that collection. That's why we talk about folder navigation next.

Navigating Folder Structures

When it comes to moving around inside folder structures that are four or more levels deep, basic navigational skills are essential. To that end, certain tools and techniques can be extremely handy. We cover these in the paragraphs that follow.

Build a mental map: If you create an organization, it should be one that makes sense to you. This will help you to keep a mental image of the folder structure in your head. Continued use and access will make this structure familiar to you.

Visual exploration: When you open one folder, look at what's inside. Check out the files that reside there. Then systematically open each subfolder, and keep going until you've seen it all—or as much as you need to know right now.

Use Back and Up buttons: The Back and Up buttons take you back to your previous location, and makes a good tool for systematic exploration of folder structures.

Searching strategies: When you can't remember a folder structure, but you know certain characteristics for the file or folder you seek, use the Windows XP Search Companion to find what you need (see Chapter 5 for details).

In the next section, we explore some of the tools and techniques you can use to inspect files within any given folder. It's a good idea to create a restore point as we will be changing folder views. That way, after you complete the next few sections, you can choose to reset Windows XP to exactly how it looks now. For help creating a restore point, see Chapter 7.

Changing the Folder View

A Windows Explorer window is split into two sections, as shown in Figure 4-3. The left side of the window displays either a series of lists (list pane), or a hierarchical listing of everything stored on your PC (folders pane). The right side of the window, called the details pane, displays the contents of a folder or drive.

To open Windows Explorer, click **start**, right-click **My Documents**, and then click **Explore** in the shortcut menu. There are six ways to view the details pane. (This applies to normal folder views as well.) Click the **Views** button on the toolbar to display each view.

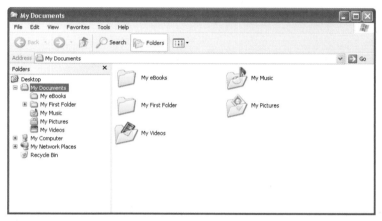

Figure 4-3 Windows Explorer.

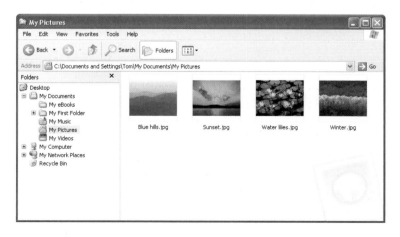

+ **Tiles view.** Displays files and folders as large icons with sorted information underneath; displayed by default the first time you open Windows Explorer (See Figure 4-3).

+ **Thumbnails view.** Handy for folders that contain pictures; displays four contained images or icons within the folder icon itself.

✦ **Icons view.**
Displays files
and folders as
icons (small
graphical
representations).

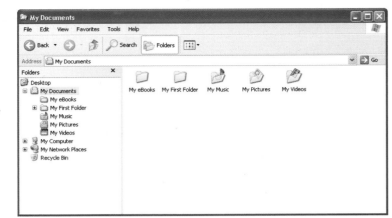

✦ **List view.**
Displays the
contents of a
folder or drive in a
list, in which each
item is preceded
by a small icon.

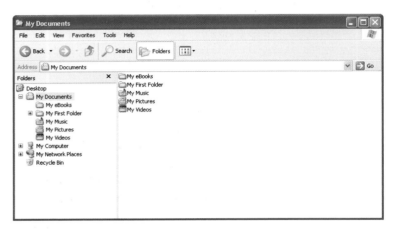

✦ **Details view.** Looks like the List view, but adds type, size, and date modified
information. Sort this view with a single click on any column name (click
once for ascending order, again for descending).

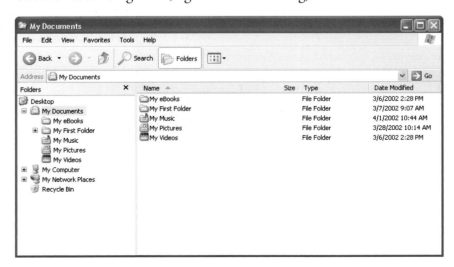

✦ **Filmstrip view.** Available only for picture folders; displays images in a single row (like a filmstrip).

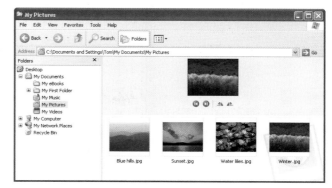

 To gain information about different folder views, go to the CD-ROM segment *Folder Views*.

Sorting the Details View

When Details view is selected in Windows Explorer, a broad range of information about each item in the selected drive or folder is available. Not only are the contents of the drive displayed, but also the size and type of each file in the drive, as well as the date each file was last modified. You can sort the contents of this window using any one of these characteristics (size, type, date modified) in ascending or descending order. For example, you might sort the files on your C: drive by file type to quickly locate files generated by a certain program.

To determine which characteristic is currently being used to sort the items in the selected drive or folder, check the column headings. The heading with an arrow next to it indicates the characteristic being used to sort the files; the direction of the arrow indicates whether files are being sorted in ascending or descending order. For example, suppose the Name column heading has an upward-pointing arrow next to it (see Figure 4-4). That indicates that items in the details pane are being sorted in ascending order by file name.

Figure 4-4: Name column heading in Details view.

To learn how to sort your files in Details view, do the following:

1 In Windows Explorer, navigate to **My First Folder** in My Documents. Click the **Views** button on the toolbar and click **Details**.

2 Click the **Size** column heading. The items in the selected drive are sorted from smallest to largest, with folders at the top of the list.

3 Click the **Size** column heading again. The items in the selected drive are sorted from largest to smallest, with files at the top of the list.

4 Click the **Type** column heading to sort the items in the selected drive in ascending order by file type; click **Type** again to sort the items in descending order.

5 Click the **Date Modified** column heading to sort the items in the selected drive in ascending order by date; click **Date Modified** again to sort the items in descending order.

6 Click the **Name** column heading to sort the items in the selected drive in ascending order by file name.

7 Click the **Close** button to close the Local Disk (C:) window.

As you learn how to view and sort files to help you find what you're looking for, you'll start to appreciate the power and flexibility of the Details view. Soon, it should become second nature to you.

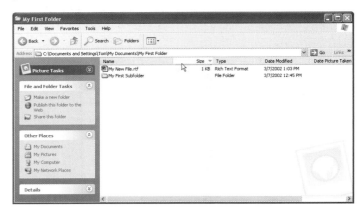

 To understand how files and folders can be used, go to the CD-ROM segment *File and Folder Tasks.*

Now that you're familiar with Windows Explorer and have changed many different settings, you can restore your PC to the way it looked and behaved before you began. To do so, however, you must have created a restore point as instructed in the "Navigating Folder Structures" section. For help restoring your system, refer to Chapter 2.

Go to the CD-ROM and select the segment:

◆ *Computer Organization* to gain information about computer organization

◆ *Folder Views* to gain information about different folder views

◆ *File and Folder Tasks* to understand how files and folders can be used

Go online to **www.LearnwithGateway.com** and log on to select:

◆ *Files: Opening with Programs* in the Beyond PC Basics course

◆ *Internet Links and Resources*

◆ *FAQs*

Gateway offers a hands-on training course that covers many of the topics in this chapter. Additional fees may apply. Call **888-852-4821** to enroll. Please have your customer ID and order number ready when you call.

4

spreadsheet2.JPG @ 100% (RGB)

Navigator Info Options

	R	S	G	K		L	M	N	O		
3	%				First	Actual	Over	Over	% over	nver	1993
						1994	(under)	(under)	(under)	under	BUDGET	cr (De
						ecember	budget	1993	1993	94 budget	FORECAST	rom 9

2,243,270	(956,730)	253,307	13%	-30%	2,990,000 ####
539,295	(210,705)	167,949	45%	-28%	720,000 ####
200,742	(9,258)	54,293	37%	-4%	270,000 ####
56,427	34,427	43,227	327%	156%	60,000 ####
60,739	(39,261)	(17,851)	-23%	-39%	50,000 ####
(450,431)	249,569	(7,523)	2%	-36%	(593,000) ####
	0	0			0
2,650,042	(931,958)	493,402	23%	-26%	3,497,000 ####
	0	0			
	0	0			82,000
161,452	101,452				
61,737	31,737	(17,821)	-22%	106%	23,000 ####
136,915	16,915	64,779	90%	14%	225,000 ####
887,473	(782,527)	(92,963)	-9%	-47%	1,200,000 ####
5,336	(664)	1,295	32%	-11%	6,000 ####
26,332	(9,668)	4,747	22%	-27%	34,970 ####
3,407	(3,593)	(918)	-21%	-51%	5,000 ####
65,795	(39,205)	3,523	6%	-37%	100,000 ####
17,175	(825)	2,761	19%	-5%	20,000 ####
10,073	73	(35,480)	-78%	1%	7,500 ####
1,275,505	(528,205)	91,375	7%	-31%	1,703,470 #####

NUM

	L	M	N	O	P	Q	R
	Actual	Over	Over	% over	% over	1995	%
	1994	(under)	(under)	(under)	under	BUDGET	cr (Dec
	ecember	budget	1993	1993	94 budget	FORECAST	rom 9

2,243,270	(956,730)	253,307	13%	-30%	2,990,000	####
539,295	(210,705)	167,949	45%	-28%	720,000	####
200,742	(9,258)	54,293	37%	-4%	270,000	####
	34,427	43,227	327%	156%	60,000	####
					50,000	####
					(593,000)	####
					0	
					497,000	####
					82,000	
					23,000	####
					225,000	####
					200,000	####
					6,000	####
					34,970	####
					5,000	####
(39,205)		3,523	6%	-37%	100,000	####
(825)		2,761	19%	-5%	20,000	####
73		(35,480)	-78%	1%	7,500	####
(528,205)		91,375	7%	-31%	1,703,470	#####

NUM

CHAPTER 5

Working With Objects

T his chapter takes your learning one step farther, explaining how to work with the objects stored on your PC. First, you'll learn about object paths; next, you'll find out how to create shortcuts. Then you'll discover how to select, print, move, copy, delete, rename, and open objects. Finally, you'll learn how to use the Search Companion to find objects stored on your PC.

Understanding Object Paths

When you send a letter to someone, you write the recipient's name and address on the envelope to ensure that the letter is delivered to the correct person. The same way an *object*—be it a file, a folder, a printer, or some other Windows resource—uses a unique "address" to identify it among all other resources on a PC, even those of the same type and name. That way, it can always be located and accessed properly. The secret to this addressing scheme is called an *object path*. An object path uses all the location information necessary to identify any object's exact location as a prefix to that object's name.

To illustrate, let's find a concrete example of an object path using Windows Explorer:

❶ Click **start**. The start menu appears.

❷ Right-click **My Computer**, and then select **Explore** from the shortcut menu that appears. The My Computer window opens in Windows Explorer format.

 Windows Explorer is discussed in detail in Chapter 4; it enables you to view information stored on the hard disk of your computer and see any network drives that are mapped to your computer.

❸ Double-click the **Local Disk (C:)** icon in the details pane (the pane on the right). My Computer displays the top-level folders on the Local Disk (C:) along with any files in the current folder.

❹ Double-click the **Documents and Settings** folder icon. My Computer displays a list of folders related to users defined on your PC.

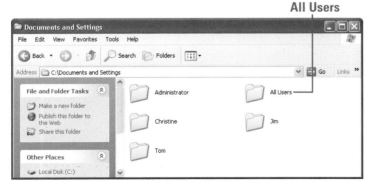

❺ Double-click the **All Users** folder icon. My Computer lists folders associated with any user who logs on to your system.

❻ Double-click the **Start Menu** folder icon. My Computer lists elements in the default start menu for all users, including the Windows Catalog and Windows Update shortcuts.

Note the text that appears in the **Address** box in the My Computer window: It reads **C:\Documents and Settings\All Users\Start Menu**. This is the object path for objects that reside inside the Start Menu folder. When you combine this information with an object's name, you have the complete address for the object. For example, the complete addresses for the Windows Catalog and Windows Update shortcuts inside the Start Menu folder are:

✦ C:\Documents and Settings\All Users\Start Menu\Windows Catalog

✦ C:\Documents and Settings\All Users\Start Menu\Windows Update

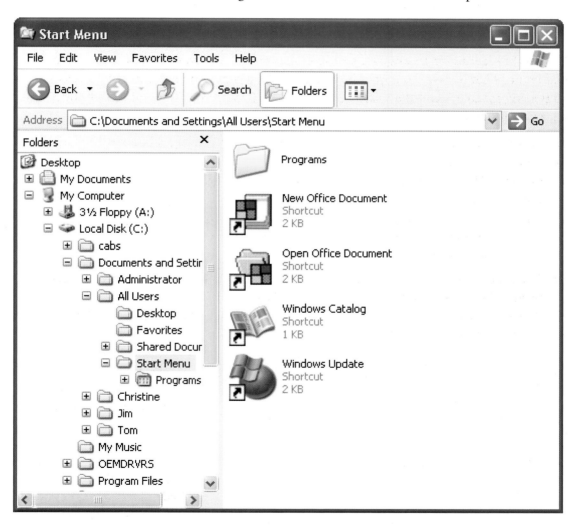

Creating and Managing Shortcuts

In the preceding section, you discovered the object path to two shortcuts that appear in Windows Explorer by default: Windows Catalog and Windows Update. A *shortcut* is a kind of Windows XP object that enables you to associate an icon on the desktop or in some other convenient location with a specific document, program, printer, or other resource.

Although a shortcut can be placed just about anywhere you like, the most common and most convenient location for shortcuts is the Windows XP desktop. For example, suppose you frequently use WordPad. To launch it, you click **start**, then **All Programs**, then **Accessories**, then **WordPad**. That's a total of four mouse clicks. To save time and effort, you could place a shortcut to WordPad on your desktop. That way, you could simply double-click the shortcut to launch the program.

Shortcuts look like ordinary program icons, but with a small arrow in a box in the lower-left corner. Figure 5-1 shows a desktop shortcut to WordPad; you'll learn how to create one for yourself in the next section.

Note that shortcuts are part of each user's desktop environment. If Tom and Christine both have accounts on a Windows XP PC, Tom's shortcuts show up only when he logs on, and Christine's only when she logs on. As you work with shortcuts you can drag and drop them onto the start menu (or its submenus).

It's a good idea to create a restore point as we will be creating multiple shortcuts. That way, when you've completed this chapter, you can easily reset Windows XP to exactly how it looks right now. For help creating a restore point, refer to Chapter 7.

Figure 5-1 WordPad shortcut icon.

Creating a Shortcut to a Program, Drive, or Folder

There are many ways to create shortcuts in the Windows XP environment; the following are just a few:

1. One is to right-click and drag the program, drive, folder or other object from the My Computer window (or other location) to the desktop and select **Create Shortcut** Here from the menu that appears.

2. You can also drag items from the start menu to the desktop.

The method illustrated here uses a right-click and drag operation to create a program shortcut (in this case, for WordPad):

❶ Click **start**. The start menu opens.

❷ Click **All Programs**. A list of programs on your PC appears.

❸ Click **Accessories** to view a list of accessory-type programs installed on your computer.

❹ Click **WordPad** and, while holding down your mouse button, drag the icon from the menu to your desktop.

❺ Release the mouse button to "drop" the WordPad icon on your desktop. A shortcut menu appears.

❻ Click **Copy Here** to create a shortcut on the desktop.

❼ Double-click the shortcut. Windows XP starts WordPad, displaying the WordPad program window on your desktop. Click the **Close** button in the upper-right corner to close this window.

Another way to create a shortcut, whether it's for a program or another type of object, is to use the Create Shortcut Wizard. Here's how:

 If you complete the steps here in addition to the ones immediately preceding, you will end up with three WordPad icons on your desktop. This doesn't cause any problems with your system, but consumes valuable desktop space. Fortunately, you'll learn how to delete shortcuts and other objects later in this chapter.

❶ Right-click an empty area on the desktop, click **New** in the shortcut menu that appears, and then click **Shortcut**. The Create Shortcut Wizard starts.

❷ Click the **Browse** button to locate the object for which you want to create a shortcut. The Browse For Folder dialog box opens.

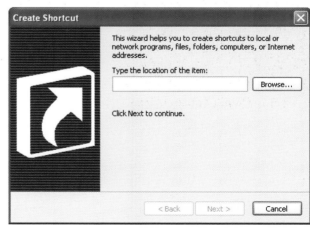

③ Click the **WordPad** shortcut icon, and then click **OK**.

④ The object's path appears in the wizard screen. Click **Next** to continue.

⑤ Windows XP provides a default name for the shortcut. To change it, you could type a preferred name over the default. In this case, leave the default name of "wordpad (2)."

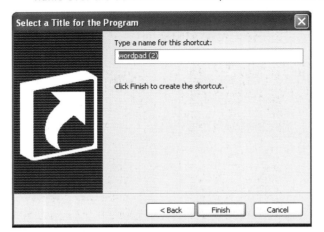

⑥ Click **Finish**. A shortcut named "wordpad (2)" appears on your desktop.

⑦ Repeat steps 1 through 6 to create a "wordpad (3)" shortcut on your desktop.

⑧ Double-click one of the new shortcuts. Windows XP starts WordPad, displaying the WordPad program window on your desktop. Click the **Close** button in the upper-right corner to close this window.

Creating a Shortcut to a File

Suppose you've decided to write your memoirs—a project that could take you weeks, months, or even years to complete. That means you'll be opening the same word-processing file to compose your masterpiece every single day for the foreseeable future. To save yourself time each day, you can create a shortcut to that file; that way, you can open the file and the word-processing program you use to work on it in one easy step.

In this example, you'll create a file in WordPad, and then create a shortcut to access it from the desktop:

① Double-click the **WordPad** shortcut icon on the desktop. WordPad starts, and its program window opens on your desktop.

② In the WordPad work area, type **My book begins with this simple sentence.**

③ Click the **Save** toolbar button (the one with a picture of a floppy disk on it). The Save As dialog box opens.

④ Double-click **My Documents** and double-click **My First Folder**. Type **MyBook** in the File name text box and click the **Save** button.

⑤ Click the **Close** button to close the WordPad window.

⑥ Click **start** and click **My Recent Documents** to view a list of documents you've accessed recently.

⑦ In the list of documents, right-click **MyBook**, click **Send to** in the shortcut menu that appears, and click **Desktop (create shortcut)** in the Send to submenu. A shortcut for the file appears on the desktop.

⑧ Click the **Close** button to close the My First Folder window.

5

Using the Desktop Cleanup Wizard

The more shortcuts you create and the more programs you install, the more likely it is that their icons begin to overwhelm your Windows XP desktop, cluttering your workspace. Of course, one way to rein in this clutter is to delete shortcuts you no longer use; then again, you can almost guarantee that the second you delete a shortcut, something will happen to make you wish it was still on your desktop.

As an alternative to deleting shortcuts, you can use the Desktop Cleanup Wizard. This wizard analyzes the shortcuts on your desktop to determine the last time each one was used. Any shortcuts that haven't been used for a while are moved to a desktop folder called "Unused Desktop Shortcuts." Here they are stored safely in case you need them again without consuming valuable desktop real estate.

To run the Desktop Cleanup Wizard, do the following:

1. Right-click an empty area on your desktop; a shortcut menu appears.
2. Click **Arrange Icons by** and, in the submenu that appears, click **Run Desktop Cleanup Wizard**.
3. The Desktop Cleanup Wizard starts, displaying its Welcome screen.

4. Click the **Next** button to put the wizard to work. The wizard lists the shortcuts on your desktop, with check marks next to those shortcuts that are seldom or never used; shortcuts with check marks next to them will be moved to the Unused Desktop Shortcuts folder. To override the wizard's selections, click a checked shortcut to clear it, or click an unchecked shortcut to select it. (For this exercise, select only the **wordpad (3)** shortcut.) When you're satisfied with the selections on the screen, click the **Next** button.
5. To confirm the selections made in the preceding screen, the wizard lists the shortcuts to be moved to the Unused Desktop Shortcuts folder. To alter these selections, click **Back**, and make changes as needed. To move the selected shortcuts to the Unused Desktop Shortcuts folder, click the **Finish** button. A shortcut for the Unused Desktop Shortcuts folder is added to your desktop, and the selected shortcuts are placed in the folder.

Manipulating Objects

One of the great things about Windows XP is how easily it allows you to manipulate the objects on your system. Do you want to copy or move a file from one folder to another? No problem. Are you finished using an object? You can easily delete it. You can also rename, open, and even print objects. Before you can manipulate the objects on your PC, however, you must learn how to select them. This section demonstrates how to select objects, and addresses all the important things you can do with objects.

In Chapter 4, you were instructed to create several folders, subfolders, and files; these same objects are used in the exercises that follow. If you did not create these objects, you can substitute folders, subfolders, and files of your own.

Selecting Objects

The first step to manipulating the objects on your PC is to select them—that is, mark them to indicate that they will be subject to some sort of user action.

Selecting a Single Object

This section demonstrates the technique for selecting a single object. As you practice, pay close attention to the changes that occur in the lists on the left side of the My Documents window.

1. With My Documents open, click **My First Folder**; the My First Folder icon becomes shaded in blue, indicating that it is selected, and the File and Folder Tasks list expands with additional options.

2. Double-click **My First Folder** to open it. "My Computer" is replaced by "My First Folder" in the window's title bar, and the contents of My First Folder are displayed.

You'll learn more about opening objects later in this chapter, in the section "Opening Objects."

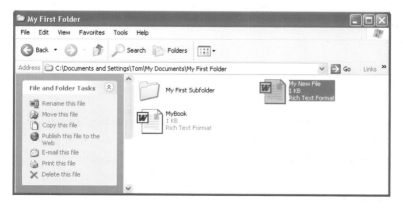

3. Click **My New File**. The My New File document becomes selected, and the File and Folder Tasks list changes, containing only those options that apply to files.

4. Click the **Back** button in the toolbar to return to the My Documents window.

Selecting Multiple Objects

There may be times when you need to perform the same action on several objects at once—perhaps to move numerous files from one folder to another. Rather than selecting each file and moving it one at a time, you can select every file that needs to be moved, and perform a single move operation on all of them at once.

Depending on whether the files you need to select are adjacent or non-adjacent, you'll use a different technique to select them; these techniques are covered next.

Selecting Adjacent Objects

There are two ways to select adjacent objects: by using the "click and drag" technique, or by pressing and holding down the SHIFT key while clicking objects with the mouse (this action is called "Shift-clicking").

To practice clicking and dragging to select multiple adjacent objects, do the following:

❶ Place your mouse pointer in the top-left corner of the details pane in My Documents, above and to the left of the My eBooks folder.

❷ Press and hold down the left mouse button, and drag the mouse pointer toward the bottom-right corner of My Documents. As you drag, a light blue box encloses the objects in the window; these objects become shaded in dark blue, indicating that they are selected.

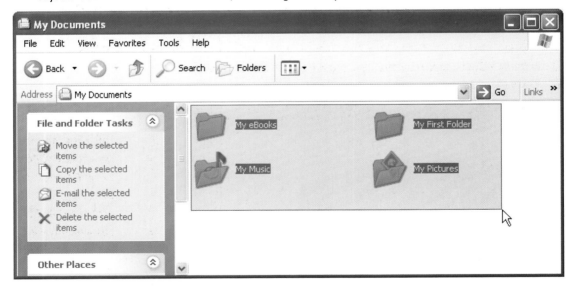

❸ When you have selected all the objects in the My Documents window, release the left mouse button. The light blue box disappears, but the objects in the window remain selected.

❹ Click a blank area in the My Documents window to deselect the objects. The objects return to their original, unshaded appearance.

To practice selecting multiple adjacent objects by Shift-clicking, do the following:

1. In the My Documents window, click the **My eBooks** folder to select it.
2. Press and hold down the **SHIFT** key on your keyboard.

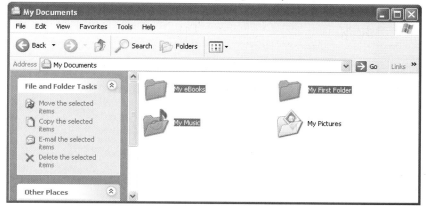

3. While holding down the SHIFT key, click the **My Music** folder in the My Documents window. The first three folders in the window, My eBooks, My First Folder, and My Music, are selected.

4. Click a blank area in the My Documents window to deselect the three folders.

Selecting Non-Adjacent Objects

To select multiple non-adjacent objects press the **CTRL** key. Not surprisingly, this operation is referred to as Control-clicking. "Control-clicking" demands that you click each object you want to select. To get used to this technique, follow these steps:

1. In the My Documents window, click the **My eBooks** folder to select it.
2. Press and hold down the **CTRL** key on your keyboard.

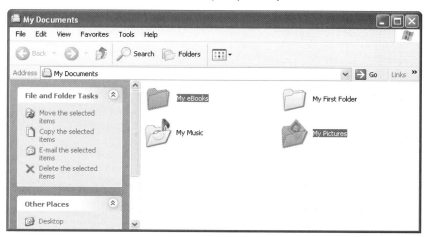

3. While holding down the CTRL key, click the **My Pictures** folder in the My Documents window. Only My eBooks and My Pictures are selected.

4. Click a blank area in the My Documents window to deselect the two folders.

Printing Objects

The simplest way to print a document is to click the Print button in a program's toolbar. This simply sends a single copy of the open document to your default printer for output.

As usual with Windows, there are other ways to print as well. If you want to access an explicit set of printing controls before you print, use the Print command in the file menu, like this:

❶ Click **start**, click **My Documents**, and then double-click **My First Folder** to display its contents.

❷ Right-click **My New File**, then **Open With**, and then click **WordPad**. My New File opens in WordPad.

❸ Click **File** and click **Print**. The Print dialog box opens. Notice the various panes and text boxes in this window. To avoid using menus, you can press **CTRL+P** on your keyboard to open the Print dialog box instead.

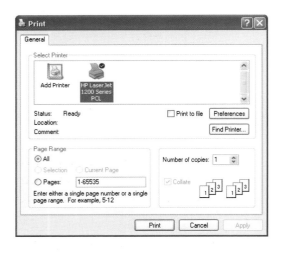

◆ The **Select Printer** pane lets you add or choose a printer, shows status information, allows you to print to a file, set preferences, or even find a particular printer.

◆ The **Page Range** pane elects to print all pages by default (notice that the All radio button is already selected), but gives options to print only a highlighted selection, the current page, and provides a number box where you can specify a page number or a range of page numbers.

◆ The **Number of copies** spin control lets you increase the number of copies you print; when you elect to print more than one, WordPad's print controls automatically collate pages for you.

❹ After making your selection in the various panes, you can click **Print** to send the document to be printed accordingly. Clicking **Cancel** closes the Print dialog box (and nothing prints). Clicking **Apply** saves your settings for this print job without printing.

❺ Click **Cancel** to close the Print dialog box. Click the **Close** button to close WordPad.

There's one big difference between using the Print button on the toolbar versus using the Print dialog box to control printing—you can change your mind and cancel printing when you use the Print dialog box. After you click the Print button on the toolbar, you can't cancel the job (except by using the controls available in the Printers and Faxes window elsewhere in Windows XP).

The same thing is true for shortcut printing, which doesn't require you to open an application to print. You can right-click a file icon inside My Computer or Windows Explorer, and print straight from the resulting shortcut menu, like this:

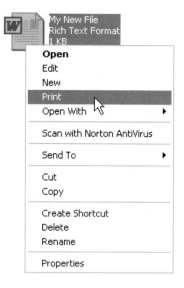

❶ Click **start**, click **My Documents**, and then double-click **My First Folder** to display its contents in the window.

❷ Right-click **My New File** and select **Print** from the shortcut menu.

❸ Microsoft Word flashes open, prints the file, and then closes automatically. It's almost too fast to follow!

Remember, because Microsoft Word is at the top of the file associations list, it's picked automatically when you double-click an icon or use shortcut commands like Print. That's why we had to use the Open With command to select WordPad two exercises back. But shortcut printing is about as easy as printing can get!

In the section that follows next, we explain how to move objects around inside Windows, and how to copy them (for safe keeping or other purposes).

Moving and Copying Objects

Now that you have learned how to select objects, you're ready to manipulate them. Some of the most common object-manipulation tasks are moving and copying objects from one location to another. For example, when you finish working on a file, you might decide to move it to a folder that contains projects you have completed.

When you move an object, it is placed in its new location, and deleted from its original location. Copying an object, on the other hand, leaves the object intact in its original location, and creates a duplicate object in the new location.

Moving Objects

Windows XP enables you to move and copy objects using a variety of techniques. For example, you can move objects using any of the following techniques:

+ Drag and drop

+ Cut and paste

+ The Move this file task in the File and Folder Tasks list

To practice moving objects using drag and drop, do the following:

1. In My Documents, double-click **My First Folder**. The My First Folder window opens.
2. Click **My New File**. The My New File document is selected, and the File and Folder Tasks list expands to include additional tasks.
3. Click and hold your mouse button on **My New File** and drag the My New File icon to the My First Subfolder icon. My New File is moved from My First Folder to My First Subfolder.
4. Double-click **My First Subfolder**. The My First Subfolder window opens, displaying the My New File icon.

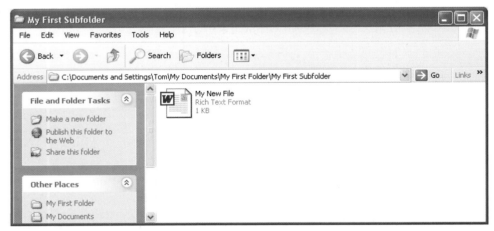

Although the drag-and-drop technique is a quick and easy way to move objects, it may not always be the most convenient—especially when the destination location is not displayed in the current window. In that case, you can use a cut-and-paste operation. Here's how:

1. In the My First Subfolder window, which you opened in the preceding steps, select the **My New File** icon.
2. Click the **Edit** menu and then click **Cut**. The My New File icon appears dimmed.
3. Click the **Back** button in the toolbar to return to the My First Folder window.
4. Click a blank area in the My First Folder window to ensure that no objects are selected.
5. Click the **Edit** menu bar and click **Paste**. My New File is moved from My First Subfolder to My First Folder.

If you need to move an object from one location to another faraway location, such as to a different drive or to another computer on your network, you can use the Move this file task in the File and Folder Tasks list. That way, you don't have to waste time navigating your PC's organizational structure to locate the destination you need. Here's how:

① In My First Folder, click **MyBook**. The File and Folder Tasks list expands to include a task named "Move this file."

② Click **Move this file**. The Move Items dialog box opens.

③ In the Move Items dialog box, select the destination location for the object (in this case, **Local Disk (C:)**).

④ Click **Move**. The Move dialog box closes, and My New File is moved to the selected location.

Copying Objects

Just as there are several ways to move objects, there are several options when it comes to copying them:

✦ CTRL drag and drop

✦ Copy and paste

✦ The Copy this file task in the File and Folder Tasks list

To learn how to copy objects using drag and drop, place a copy of My New File in My First Subfolder by doing the following:

① With the My First Folder window open on your desktop, press and hold down the **CTRL** key.

② With the CTRL key still pressed down, click and hold the **My New File** icon and drag it to My First Subfolder.

 As you CTRL drag and drop, watch the bottom-right corner of the mouse pointer. A plus sign should appear, indicating that a copy, not a move, is being performed.

③ Release the mouse button and CTRL key. Notice that the My New File icon still appears in the My First Folder window. Double-click **My First Subfolder** to open the My First Subfolder window.

④ After verifying that My First File is indeed in My First Subfolder, click the **Back** button in the toolbar to return to the My First Folder window.

If you want to copy an object to a destination that is not displayed in the current window, you can perform a copy-and-paste operation. Instead of using the Edit menu to issue these commands, however, this section demonstrates the use of shortcut menus to accomplish this task:

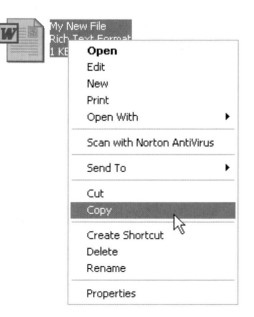

① With the My First Folder window open on your desktop, right-click **My New File**, and then click **Copy** in the shortcut menu that appears.

② Click the **Back** button to navigate to the My Documents folder.

③ Right-click a blank area in the My Documents window, and then click **Paste** in the shortcut menu that appears. A copy of My New File appears in the My Documents window.

④ Click the **Forward** button in the toolbar to return to the My First Folder window. Notice that this window still contains an icon for My New File.

Just as you can use the Move this file task to move an object from one location to another far away, such as a different drive or another computer on your network, you can use the Copy this file task to copy an object. Here's how:

1 In My First Folder, click **My New File**. The File and Folder Tasks list expands to include a task named "Copy this file."

2 Click **Copy this file**. The Copy Items dialog box opens.

3 In the Copy Items dialog box, select the destination location for the object (in this case, **Local Disk (C:)**).

4 Click **Copy**. The Copy dialog box closes, and My New File is copied to the selected location.

Deleting Objects

When you delete objects on your computer, you are temporarily placing them in the Recycle Bin. Doing so frees valuable disk space, and can help keep you organized. If you delete an object, but decide you did so in error, you can retrieve it from the Recycle Bin as long as the Recycle Bin hasn't been emptied (or until the Recycle Bin runs out of room and deletes it permanently).

Deleting objects is a relatively simple process, and there are several ways to accomplish the task. For example, you can use the menu system, a shortcut menu, or the DELETE key on your keyboard to delete objects. Alternatively, you can drag objects to the Recycle Bin icon on your desktop to delete them. This section steps you through the process of deleting files and folders, shortcuts, as well as working with the Recycle Bin.

Deleting Files and Folders

Deleting files and folders are virtually the same; you have several deletion methods at your disposal. Deleted files and folders are placed in the Recycle Bin. Furthermore, folders need not be empty to be deleted. To learn how to delete files, deleting folders uses the same method, let's delete the files you moved and copied to the C: drive in the preceding section:

1 Click **start** and click **My Computer**.

2 Navigate to the Local Disk (C:) window.

3 In the Local Disk (C:) window, click **MyBook** to select it.

4 Click the **File** menu and click **Delete**. The Confirm File Delete dialog box opens.

5 Click **Yes**. A dialog box opens briefly to indicate the progress of the deletion. When the deletion is complete, you are returned to the Local Disk (C:) window, which no longer lists MyBook.

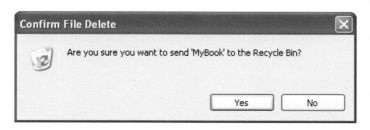

6. Click the **Close** button to close the Local Disk (C:) window and return to the desktop.
7. Click **start** and click **My Documents**. The My Documents window opens.
8. Double-click **My First Folder**. The My First Folder window opens.
9. Click **My New File** to select it.
10. Press the **DELETE** key on your keyboard. Once again, the Confirm File Delete dialog box opens.
11. Click **Yes**. As before, a dialog box opens briefly to indicate the progress of the deletion. When the deletion is complete, you are returned to the My First Folder window, which no longer lists My New File.

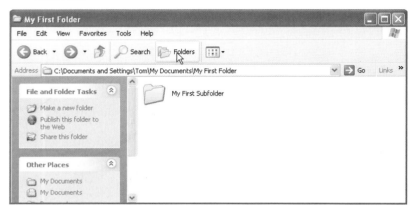

12. Click **My First Subfolder** and press the **DELETE** key on your keyboard to delete it.
13. Click **Yes** in the Confirm Folder Delete dialog box. The folder no longer exists in My First Folder.

Deleting Shortcuts

Are there shortcuts littering your desktop that you never use? One way to eliminate them is to simply delete them from your system. Doing so is simple: Just right-click the icon of the shortcut you want to delete and select **Delete** from the shortcut menu that appears. The shortcut is removed from the desktop.

To practice deleting shortcuts, do the following:

1. Right-click the wordpad (2) shortcut on your desktop.
2. Click **Delete** in the shortcut menu that appears.
3. A Confirm Delete dialog box appears. Click **Yes** to confirm deletion of the shortcut.
4. The shortcut is deleted.

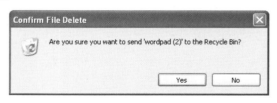

 Deleting a shortcut does not delete the actual file.

Working with the Recycle Bin

If you realize you've deleted an object in error, you'll probably be able to recover it from the Recycle Bin. Sometimes the Recycle Bin has been emptied, has run out of room and deleted the object permanently, or files deleted using third-party software might not be placed in the Recycle Bin.

Restoring Deleted Items

The act of recovering objects from the Recycle Bin is called restoring; to restore objects, do the following:

 These steps assume the My First Folder window is still open on your desktop.

1 Double-click the **Recycle Bin** icon in the lower-right corner of the desktop. The Recycle Bin window opens.

2 In the Recycle Bin window, double-click **My First Subfolder**. The My First Subfolder Properties dialog box opens.

3 Click the **Restore** button.

4 Click **OK** to close the My First Subfolder Properties dialog box and restore the folder to its original location (that is, in My First Folder).

⑤ Arrange the Recycle Bin window and My First Folder window so that the Recycle Bin window is on top, but the contents of both are visible.

⑥ In the Recycle Bin window, click **My New File** to select it.

⑦ Click the **File** menu and click **Restore**. My New File is moved from the Recycle Bin window to the My First Folder window.

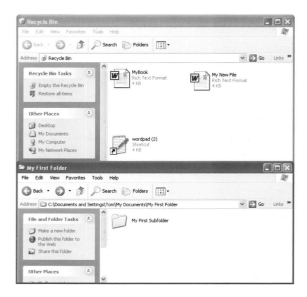

 Other ways to restore objects in the Recycle Bin include dragging them from the Recycle Bin window to the location where they belong, or right-clicking them in the Recycle Bin window and clicking **Restore** in the shortcut menu that appears.

Emptying the Recycle Bin

To free up hard-drive space in a pinch, you can empty the Recycle Bin. Here's how:

① In the Recycle Bin window, click the **File** menu and click **Empty Recycle Bin**. The Confirm Multiple File Delete dialog box opens.

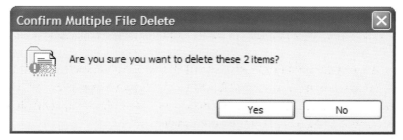

② Click **Yes**. The Confirm Multiple Delete dialog box closes, and the Recycle Bin is emptied.

 ③ Click the **Close** button to close the Recycle Bin window. Notice that the Recycle Bin desktop icon has changed to reflect the fact that the Recycle Bin is now empty.

Renaming Objects

As you know, an object is an entity, defined by a set of attributes. One of the most important attributes is an object's name. Although default names are supplied by Windows XP or the program being used to create the object, these names may not adequately describe the object. For example, when you create a file using WordPad, that file is named "Document" by default. Although this name describes the file's type, it doesn't indicate the file's contents. A better name for the WordPad file might by "Memoirs" or "Work Schedule" or "Great American Novel."

There are a few ways to rename objects: using the File menu, using shortcut menus, and so on. To learn how to rename objects, let's create a few new documents and rename them:

❶ Click **start** and click **My Documents**. The My Documents window opens.

❷ Right-click a blank space in the window. In the shortcut menu that appears, click **New**, and then click Text Document.

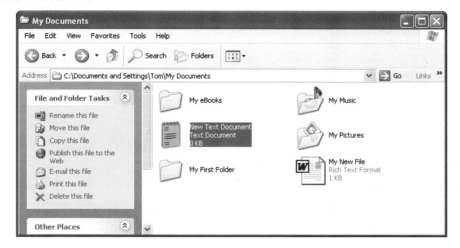

❸ An icon for a new text document appears in the My Documents window; notice that its default name, "New Text Document," is selected. To accept the default name, press **ENTER**.

❹ Repeat steps 2 and 3 to create a second document. Notice that this document's default name is "New Text Document (2)," making it unique in the folder.

❺ Click **New Text Document** to select it.

❻ Click the **File** menu and click **Rename**. The New Text Document name is selected.

❼ Type **File1**, and press **ENTER**.

❽ Right-click **New Text Document (2)** and click **Rename** in the shortcut menu that appears. The New Text Document (2) name is selected.

❾ Type **File1**, and press **ENTER**. The Error Renaming File or Folder dialog box opens, indicating that you must specify another name for this file.

Error Renaming File or Folder

Cannot rename New Text Document (2): A file with the name you specified already exists. Specify a different file name.

[OK]

⑩ Click **OK**. The original name of the file is restored, and is selected to be accepted or changed.

⑪ Type **File2**, and press **ENTER**. The file's name is changed.

To rename a desktop shortcut, right-click it and click **Rename** in the shortcut menu that appears. The shortcut's name is selected; type the name you want, and press **ENTER**.

Opening Objects

You can open any object accessible through My Computer or the Windows Explorer by right-clicking it and choosing Open from the shortcut menu that appears. Selecting this command starts whatever application is associated with the object and displays that object's contents in a window for you to view—or for further work, if you're so inclined.

You can use this technique to access or edit the objects you've worked with in previous sections. Here's how:

① In the My Documents window, right-click **File1** (created in the preceding section) and click **Open** in the shortcut menu that appears.

② Notepad starts with File1 open in the workspace for your inspection—or further work.

③ Click the **Close** button to close Notepad.

④ Click the **Close** button to close My Documents.

To learn more about opening and using objects in Windows, go to the Web segment *Objects: Manipulating* in the Beyond PC Basics course.

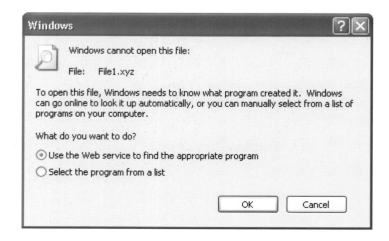

If you try this technique on an object that Windows XP doesn't recognize—for example, a file named File1.xyz, Windows XP displays a dialog box indicating that it doesn't know what program to use to open the object.

Windows

Windows cannot open this file:

File: File1.xyz

To open this file, Windows needs to know what program created it. Windows can go online to look it up automatically, or you can manually select from a list of programs on your computer.

What do you want to do?

◉ Use the Web service to find the appropriate program

○ Select the program from a list

[OK]   [Cancel]

This dialog box gives you two options:

✦ **Use the Web service to find the appropriate program.** Click **OK** to search Microsoft's File Associations database on the Web to determine whether a program is known to be associated with files of type xyz. Results of the search appear in a Web browser window. You must have a working Internet connection for this to work. If no match is found, you'll see a display like the one shown here.

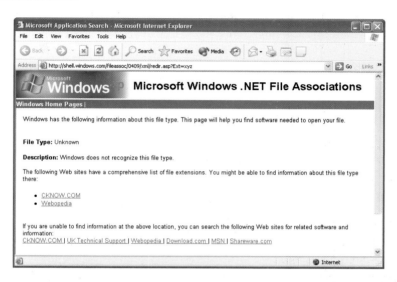

✦ **Select the program from a list.** To specify which program should be used to open the file, click the **Select the program from a list** option button and click **OK**. The Open With dialog box opens; from here, you can select any program already installed on your PC (we often use NotePad or WordPad for mystery files, just to see what they contain).

Using the Search Companion

You can use Windows XP's Search Companion feature to sniff out just about any object, no matter where it is, using all kinds of different attributes to help narrow or qualify your searches.

For example, when searching for a file or folder, the Search Companion lets you specify the following kinds of information to help narrow your searches:

✦ **File name.** Enter complete or partial file names to look for specific files by name.

✦ **Text contents.** Specify text that must occur within a file for it to be selected during a search.

✦ **Location.** Specify search targets, from individual *containers* (default folders like My Documents or drives on your PC) to My Computer (to search every accessible location on your PC).

Other search options enable you to further narrow your search, including restrictions on file dates, file types (such as word processing, spreadsheet, picture, music, or video files), file sizes, and other controls. In addition to enabling you to search for objects on your own PC, Search Companion also allows you to search for computers on your network, if applicable, people in your address book, and information in the Help and Support Center. You can even use Search Companion to search for information on the Internet (if an Internet connection exists).

 To be able to locate files and folders you have worked on, go to the Web segment *Files and Folders: Finding* in the Beyond PC Basics course.

Now that you're familiar with using objects in Windows XP, you might want to restore your PC to the way it looked and behaved before you began. To do so, however, you must have created a restore point as instructed earlier in this chapter. For help restoring your desktop, refer to Chapter 7.

5

Using Multimedia Features and a CD Burner

Your PC can support several multimedia activities, such as playing music and movies. Understanding how to use CDs and DVDs, where much of this multimedia content originates, is essential to getting the most out of your PC. In this chapter, you'll discover how to use the CD and DVD drives and be introduced to various types of CD and DVD media. You'll even explore a few popular media playback tools. Finally, you'll learn how to use CDs and DVDs to install new software on your computer. By the time you finish this chapter, your PC's multimedia features will no longer be a mystery.

Utilizing CD/DVD Drives and Media

Your PC allows you to play back CDs and/or DVDs, just as you do using your stereo and home theatre. However, your PC may also give you the added advantage of being able to burn your own CDs and DVDs.

A *CD* can contain music, data, or both. Some audio CDs include multimedia files (audio, video, animation, movies, software, etc.) that go along with the music, while data CDs typically contain data files, multimedia files, or software. For example, many software programs—including Windows XP—come on data CDs, from which they can be installed. A *DVD,* on the other hand, can contain a movie, data, or both. As with data CDs, DVDs can be used to store data files, multimedia files, and software. Unlike CDs, however, which max out at between 650 and 700 MB of data, DVDs can hold as much as 7 GB of data.

 Data CDs and DVDs can also contain music files, but these differ from the types found on audio CDs. Music files require PC software for playback, while audio CDs can be played in a typical CD player.

The discs you place in a CD/DVD drive are typically referred to as media. You'll need to pay close attention to the type of media you use to ensure it supports the task you want to perform. For example, if you want to burn a DVD, you'll need to make sure you're using a DVD-R or DVD-RAM and not a DVD-ROM. Also, make sure your drive can read that media type—you won't be able to burn a DVD in a CD-ROM drive. Because many CDs and DVDs are exactly the same size and color (see Figure 6-1), you might not be able to identify a disc's media type simply by looking at it. If the media type is not printed on the disc itself, look at the original packaging to determine whether the disc is a CD-ROM, CD-R, CD-RW, DVD-ROM, DVD-R, or DVD-RAM.

As mentioned in Chapter 1, there are three types of CD drives and three types of DVD drives:

♦ **CD-ROM drive.** A CD-ROM drive reads information on CD-ROMs. CD-ROMs can be read, but not written to.

♦ **CD-R drive.** A CD-R drive can read information on CD-ROMs and write information to CD-Rs. A CD-R can be written to, or burned, only once.

♦ **CD-RW drive.** A CD-RW drive can **Figure 6-1** CD/DVD media.
read information on CD-ROMs and write information to CD-Rs and CD-RWs. A CD-RW is a CD that you can write to several times.

♦ **DVD drive.** A DVD drive reads information on DVD-ROMs. Like CD-ROMs, DVD-ROMs can be read, but not written to.

♦ **DVD-R drive.** A DVD-R drive can read information on DVD-ROMs and write information to DVD-Rs. A DVD-R can be written to, or burned, only once.

♦ **DVD-RAM drive.** A DVD-RAM drive can read information on DVD-ROMs and write information to DVD-Rs and DVD-RAMs. A DVD-RAM is a DVD that you can write to many times.

6

Your computer might have a drive that plays CDs, burns CD-Rs or CD-RWs, plays DVDs, or burns DVD-Rs or DVD-RAMs. Many CD/DVD drives are combination players. For example, some CD-RW drives can also play DVDs.

You need to know what kinds of CD or DVD drives your PC has because that determines what types of media your computer can read. If you have a plain CD-ROM drive, you can read CDs, but you can't burn your own CDs or play DVDs. If you have a DVD drive, you can play CDs, but cannot burn CD-Rs or CD-RWs. Table 6-1 lists uses for each type of CD or DVD drive.

Table 6-1 Types of CD/DVD drives and their uses.

TASK	CD-ROM	CD-R	CD-RW	DVD	DVD-R	DVD-RAM
Play CDs	✔	✔	✔	✔	✔	✔
Read data CDs	✔	✔	✔	✔	✔	✔
Burn CD-Rs		✔	✔			
Burn CD-RWs			✔			
Play DVDs				✔	✔	✔
Read data DVDs				✔	✔	✔
Burn DVD-Rs					✔	✔
Burn DVD-RAMs						✔

Using Your CD/DVD Drive

No matter what type of media you plan to use in your CD/DVD drive, the procedure is essentially the same. Only a few simple steps are required. Before you use your drive, however, there are a few precautions you should take:

✦ Always use the button on the CD/DVD drive to open and close the drawer. Never force the drawer in or out.

Some multimedia programs include an Eject button or command you can use to open the CD/DVD drive drawer.

+ Make sure the CD/DVD media you place in the CD/DVD drive drawer is centered within the grooves, notches, or depression in the drawer.

+ Never place anything other than CD/DVD media in or on your CD/DVD drive drawer. Doing so could damage the drive.

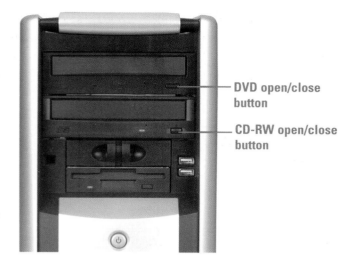

DVD open/close button

CD-RW open/close button

+ Always place CD/DVD media with its label face up.

+ Always hold CD/DVD media by the edges or stick your finger in the center hole. Fingerprints and smudges on the data side of the CD/DVD media might cause skipping or prevent reading or writing.

6

To use your CD/DVD drive, follow these steps:

1. Press the open/close button on the front of your CD/DVD drive. The CD/DVD drive drawer opens.
2. Pick up the CD/DVD media by its edges only or by placing a finger in the center hole.
3. Place the CD/DVD media in the tray with the label facing up. Move the media into the center of the drawer so that it fits within the defined holding area.
4. Press the open/close button on the front of your CD/DVD drive. The CD/DVD drive drawer closes.

The PC scans the CD/DVD disc to see what type of media it is. Depending on the speed of your drive, this may take a few moments.

Opening a File on a CD

Though the storage capabilities of a CD pale in comparison to a DVD, CD's still hold a tremendous amount of data. Because no network or INternet connection is required to use them, they are often employed by software companies to distribute their products. Unlike hard drives or floppy disk, however, your ability to copy files to a CD depends on what type of CD drive your PC has and what types of CD media are at your disposal. The section "Storing Data Files on CDs" later in this chapter will show you how to store files and folders to a CD. First, you'll learn how to access the data on your CDs.

If the CD does not have autorun, or if you want to open a file other than the one that is opened automatically, do the following:

❶ Click **start** and click **My Computer**. The My Computer window opens.

❷ Under Devices with Removable Storage, double-click the **CD-RW Drive (D:)** (or similarly named) icon. The window for that drive opens, containing one or more icons representing files.

❸ Double-click the file you want to open. The program used to create the file starts, displaying the contents of the file in the program window.

❹ Close the file.

Playing Audio CDs

The first time you insert a CD or DVD into your PC, Windows XP displays a dialog
box asking you what you want to do next. For example, if you insert an audio CD, Windows XP displays the Audio CD dialog box, shown in Figure 6-2.

Figure 6-2 The Audio CD dialog box.

The default CD player may vary from machine to machine. Windows Media Player is a common one, but your machine might use a different program to play CDs, such as MusicMatch® Jukebox. (We'll cover Windows Media Player and MusicMatch Jukebox in more detail in a moment.) If your PC uses a different CD player, read its user manual or open the help menu on the program's menu bar to learn how to operate it.

This dialog box lists three options:

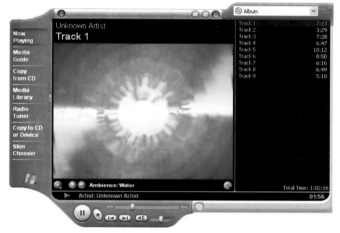

Figure 6-3 The Windows Media Player.

✦ **Play Audio CD.** Select this option to play the audio CD using the default player (in this case, Windows Media Player, shown in Figure 6-3).

✦ **Open folder to view files.** This option is used to view the files on the disc in a Windows Explorer window (see Figure 6-4).

✦ **Take no action.** When choosing this option, the dialog box will close and no action is taken on the CD.

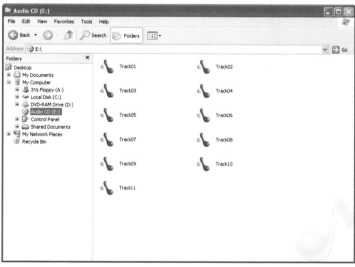

Figure 6-4 Windows Explorer window with audio track file icons.

Select the action you want to perform on the audio CD. If you know that you'll want to take the same action each time you insert an audio CD into your PC, check the **Always do the selected action** check box at the bottom of the dialog box, and then click **OK**. That way, the next time you insert an audio CD into the CD drive, Windows will automatically play back the CD without displaying the Audio CD dialog box first.

If you select the **Always do the selected action** check box for one type of media, such as an audio CD, it applies only to that type of media. If you insert a different type of media into the drive, such as a DVD-ROM, Windows XP will display a dialog box similar to the one for audio CDs, asking you what action you want to take. Make your selection just as you did for audio CDs.

More About . . . Resetting Your AutoPlay Options

When you select the **Always do the selected action** check box, you are defining an *AutoPlay option,* which tells the PC what action to take automatically when a disc of a specific type is inserted in a drive. If you make the wrong selection or change your mind later, you can change your AutoPlay settings. Here's how:

1 Click the **start** button, and then click **My Computer**. The My Computer window opens.

2 Right-click the CD/DVD drive icon. A shortcut menu appears.

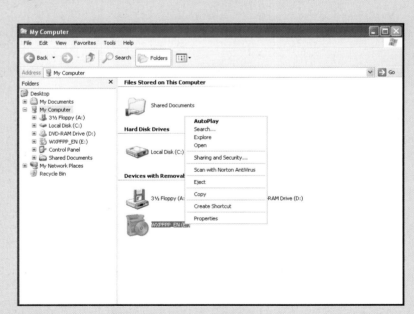

3 Click **Properties** in the shortcut menu. The CD Drive Properties dialog box opens.

More About . . . Resetting Your AutoPlay Options continued

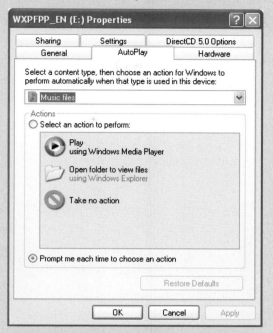

④ Click the **AutoPlay** tab.

⑤ Click the drop-down arrow, and select a type of CD/DVD media (for this example, choose Music CD). There are several to choose from:

+ **Music files.** A CD/DVD with one or more types of music files, such as MP3, WMA, CDA, or WAV.

+ **Pictures.** A CD/DVD with one or more types of image files, such as GIF, JPG, or TIF.

+ **Video files.** A CD/DVD with one or more types of video files, such as MPG, AVI, or MOV. This can also be a standard movie DVD.

+ **Mixed content.** A CD/DVD with multiple types of files, including music, images, and video.

+ **Music CD.** A standard audio CD.

⑥ In the Action section, click the **Select an action to perform** option button, and then click the desired action.

⑦ If you prefer to be prompted for an action to take each time an audio CD is inserted, select the **Prompt me each time to choose an action** option button.

⑧ Click **OK**.

 If you want to restore the settings to their defaults, click **Restore Defaults**.

Using Windows Media Player

You can use Windows Media Player (see Figure 6-5) to play audio CDs, music files, and video files, as well as to access Internet radio, television, and movie programs. You can even use Windows Media Player to copy music from CDs to your hard drive, create custom playlists, burn new audio CDs, and transfer music files to portable audio players.

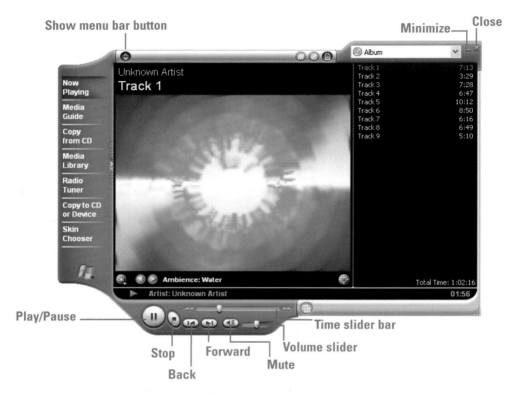

Figure 6-5 The Windows Media Player.

The controls built into Windows Media Player for listening to audio CDs are similar to those on your portable, car, or home CD player. Table 6-2 lists the common controls in a typical Windows-based CD player.

Table 6-2 The common CD player controls.

USE THIS BUTTON	TO
Play	Start the music. Once the CD is playing, the Play button becomes the Pause button.
Pause	Pause the music. To restart the music, click the Play/Pause button.
Stop	Stop the music.
Back	Skip to the previous song.
Forward	Skip to the next song.
Mute	Turn off the sound.
Volume	Change the volume. Drag the slider bar up or down to adjust volume levels.
Time	Move ahead or back within a song. Drag the slider bar to jump to a specific spot.

To learn more about the controls of your player go to your player's help menu.

To use Windows Media Player to play CDs, do the following:

❶ Insert the CD you want to listen to in your CD/DVD drive.

❷ If Windows Media Player does not start automatically, click the **start** button, point to **All Programs**, and click **Windows Media Player** (or click the **Windows Media Player** icon on the left side of the start menu).

 If a program other than Windows Media Player starts when you insert the CD, simply click the program window's **Close** button to close the program.

❸ Click **Play** to start the music.

In addition to these common playback buttons, the Windows Media Player window has the same controls as any other program window, including Minimize and Close. The normal rectangular workspace area, however, is hidden. Click the **Show menu bar** button to reveal this area.

Show menu
bar button

When you are finished listening to your CD, click the **Close** button to exit Windows Media Player. You can leave your audio CD in the CD/DVD drive or remove it. To remove the media from the drive, do the following:

1. Press the open/close button on the front of your CD/DVD drive. The drive drawer opens.
2. Pick up the CD by its edges or by placing a finger in the center hole, and remove it from the tray.
3. Press the open/close button on the front of your drive. The drive drawer closes.

Using MusicMatch Jukebox

MusicMatch Jukebox, shown in Figure 6-6, is as versatile as Windows Media Player. In fact, their capabilities are similar.

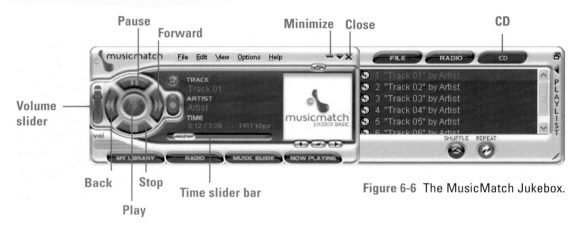

Figure 6-6 The MusicMatch Jukebox.

The controls built into MusicMatch Jukebox for listening to audio CDs are similar to the ones used by Windows Media Player. Table 6-2 (in the preceding section) lists the common controls in a typical Windows-based CD player.

To use MusicMatch to play CDs, do the following:

1. Insert the CD you want to listen to in your CD/DVD drive.
2. If MusicMatch does not start automatically, click the **start** button, point to **All Programs**, point to **MusicMatch**, and then click **MusicMatch Jukebox**.

 If a program other than MusicMatch starts when you insert the CD, simply click the program window's **Close** button to close the program.

③ Click the **CD** button on the MusicMatch toolbar to switch to the CD drive as your audio source.

④ Click **Play** to start the music.

⑤ When you finish listening, click the **Close** button to exit the player. You can leave your audio CD in the drive or remove it. To remove it, follow the steps outlined in the preceding section.

Playing DVDs

Playing DVD movies is almost as easy as playing an audio CD, but you may need to install a DVD compression and encryption decoder driver first.

 Some DVD movies include a playback tool. In that case, you can simply play the DVD using this simple tool.

One easy way to get the driver you need is to purchase and install a third-party DVD player program such as WinDVD from InterVideo or PowerDVD from CyberLink. In doing so, you'll install the compression and encryption decoder driver needed to play DVDs.

Alternatively, if you bought your PC from a large computer company, such as Gateway, it most likely came pre-installed with a DVD player program of some kind. Additionally, many DVDs themselves include the PCFriendly DVD player (see Figure 6-7). If you don't already have a DVD player installed, select to install the DVD player from the DVD media when prompted.

Figure 6-7 The PCFriendly DVD player.

Once you have a DVD compression and encryption decoder installed, you can use a third-party DVD player or Windows Media Player to play your movies. Most third-party DVD players have simple controls, including play, pause, stop, fast forward, skip forward, rewind, and skip backward. If you aren't sure how to use your specific third-party player, consult its user guide or the software's help menu.

To use Windows Media Player to play a DVD movie, do the following:

1 Insert the DVD media into the DVD drive.

2 If any program windows or dialog boxes open other than Windows Media Player, click the **Close** button to exit them.

3 Click **start**, point to **All Programs**, and then click **Windows Media Player** (or click **Windows Media Player** on the left side of the start menu). The Windows Media Player window opens.

4 In the left column of buttons, click **Now Playing**.

5 Click the drop-down arrow in the upper-right corner, and select the DVD drive.

6 Once the DVD drive is selected, Windows Media Player should play the DVD automatically. If it doesn't, click the **Play** button.

7 To view the movie in full-screen mode, click the **View Full Screen** button located in the lower-right corner below the video image. The movie is resized to the maximum size possible for your screen. Windows Media Player controls appear as tabs at the top and bottom of your screen; after a few seconds, these disappear.

 To regain access to the Windows Media Player controls during movie playback, simply move the mouse. If the controls don't reappear immediately, click the mouse near the bottom of the screen.

8 Navigate the DVD control menu using the mouse. Just point and click to the option of your choice, such as playing the movie, changing audio settings, viewing scene outlines, or accessing the bonus material on the DVD.

9 When you finish watching the DVD movie, click the **Close** button in the Windows Media Player window.

10 Remove the DVD media from the DVD drive, as described in the section "Using Windows Media Player."

Installing Software from a CD or DVD

Because CDs enable a software company to include as much as 700 MB of files on a single disc, software is often distributed on CDs. To store the same amount of data that fits on a single CD, you'd need 487 floppies!

Most software products use less than half a CD's capacity, even when lots of extras and bonuses are included. A few software products and several games, however, do come on multiple CDs or on a single DVD disc.

Although you install and load programs from a CD and a DVD the same basic way, the specific steps of an installation process will vary by program. For this reason, it's wise to read the program's installation manual and user guide before inserting CD/DVD media into your PC. Then, follow these general steps to install software from a CD/DVD (remember, you must be logged on to a computer administrator user account to install programs):

 If the steps in your software CD/DVD's user manual differ from the ones shown here, follow the ones in the user manual.

① Close any programs that are currently open on your PC, including your anti-virus software.

② Insert the CD/DVD into the appropriate drive.

③ If this is the first time the program CD/DVD has been inserted into your PC, Windows XP will look for a special file called autorun; if it finds this file, the operating system then executes its instructions. Typically, a Welcome screen with the company and product name appears; look for a Next, Continue, or OK button on the screen, and click it.

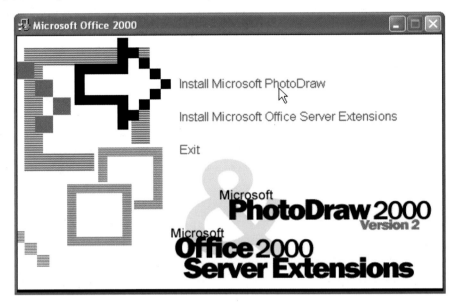

④ You should see a list of options; look for one labeled "Install" or "Setup." When you find it, click it.

 Most software CD/DVDs, in addition to offering an install option, include other options such as view samples, watch demos, work through a tutorial, see advertisements, or read documentation.

⑤ Follow any additional on-screen prompts.

 In most cases, you can accept default selections on any subsequent setup screen. However, it's always a good idea to review the installation manual before initiating an install.

If no Welcome screen appears when you insert the CD or DVD, follow these steps:

① Click the start button, and then click My Computer to open My Computer.

② Double-click the CD or DVD drive icon.

③ In the top level of the CD or DVD drive, look for a Setup or Install program icon. When you find it, double-click it.

 If you don't see a Setup or Install icon, consult the software's user manual for details on how to install the product.

④ Follow the on-screen prompts or the steps in the installation user guide.

During the course of installing a software product, you'll often be prompted to perform several common activities, including

✦ **Agree to a user license.** This typically requires you to read a lengthy legal document and click the **I Agree** button to proceed with the installation.

✦ **Provide a product key.** A *product key* is a string of letters and/or numbers that uniquely identifies a product you've purchased; these are used to prevent software piracy. Without a product key, most software will not install or function properly. You can usually find the product key on your software packaging.

✦ **Indicate an install path.** An *install path* is a folder on a local hard drive where the bulk of the software product will be installed. In most cases, you'll want to install the program in c:\Program Files*product name,* where *product name* is the exact or representational name of the software product. The setup routine usually suggests a location; it's a good practice to stick with the suggested location.

✦ **Restart.** Some programs require you to restart your system to complete the installation process.

Once your software is installed, an icon for the product should appear in the start menu, on the desktop, or both. To start the program, click the software's icon in the All Programs menu, or double-click the software's desktop icon.

Storing Data Files on CDs

Just a few years ago, storing data to CD was expensive and frustrating. Today, it is fast, reliable, and relatively inexpensive.

In addition to a CD-R or CD-RW drive, you will need a special CD recording software in order to "burn" a CD. A reliable and powerful program is Roxio's Easy Cd Creator, a program that provides quick access to most of the CD creation tools you will need. Once installed, Easy CD Creator starts automatically when a disc is inserted into your CD-RW drive.

If you chose the program's setup defaults when you installed it, you will find Easy CD Creator in the start menu's **All Programs** menu. To launch the program, point to **Roxio Easy CD Creator 5** and click **Project Selector.** From the Select a Project window, you can choose any of the following options (as shown in Figure 6-8):

+ **Make a music CD** to copy tracks from one or more audio CDs to a blank CD.

+ **Make a data CD** to format a blank CD so it can store files and folders from your computer.

+ **Make a photo or video CD** to store digital photos or video clips on a CD.

Figure 6-8 Roxio Easy CD Creator 5 Select a Project window.

 The suboptions under Make a photo or video CD are available in the Platinum edition only. To upgrade to the Platinum edition (at an additional cost), point to **Upgrade** in the Select a Project window, click the **Upgrade** button, and then click the **Upgrade Now** button. You must have Internet access to upgrade in this manner.

+ **CD copier** to create an exact duplicate copy of a CD you already own.

With Easy CD Creator, you simply *format* a disc, and then copy or save files to the disc just as if it were a floppy or hard disk.

To format a blank disc to make it readable by almost any CD drive:

1. Insert a recordable disc (a CD-R) into your disc drive. Unless AutoPlay is set up to automatically format blank CDs, Windows displays the CD Drive dialog box listing the actions you can perform with this disc. If **Create a CD using Roxio Easy CD Creator** is not selected, click the option to select it.

2. Click the **OK** button to start the formatting process. The Select a Project window opens.

③ Point to the **make a data CD** button to format this disc for ordinary data file recording. Three options appear to the right (directCD, dataCD project, and take two, which is dimmed). Move your mouse pointer to the **directCD** button and click it.

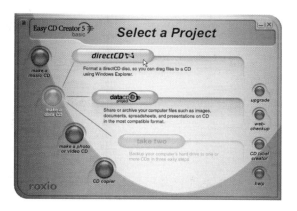

④ The directCD format utility window opens. Click the **format CD** button.

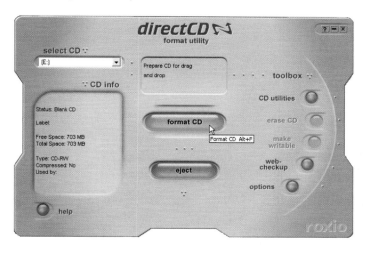

⑤ The DirectCD Format dialog box opens asking you to name the disc. Type a name in the Label field (such as MyBestFiles). This name can contain as many as 11 characters and can include spaces. The following characters, however, are not allowed: [ ] . , / \ ? : ; * " < > + = |.

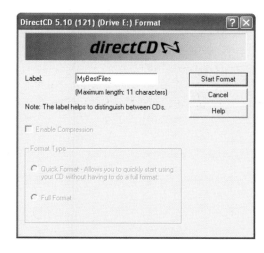

Give the CD a unique name that will help identify its contents. The CD's name will appear in My Computer whenever you insert the CD.

⑥ Click the **Start Format** button.

⑦ DirectCD displays a dialog box indicating the amount of time the formatting operation requires and asking if you want to proceed. Click **OK**.

⑧ As DirectCD formats the disc, it displays a dialog box showing the progress of the format operation. When formatting is complete, Windows displays the contents (none) of the disc in the drive.

⑨ Click the **Close** button to close the empty disc window. Click **OK** to close the DirectCD (CD Ready) dialog box. Click the **Close** button to close the directCD format utility window.

Copying Files to CD-RWs

Your recordable disc now acts like any other disk. You can write files or folders to the disc using any of the following methods:

✦ Using a program's **File, Save** or **File, Save As** command to save a document to the disc

✦ Dragging and dropping files or folders you want to copy to the disc's icon in My Computer or into a My Computer window that displays the contents of the recordable disc

✦ Selecting the file(s) and/or folder(s) you want to copy to the disc, right-clicking one of the selected files or folders, pointing to **Send To** in the shortcut menu that appears, and clicking **DirectCD Drive**

The easiest way to copy folders and files to a formatted recordable disc is to use My Computer to send the objects from your computer's hard drive to the disc. Here's what you do:

① Insert a formatted, recordable disc into your recordable drive. Windows Explorer displays the CD Drive folder.

To erase a CD-RW disc in order to re-use it, insert it in your PC's recordable drive. Then, in My Computer, right-click the disc drive icon and click **Erase this CD-RW**.

② Click the **start** button and click **My Computer**. The My Computer window opens.

③ In My Computer, navigate to the drive and folder in which the items you want to copy to disc are stored.

④ Select the folders and files you want to copy. The selected items appear highlighted.

⑤ Right-click one of the selected files or folders, point to **Send To**, and click **DirectCD Drive**. Windows copies the items onto the disc.

 Want to record music CDs and learn more about digital music in general? See the table at the end of the chapter for more information.

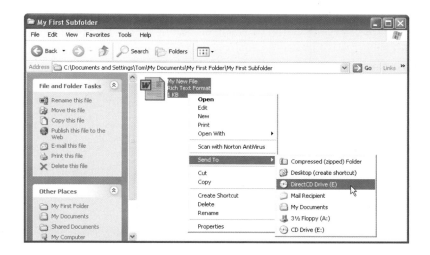

Ejecting and Closing a Disc

When you have finished copying files to a CD-RW disc, you can eject the disc and put it away in its case. You can then read the disc in most CD-RW drives and any CD-ROM drives that support CD-RW media. CD-R discs are a little different. CD-R discs cannot be read by another drive until the disc is *closed*. Closing a disc specifies the storage standard that the disc follows, thus determining the type of drive(s) that can read the disc. To eject a CD and (optionally) close the CD, take the following steps:

① Press the **Eject** button on the CD drive.

② The DirectCD Eject Options dialog box opens. Select the desired option:

    ✦ **Leave As Is.** This leaves the CD open, so you can continue to copy files to it. You can open files stored on the CD and use the CD in your recordable drive, but you will not be able to use the disc in a standard CD-ROM drive or give the disc to someone else to use in their CD-ROM drive.

+ **Close to UDF v.1.5.** This closes the CD to the *UDF (Universal Disc Format)* standard, so that anyone who has Easy CD Creator or another UDF reader installed can read the disc using a standard CD-ROM drive.

+ **Close to Read on Any Computer.** This option closes the CD, which makes the disc readable by any CD-ROM drive. It uses about 22 MB of space on the CD.

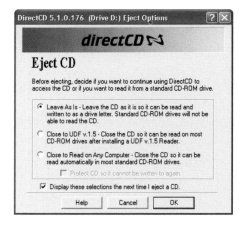

❹ If you selected the Close to Read on Any Computer option, you can also select the **Protect CD So It Cannot Be Written To Again** option. This closes the CD permanently, so nobody can modify the CD in the future.

❹ Click **OK**. DirectCD writes the data to the disc and ejects the CD using the option you selected.

❺ A dialog box opens indicating that the CD was ejected. Click **OK**. Then close any open windows.

Avoiding CD-Burning Pitfalls

Burning CDs is not always trouble-free. In fact, it's possible to ruin many recordable discs trying to copy your favorite files. If you run into trouble burning your own CDs, consider the following:

+ Make sure the speed range for the recordable discs you purchase matches or exceeds the speed range for your recordable drive.

+ If you have trouble burning files onto 80-minute discs, use 74-minute discs instead.

+ Before starting the copy process, close any unnecessary programs and turn off the screen saver. Once you start the copy operation, leave your PC alone and avoid moving near your computer. Motion can cause slight vibrations in the recorder that might negatively affect the copying operation.

Go online to **www.LearnwithGateway.com** and log on to select:

◆ *Internet Links and Resources*
◆ *FAQs*

Gateway offers a hands-on training course that covers many of the topics in this chapter. Additional fees may apply. Call **888-852-4821** to enroll. Please have your customer ID and order number ready when you call.

6

Customizing Windows XP

Every person is unique, with his or her own styles and preferences. With Windows XP, you can configure your PC to reflect your uniqueness! This chapter explores the many customization options available to you and how to use them. You'll learn how to apply desktop themes and backgrounds, customize the appearance of the desktop and windows, and change your color scheme. Then, you'll take a closer look at the start menu and taskbar, originally introduced in Chapter 1. Finally, you'll explore the Control Panel, which houses a set of tools designed to help you manage just about everything in the Windows XP environment and on your PC, from hardware to software and everything in between.

Customizing Your Desktop

There are many ways you can make Windows XP your own. On the desktop for instance, you can apply a theme or a background image, add icons, change the appearance of program windows, or use a screen saver. You can also customize your start menu and taskbar, and tweak and tune the way your desktop looks and feels to your heart's content.

Creating a Restore Point

In this section, you'll step through the process of changing all sorts of Windows settings. When you're finished, you may or may not like what you see. Undoing each step in every process to restore your system to its starting point can be tedious at best; fortunately, there's a better way. If you take the following steps, you can create a *restore point* for your PC. When you've completed this section, you can easily reset Windows XP to its current looks and behavior, no matter what changes you may be inspired to make!

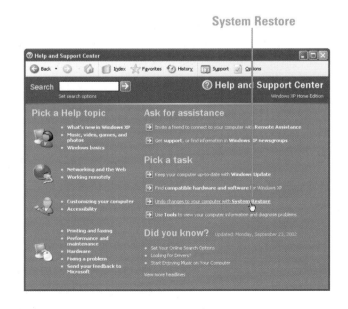

System Restore

① Click **start**. The start menu appears.

② Click **Help and Support**. The Help and Support Center window opens.

③ Click the **System Restore** button in the upper-right corner of the window. The System Restore window opens.

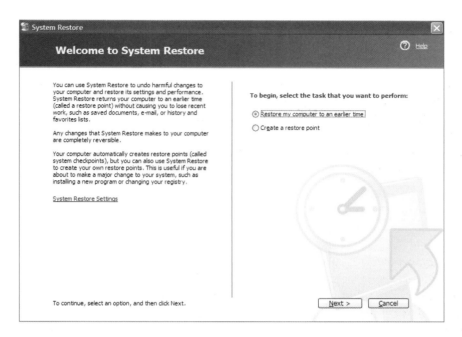

④ Click the Create a restore point option button, and then click Next.

⑤ In the Restore point description text box, type Before Customizing Your Desktop, and then click Create.

⑥ Click Close to close the System Restore window.

⑦ Click the Close button to close the Help and Support Center window.

What you've just done is to take a snapshot of your system's current settings, preferences, and so forth, to which you'll now be able to return at will. Think of this as a form of insurance against making changes to your system that you don't like or don't want to keep around. You can now return to your initial point of departure down the customization trail any time you like.

In the sections that follow next, you explore some of the kinds of changes you can make to your Windows XP desktop. We start you off with a restore point to allow you to experiment with these various capabilities, and know that you can easily restore the original desktop.

Managing Windows XP Display Properties

The key to managing much of the way your desktop looks lies within the frame of the Display Properties dialog box. This powerful and useful tool is accessible in all kinds of ways, but always looks and acts the same. Figure 7-1 depicts the Display Properties dialog box.

7

Figure 7-1: The Display Properties dialog box shows the Themes tab by default.

In this window you see a set of tabs across the top of the display area. Each of these tabs covers its own desktop or display related controls. In the sections that follow next, we'll cover these in their order of appearance. Here's a quick overview from which we'll launch this tour:

✦ **Themes:** Lets you choose named combinations of sounds, icons, and visual elements called themes.

✦ **Desktop:** Lets you choose, position, and stretch a background or image for your desktop.

✦ **Screen Saver:** Activates an image or display after your PC is idle for some time.

✦ **Appearance:** Gives you down-and-dirty control over the way individual Windows and desktop elements look and act.

✦ **Settings:** Supplies controls for monitors or displays you use with Windows XP.

Applying Themes

You manage themes through the Themes tab in the Display Properties window. Here, a *theme* is a set of appearance options that work as a named group, and that create a quick and easy way for you to personalize Windows XP. At any time, you can also save whatever set of customizations you may have made to your desktop, and save it as a named theme for later re-use.

Themes gather up all the options that control your desktop's appearance inside a single, named collection of settings that covers color schemes, how windows and buttons look, font selections and sizes, and all kinds of detailed controls over all kinds of desktop objects.

 With a standard installation of Windows XP, there are only a few themes to choose from. If, however, your PC has the +Plus Pack® for Windows XP installed, you have many more themes available to you.

To apply a theme to your desktop, do the following:

1 Right-click a blank area on your desktop. A shortcut menu appears.

2 Click Properties in the shortcut menu. The Display Properties dialog box opens.

3 Click the Theme list, and then click Windows XP. Notice how the background changes in the Sample preview box; this background is called "Underwater."

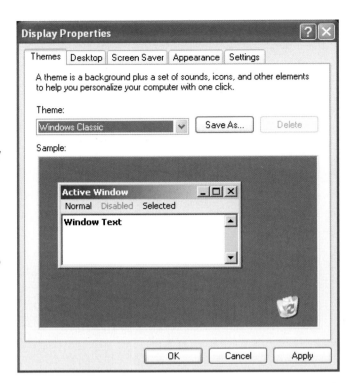

④ Click the Theme list again and click Windows Classic. The background in the Sample preview box changes yet again to resemble previous versions of Windows. Notice the squared off windows and 2-D shading and color schemes in use.

⑤ Click through your list of themes to see what each one looks like inside the Sample preview box. Click Windows XP and click OK to close the Display Properties dialog box and apply the theme to your desktop.

Changing the Desktop

Instead of using a theme, which changes numerous appearance options at once, you can change individual options separately. The Desktop and Appearance tabs are where you'll find such controls. For example, using the Desktop tab you can apply a new background without affecting other desktop appearance options.

The Desktop tab also provides various ways to place and manage icons on your desktop using its Customize Desktop button. We cover this later in this chapter in a section entitled "Using the Customize Desktop Button.

In fact, Windows XP offers at least three different ways to choose a background for your desktop:

✦ You can select a pre-defined background in the Desktop tab of the Display Properties window.

✦ You can browse your file system for a background file of your own choosing in the Desktop tab of the Display Properties window.

✦ By right-clicking on an image in Internet Explorer, you can click the Set as Background menu selection to use whatever image you've selected as your background.

We explain each of these methods step by step in the sections that follow next.

Select a Pre-defined Background

To choose from a list of pre-defined choices to select the background for your desktop, do the following:

1 Right-click a blank area on your desktop and click Properties in the shortcut menu that appears. The Display Properties dialog box opens.

2 Click the Desktop tab. The Display Properties dialog box displays a list of backgrounds to choose from in the Background list.

③ Scroll through the Background list, and click any that interest you. Note that as you select various background names, corresponding patterns appear in the monitor preview area above the list box.

④ When you find a background you like, click OK to close the Display Properties dialog box and apply the background to your desktop.

Browse your PC for a Background

To select an image from your PC's file system as the background for your desktop, do the following:

① Right-click a blank area on your desktop and click Properties in the shortcut menu that appears. The Display Properties dialog box opens.

② Click the Desktop tab, and then click the Browse button. By default, this opens a Browse window for the My Pictures folder on your PC.

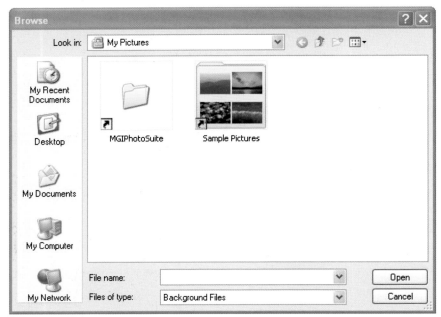

③ Double-click the Sample Pictures folder to find a usable background image; click any file that appears to select a corresponding image for your background. On the other hand, If you've got a digitized family or vacation photo, or some other favorite image, you could pick that as your background instead.

④ When you find a background you like (such as Water lilies), click Open to select that file. It shows up in the monitor frame in the Desktop tab immediately thereafter.

⑤ Click Apply to select that background for your desktop. Then click OK to close the Display Properties dialog box. Notice how your desktop changes to the new image.

Using the Customize Desktop Button

If you've used previous versions of Windows, you may miss the many icons that used to appear on the desktop by default, such as My Documents, My Computer, My Network Places, and Internet Explorer. To add any of these icons to your Windows XP desktop, you use the Customize Desktop button, as follows:

1. Right-click a blank area on your desktop and click Properties in the shortcut menu that appears. The Display Properties dialog box opens.

2. Click the Desktop tab, then click the Customize Desktop button under the Background list. The Desktop Items dialog box opens.

3. Click any or all of the Desktop icons check boxes to place the corresponding icon on your desktop. For example, select the My Documents check box to make that folder appear on the desktop. Notice also that if you click the My Documents icon and then the Change Icon button, you can then change the icon associated with My Documents (you can even use the Browse button to pick from other icon collections). The Change Icon dialog box opens.

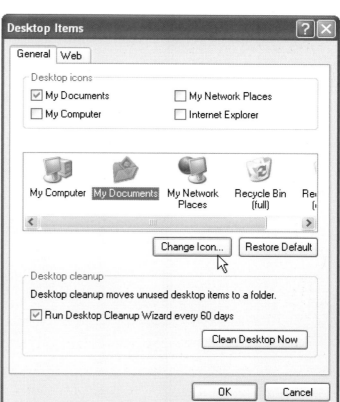

Look for icons in this file:

C:\WINNT\SYSTEM32\mydocs.dll Browse...

Select an icon from the list below:

OK   Cancel

④ Click the first icon, and then click OK to close the Change Icon dialog box. Click OK to close the Desktop Items dialog box and return to the Display Properties dialog box. Any changes you make will not yet take effect.

⑤ Click OK to close the Display Properties dialog box and add any icons you may have selected or changed to your desktop.

Your desktop should appear similar to Figure 7-2.

Figure 7-2: Modified Windows XP desktop.

Using a Screen Saver

In the Display Properties window, the third tab from the left is the Screen Saver tab. Inside this tab, you can not only select and control the behavior of various screen savers, you can also manage monitor and other power controls as well. That's because screen savers activate once a PC has been idle for some time—because idle PCs use electrical power to nobody's benefit, it makes sense that managing energy saving options for your PC's display appear in the same place.

Screen savers are utilities that display various types of images on screen after a specified period of inactivity has elapsed. These utilities were originally designed to protect computer monitors from damage caused by an image being displayed without interruption over long periods of time. Although innovations in monitor design fixed the problem that could cause this type of damage, screen savers remain very popular. Some screen savers show a blank screen, others move two or three-dimensional images around on the monitor.

Follow these steps to apply a screen saver to your Windows XP desktop:

1. Right-click a blank area on your desktop and click **Properties** in the shortcut menu that appears. The Display Properties dialog box opens.

2. Click the **Screen Saver** tab. The Display Properties dialog box lists available screen savers and settings.

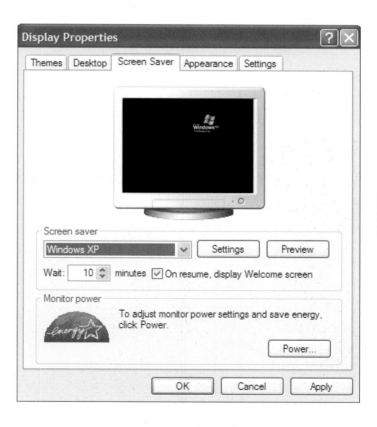

③ Click the Screen Saver list and click 3D Flying Objects. The monitor in the Screen Saver tab displays a reduced-size version of the selected screen saver.

④ Click the Preview button to view a full-screen preview of the screen saver. Click or move the mouse to stop the preview phase and return to the Display Properties window.

⑤ Click the Settings button. The Settings dialog box opens for whatever screen saver you select (3D Flying Objects Settings, in this case). Note that for some screen savers—such as 3-D Flying Objects default Style (Windows logo)—other settings (Color Usage, Resolution, and Size) are dimmed and inactive. If you click the Style list (and click Ribbon, for example), other settings in the dialog box become active, as shown in Figure 7-3. Click OK to preview your settings or Cancel to ignore them.

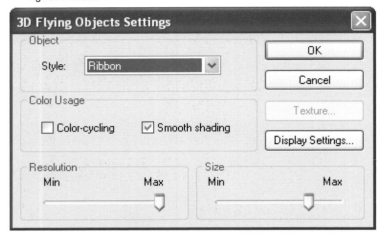

Figure 7-3: Select the Ribbon style in the 3D Flying Objects Settings window to activate most controls.

⑥ Preview several screen savers until you find one you like, and then select it.

⑦ Click OK to close the Display Properties dialog box and apply the screen saver to your desktop. You may see a "Please Wait" message box pop up; if so, you'll have to wait until you regain control over your desktop to proceed. This may take a half a minute or more—please be patient.

Screen savers can be a source of entertainment and visual interest on an otherwise idle desktop.

 If others access your computer across a network, some PC experts recommend you avoid the 3-D screen savers. That's because they crunch lots of numbers in the background to calculate changing shapes, sizes, and colors. Number-crunching screen savers use CPU cycles that others may prefer to use for more productive purposes! In such cases, you're best off choosing the Blank screen saver, boring though it may be.

At the bottom of the Screen Saver tab, you see a section labeled Monitor Power. Inside that section is the Power button. Click that button to manage various aspects of how your Windows XP PC uses electricity. The Power Option Properties window lets you manage power schemes, control how power-saving settings are used, where your PC stores data on a hard disk when it hibernates, and lets Windows XP know if your PC is attached to an uninterruptible power supply (UPS). Because they're so concerned with conserving battery power, laptop users will probably be a lot more inclined to explore this window than users on normal desktop PCs.

Changing Your Windows Appearance

The fourth tab from the left in the Display Properties window is labeled Appearance. This tab provides item-level controls over all kinds of Windows appearance elements, including:

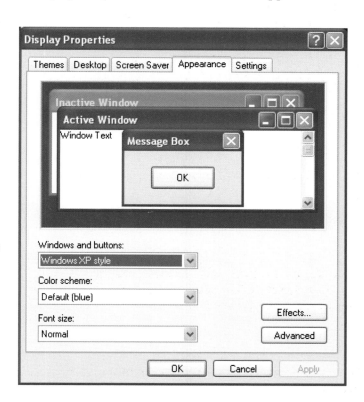

✦ **Windows and buttons:** Control how windows and buttons look on your desktop when they're active or inactive.

✦ **Color scheme:** Control what colors appear in window title bars, borders, and so forth.

✦ **Font size:** Choose from Large Fonts, and Extra Large Fonts to manage text readability on screen.

✦ **Effects:** Control various kinds of animations, shadows, or transitions for desktop elements on the move.

✦ **Advanced:** Control individual aspects of themes to be managed individually.

In practice, it's easy to use the three drop-down list controls (Windows and buttons, Color scheme, and Font size). Because default settings are customized during Windows XP installation, the settings behind the Effects button seldom need to be changed.

If your PC starts running slowly, you can improve performance somewhat by clearing most boxes in the Effects window (and selecting "Use large icons"). It might not make a huge difference, but it can help.

When it comes to the Advanced button in the Appearance tab, you could spend *hours* setting each Windows XP desktop item's appearance individually. To get a sense of how much there is to tweak, click the Item list in the Advanced Appearance window (we count 18 items). Because themes do all this for you in one go, this explains why they're popular for those with a keen sense of style but who don't have lots of free time on their hands.

Changing the Color Scheme

There are many specialized settings that change how Windows XP looks and behaves. Some are simply for the sake of personalization, allowing you to choose the settings you like best. Others are designed to help people who have trouble reading the on-screen text or using the mouse. For some viewers, choosing a color scheme may be a form of pure personalization; for other viewers (especially those who may be insensitive to certain colors or shades) selecting workable color schemes may offer significant readability improvements.

This section explores using the Appearance tab to change a simple Windows XP desktop setting: the color scheme. Here's how:

① Right-click a blank area on your desktop and click Properties in the shortcut menu that appears. The Display Properties dialog box opens.

② Click the Appearance tab. The Display Properties dialog box displays several specialized settings.

③ Click the Color scheme list, and then click Olive Green. The preview window displays how various types of windows (active, inactive, message box) appear within that selected color scheme. It takes about two seconds for the preview of a new color scheme to appear.

④ Click the Color scheme list, and then click Silver; the preview window changes again to show the new scheme.

⑤ If other color schemes are available, click them individually to view them.

⑥ Click Default (blue) and then click OK to close the Display Properties dialog box and apply your chosen color scheme to your desktop. Click Cancel to maintain your current settings, if you prefer.

Managing Display Settings

The rightmost tab in the Display Settings window is labeled Settings. This is where you manage settings for your Windows XP display device (or devices, if you're lucky enough to use more than one monitor on your PC). The key settings in this tab, shown in Figure 7-4, cover two important display characteristics: screen resolution and color quality.

Figure 7-4 The Settings tab provides controls for screen resolution and color quality.

Screen resolution is important because it literally controls how many individual pieces of information (called *picture elements*, or *pixels* in computer lingo) your PC's display can handle. Most people who read this book will use display devices whose resolution falls somewhere in the range from 800 x 600 and 1280 x 1024. The first number in the table is the horizontal pixel count or width; the second the vertical pixel count or height.

The higher the resolution to which a display is set, the more information it can fit on the screen (but the smaller that information appears). High resolutions work best when you've got a lot of material to examine in a single view—such as larger photos or Web pages—or when you want to fit as many items on your monitor as possible. Lower resolutions may work better for those whose vision is less acute, or who don't need as much space on their desktop at any one time.

Color quality is another key aspect when establishing settings for PC displays; this value is determined by the PC's video card or graphics adapter. Such settings vary across three typical values:

✦ Medium: This technique uses 16 bits of information to represent individual colors, so 65,535 distinct colors may be specified.

✦ High: This technique uses 24 bits of information to represent individual colors, so over 16 million distinct colors may be specified.

✦ Highest: This technique uses 32 bits of information to represent individual colors, so over 4 billion distinct colors may be specified.

The greater the number of colors a graphics adapter can handle, the more RAM it must contain, which usually means a more expensive adapter. Typically, most modern graphics adapters handle medium and high color quality; only the highest-end and most expensive adapters can handle 32-bit color, however.

Other controls on the Settings tab include the Identify, Troubleshoot, and Advanced buttons. When you have multiple monitors installed, Identify displays the monitor number (used to identify individual devices) on each display. Use the former to help you solve display problems; use the latter to manage monitor and graphics display settings at the highest possible level of detail (you shouldn't need to do this very often, if at all).

This concludes our tour of the Display Properties window. Though you will encounter other aspects of this important Control Panel icon elsewhere in this chapter, we now turn our attention toward various ways to customize your Windows XP environment.

 To learn how to customize your PC, go to the CD-ROM segment: *Customizing Your PC*

Customizing the Start Menu

You learned in Chapter 2 that the start menu is an important tool you can use to start programs, find files and folders, configure Windows XP, and much, much more. As you can see, the start menu is divided into two columns. The left-hand column includes two sections: *pinned* programs on top, and recently used programs on the bottom. Pinned programs are always available for you to choose, whereas the list of recently used programs changes to reflect—you guessed it—whatever programs you have used most recently.

Adding to the Start Menu

The first time you use Windows XP, the area where recently used programs normally appear is filled with pre-defined icons for several Microsoft programs, including MSN® Explorer, Windows Media Player, Windows Movie Maker, Tour Windows XP, and the Files and Settings Transfer Wizard. By default, these pre-defined icons remain in this area of the start menu for seven days; after that, they will be replaced by icons for those programs you've used recently.

Moving and Removing Start Menu Items

As you know, the list of recently used programs changes to reflect what programs you have used most recently. To move a program to the left column of your start menu permanently (at the top of the menu), you must *pin* it. Here's how:

1. Click the start button and navigate to a program you want to pin to the left column of the start menu.
2. When you find the program you want, right-click its icon in the start menu and click Pin to Start menu in the shortcut menu that appears. The program is pinned to the left column of the start menu, and appears above the line in the left-hand column thereafter.

    If a program you wish to pin to the start menu appears in the list of recently used programs, you can drag it up into the pinned-items list.

3. Close the start menu by clicking your start button again.

    To unpin a pinned start menu item, simply right-click the program's icon and select Unpin from Start menu in the shortcut menu.

Any program you use regularly—perhaps even programs you use daily—can be handy to put into the pinned items list. But before you jump to do this, read through the next sections in this chapter. There, you learn how to put programs in the Quick Launch area of the Taskbar where you can launch them without having to click the start menu first. Since this involves one less click than the start menu technique, this is even more direct than pinning those programs!

Open
Pin to Start menu
Send To ▶
Cut
Copy
Create Shortcut
Delete
Rename
Sort by Name
Properties

7

You can clear programs manually from the recently used programs area in the left-column of the start menu. Here's how:

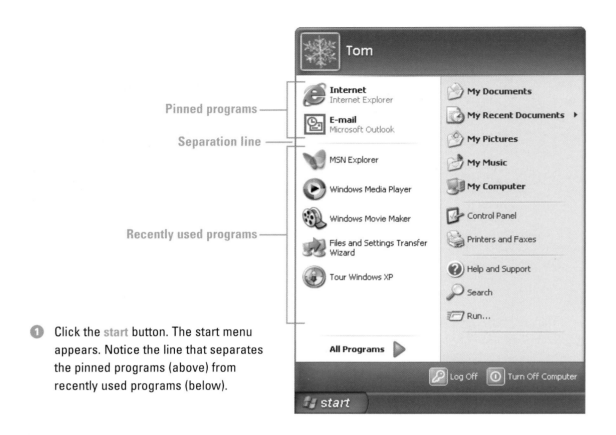

Pinned programs

Separation line

Recently used programs

1 Click the start button. The start menu appears. Notice the line that separates the pinned programs (above) from recently used programs (below).

2 Right-click the start button. A shortcut menu appears.

③ Select **Properties** from the shortcut menu. The Taskbar and Start Menu Properties dialog box opens.

④ Click the **Customize** button. The Customize Start Menu dialog box opens.

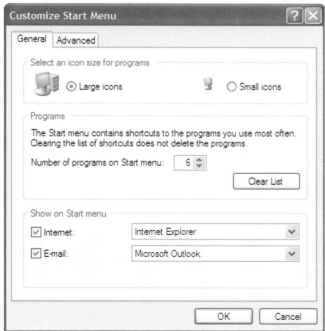

⑤ In the Programs pane, click **Clear List**, then click the **OK** button.

6 You are returned to the Taskbar and Start Menu Properties dialog box. Click OK to apply your changes.

7 Click the start button. Notice that all the items in the recently used programs area are removed.

After you've cleared the items in the recently used programs area, you can quickly fill that area with the programs of your choosing. In this example, You'll populate the recently used programs area of the start menu with Solitaire, Windows Media Player, and Calculator:

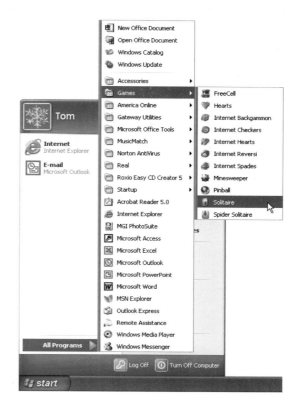

1 Click start, point to **All Programs**, point to **Games**, and click **Solitaire**.

2 The Solitaire window opens, and the start menu disappears. Click the Close button in the Solitaire window to close the game.

3 Click the start button, point to **All Programs**, point to **Accessories**, and click **Calculator**. The Calculator program opens on your desktop.

4 Click the Close button in the Calculator window to close it.

5 Click the start button, point to **All Programs**, and click **Windows Media Player**. The Windows Media Player program is started.

6 Click the Close button in the Windows Media Player window to close the program.

7 Click the start button. The start menu appears. Notice that Solitaire, Calculator, and Windows Media Player have been added to your recently used program list.

To remove a program from the list of recently used programs, right-click it in the start menu and choose Remove from This List in the shortcut menu that appears. This will remove only that item from the list.

To learn how to customize the start menu on your PC, go to the CD-ROM segment: *Start Menu: Customizing*

Customizing the Taskbar

The taskbar can appear and behave in many different ways. By default, the taskbar appears on top of other programs that may be active, groups similar items together, and is locked in place. Any of these defaults can be altered, however. In addition, other options are available—and sometimes recommended—to better meet your needs.

Auto-Hiding the Taskbar

Although the taskbar is an important tool, it requires a small but constant amount of precious real estate on your screen. To *auto-hide* the taskbar so that it disappears from view when it's not in use, do the following:

1. Right-click a blank area on the taskbar and choose Properties from the shortcut menu that appears. The Taskbar and Start Menu Properties dialog box opens with the Taskbar tab

2. In the Taskbar appearance area, click the Lock the taskbar check box to disable it. (The check mark should be cleared.)

3. Click the Auto-hide the taskbar check box to enable it.

4. Click OK. The Taskbar and Start Menu Properties dialog box closes, and you are returned to the desktop. Notice that the taskbar has been removed from the screen.

5. Move the mouse pointer to the bottom of the screen, where the taskbar was previously located; the taskbar pops into view.

6. Move the mouse pointer away from the taskbar area, and the taskbar disappears again.

Moving, Resizing, and Locking the Taskbar

For some people, the default position for the taskbar—stretched across the bottom of your screen from left to right—doesn't work. It might be because of the way their monitor is set up (perhaps the bottom of the screen is occluded or hard to see) or because some of the programs they use want that portion of the display to themselves. Whatever the reason, you can reposition and change the size of the taskbar to meet your particular needs or situation.

You must unlock the taskbar before you can move or modify it. We described how to unlock the taskbar in the preceding section.

Here's how to customize the location and size of the taskbar:

❶ Press and hold the left mouse button on a blank area on the taskbar and drag the taskbar to either side or to the top of your screen. (If your taskbar is set to auto-hide, simply position your mouse pointer on an area of the desktop where it's hiding, and it pops right up.)

❷ Move your mouse pointer to the edge of a blank area on your taskbar; the mouse pointer changes to a double-headed arrow. Press and hold the left mouse button and drag the edge of the taskbar to make it larger. Your screen may look like the one in Figure 7-5.

_____ Taskbar

_____ Notification area

Figure 7-5 A desktop with a customized taskbar.

❸ To lock the taskbar in its new location, right-click any blank area on the taskbar and click Lock the Taskbar in the shortcut menu that appears. After that, you can no longer move or resize the taskbar.

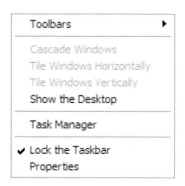

❹ To return the taskbar to its default position, repeat these steps in reverse order, and then lock the taskbar into place.

Customizing the Taskbar Notification Area

As mentioned in Chapter 2, the notification area displays small icons to represent programs that are active, but that do not appear on your desktop. Typically these include items such as anti-virus software, audio controls, CD-ROM burner programs, and the like. The notification area also conveys information about various system conditions and operations.

 To learn more about options available on your taskbar, go to the CD-ROM segment go to the Web segment *Taskbar Options* in the Beyond PC Basics course.

Customizing Toolbars

In addition to housing the start button and notification area, as well as taskbar buttons for any programs or windows currently on your desktop, the taskbar can display its own toolbars. These toolbars give you quick access to URLs and links to Web sites, shortcuts on the desktop, and programs.

Windows XP includes four pre-defined taskbar toolbars, but you can also create your own customized toolbars. The pre-defined taskbar toolbars include:

✦ **Address:** Shows the address for the Internet Explorer window currently open on your desktop, or it is blank if none is open.

✦ **Links:** Shows the contents of the Links folder in Internet Explorer's Favorites menu (these include pre-defined links supplied with the program, but can also include custom links added afterward).

✦ **Desktop:** Lists the icons visible on the Windows XP desktop, along with top-level icons available in My Computer or Windows Explorer (My Computer, My Documents, Recycle Bin, and so forth).

✦ **Quick Launch:** Defines an area on the taskbar to which you can drag program files (and into which some installer software inserts icons automatically) where you can launch programs with a single mouse click.

All of these toolbars can come in handy, so they're worth getting to know.

To add a toolbar (in this case, the Desktop toolbar) to your taskbar, do the following:

1. Right-click a blank area of the taskbar to display the shortcut menu, click Toolbars, and then click Desktop. (If your taskbar is set to Auto-hide, simply move your mouse pointer to the area of the desktop where it's hiding, and it pops up.)

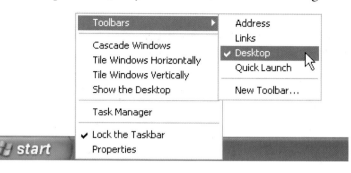

2. The Desktop toolbar appears in the taskbar. To get the hang of using this toolbar, click the right-pointing double arrows on the toolbar to open the toolbar menu, point to My Computer, and then point to Control Panel.

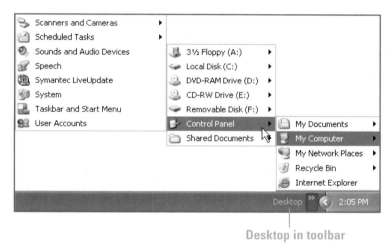

Desktop in toolbar

3. The Control Panel menu (partially shown) contains many tools you can use to configure Windows XP, many of which are introduced in the next section of this chapter. To close this menu and its two submenus, click a blank area on the desktop.

Experiment with the other toolbar selections as well. The Quick Launch facility can be particularly helpful as it provides access to our most-used applications with only a single click of the mouse, and in most cases it is always visible.

Restoring Your Desktop

Now that you know how to customize the Windows XP desktop and have made changes to many different settings, let's turn back the clock to see how the computer looked and behaved before you began.

 To complete these steps, you must have defined a restore point; that's why you created one at the outset of this chapter.

1 Click start, and then click Help and Support. The Help and Support Center window opens.

2 Click System Restore (in the upper-right corner of the window). The System Restore window opens.

3 Verify that Restore my computer to an earlier time is selected, and then click Next.

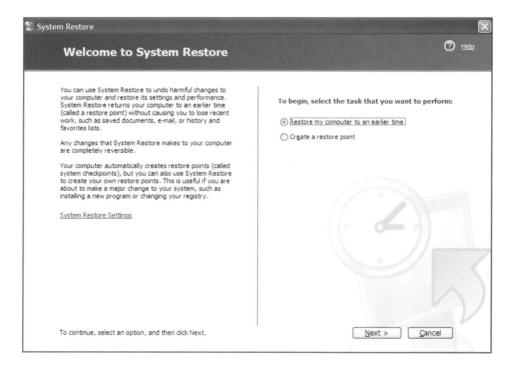

4 In the calendar, click the date on which you created the restore point.

5 In the list, click the Before Customizing Your Desktop restore point, and then click Next.

⑥ In the Confirm Restore Point Selection screen, click Next. The System Restore process restores files and settings, and then shuts down Windows XP and restarts the computer.

⑦ After the computer restarts, log on to Windows XP; please supply a valid user name and/or password if necessary.

⑧ The System Restore window opens, indicating that the restoration is complete. Click OK. Windows XP now looks and behaves as it did when you began the steps in this chapter.

 While you're making various changes to your desktop, taskbar, and related Windows XP controls, consider creating specific restore points to capture various aspects of your desktop configuration. That way, instead of an "all or nothing" approach like the one forced by the previous steps, you can pick and choose among the various settings that you might most like to keep.

 To learn more about different things you can do with your desktop, go to the Web segment *Desktop Options* in the Beyond PC Basics course.

Configuring Windows XP with Control Panel

Unlike customizations, which make Windows XP more fun to use, *configuration changes* are sometimes required to enable a computer to function properly and to work with various peripheral and internal devices. The next section discusses several different configuration options, and how to set them using tools found in Control Panel. Control Panel has been redesigned in Windows XP, grouping similar functions into categories.

7

Each category contains tools (and sometimes wizards) to configure some aspect of your computer, such as hardware, software, or networking. To open Control Panel, click start, and then click Control Panel. Figure 7-6 depicts the category list for Control Panel.

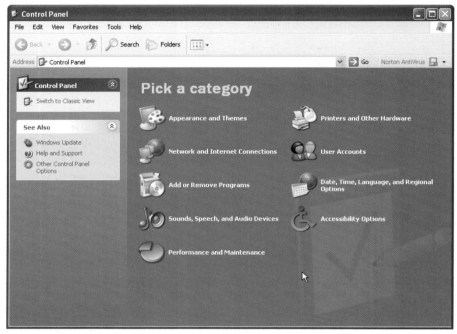

Figure 7-6 The default Category view for Control Panel lists nine categories for tasks and activities.

+ **Name/Description:** Name provides a name for the category involved and Description covers the general functions and capabilities associated with the named category.

+ **Tasks:** Describes the task entries in the corresponding category window.

+ **Control Panel Icons:** Names the associated control panel icons accessible through this category in alphabetical order, where applicable (all but two of the nine categories that appear have related icons; the other two list other accessible objects or functions).

Table 7-1 describes the function and contents for each category, where each table entry follows the same structure:

Table 7-1 Windows XP Control Panel categories and information.

NAME/DESCRIPTION	TASKS	CONTROL PANEL ICONS
Appearances and Themes Handles desktop themes and desktop appearance settings	Change theme, change desktop background, choose screen saver, change display settings.	Display, Folder Options, Taskbar and Start Menu
Network and Internet Connections Handles local and Internet setup and configuration	Set up or change your Internet connection, create connection to network at workplace, set up or change home or small office network	Internet Options, Network Connections
Add or Remove Programs Install or remove programs or Windows components	Change or remove (existing programs), add new programs, add/remove Windows components	Add or Remove Programs (separate lists for each of the three tasks mentioned)
Sounds, Speech, and Audio Devices Handles speech or sound related settings and hardware	Adjust system volume, change sound scheme, change speaker settings	Sounds and Audio Devices, Speech
Performance and Maintenance Provides access to system information, tuning, and upkeep	See basic PC information, adjust visual effects, free up space on your hard disk, back up your data, rearrange items on your hard drive to make programs run faster	Administrative Tools, Power Options, Scheduled Tasks, System
Printers and Other Hardware Manages printers, faxes, game controllers, keyboards, etc.	View installed printers or fax printers, Add a printer	Game Controllers, Keyboard, Mouse, Phone and Modem Options, Printers and Faxes, Scanners and Cameras
User Accounts Creates and manages user accounts and settings for Windows XP	Change an account, create a new account, change the way users log on or off	None (Can pick from a list of already created accounts to access or change data)
Date, Time, Language, and Regional Options Manages various system context data	Change the date and time, change the format of numbers, dates, and times, add other languages	Date and Time, Regional and Language Options
Accessibility Options Manages special user access tools to improve access for the impaired	Adjust contrast for text and colors on your screen, configure Windows to work for your vision, hearing, and mobility needs	Accessibility Options (tabs for Keyboard, Sounds, Display, Mouse, and General behaviors)

7

While we don't cover all nine categories in detail in this chapter, you'll find many of them covered in the sections that follow.

To tour the Control Panel, go to the CD-ROM segment *Introduction to the Control Panel*.

 To understand how the Control Panel can be configured for different accessibility options, go to the Web segment *Control Panel: Accessibility Options* in the Beyond PC Basics course.

Using the Add or Remove Programs Category

Your PC most likely arrived with the Windows XP operating system and a large array of software programs already installed. The Add or Remove Programs tool in Control Panel allows you to change or remove these programs, add new programs, and add or remove additional pieces of the operating system, called *Windows components*. You can use this tool to see what programs are installed on your PC. Here's how:

Figure 7-7: The Add or Remove Programs window.

1. If Control Panel is not already open, click start and click Control Panel.

2. Click Add or Remove Programs. The Add or Remove Programs window opens, as shown in Figure 7-7.

3. Scroll through the list of currently installed programs, and then click Close. You are returned to the Control Panel.

Exploring the Performance and Maintenance Category

The design of Windows XP's Control Panel places most of the tools you need most often within easy reach. However, you may occasionally need a tool to help you clean up or manage your PC, or to tackle a more complex system management or configuration task. The Performance and Maintenance category in Control Panel puts the necessary activities and icons at your fingertips, to help you get the most out of your system.

Tasks available in this category include these important basic PC inspection and maintenance activities (and provide easy access to related system tools):

See basic PC information. Shows the System Properties window, whose many tabs provide access to all kinds of information about your PC, including hardware, computer name, and other data.

Adjust visual effects. Provides access to all kinds of built-in Windows desktop display behaviors. The default setting is Let Windows choose what's best for my computer. This seldom needs tweaking.

Free up space on your hard disk. Allows you to select a hard drive and then run Disk Cleanup. It's highly recommended that you do this at least once a month.

Back up your data. Allows you to run the built-in Windows Backup or Restore Wizard, which guides you through copying (backing up) data from your system or restoring that data as you direct.

Rearrange items on your hard drive to make programs run faster. This runs a built-in Disk Defragmenter program, which reassembles pieces of big files that may be scattered around your hard disk. By rearranging such files, your system may run faster. Again, it's highly recommended that you do this at least once a month.

Exploring the Printers and Other Hardware Category

Control Panel's Printers and Other Hardware category contains several tools to help you configure your printer and other required hardware (keyboard and mouse) as well as some of the optional hardware (game controllers, scanners, and cameras) installed on your PC.

This category gets its name in part from its controls for faxes and printers. In fact, this category's set of tasks appears as follows:

✦ View installed printers or fax printers

✦ Add a printer

7

Use the first activity to open the Printers and Faxes window, as shown in Figure 7-8. From within this window, users can inspect all available print and fax devices. They can also manage (pause, restart, or delete) their own print jobs on any such devices, and administrators can manage any and all print jobs. The second activity opens the Add Printer Wizard, which guides administrators through the process of adding and naming a printer to a Windows XP machine. See the table at the end of this chapter for a pointer to more information about installing a printer.

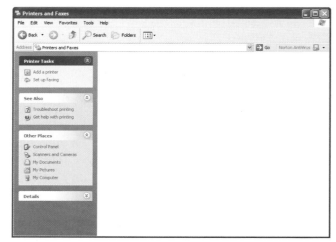

But as the "other hardware" part of the name for this Control Panel category indicates, there's more to this collection of tasks and Control Panel icons than printers and faxes.

Other Control Panel icons in the Printers and Other Hardware category include:

Figure 7-8 The Printers and Faxes Control Panel window.

✦ **Game Controllers:** Click this icon to add, remove, or manage a game controller on your PC.

✦ **Keyboard:** Click this icon to manage keyboard repeat delay and repeat rates, and the cursor blink rate on screen (on the Speed tab), or to inspect or troubleshoot keyboard hardware properties (on the Hardware tab).

✦ **Phone and Modem Options:** Click this icon to set dialing rules for your phone line, to add or remove modems and inspect their properties, or to manage various telephony providers (Windows services related to using telephones and modems) on your PC.

✦ **Scanners and Cameras:** Click this icon to add or remove imaging devices like scanners and cameras on your PC, or to inspect their properties and status.

The Control Panel is a powerful facility to help you manage and control your PC. As you get more familiar with its capabilities, it will become a part of your essential Windows XP toolkit.

 To learn more about folders from the Control Panel, go to the CD-ROM segment *Control Panel: Folder Options.*

TO KEEP ON LEARNING . . .

Go to the CD-ROM and select the segment:

◆ Customizing Your PC

◆ Start Menu: Customizing

◆ Introduction to the Control Panel

◆ Control Panel: Options

Go online to www.LearnwithGateway.com and log on to select:

◆ *Taskbar Options* in the Beyond PC Basics course

◆ *Desktop Options* in the Beyond PC Basics course

◆ *Control Panel: Accessibility Options* in the Beyond PC Basics course

◆ *Internet Links and Resources*

◆ *FAQs*

Gateway offers a hands-on training course on many of the topics covered in this chapter. Additional fees may apply. Call 888-852-4821 to enroll. Please have your customer ID and order number ready when you call.

7

CHAPTER **8**

Working in a Network Environment

In the 1960s and 1970s, free-spirited youths gathered in communes, pooling their resources, sharing their property, and working together for the common good. A *network* is the computer world's equivalent of a commune. Using network cable connections or wireless devices, computers can establish their own electronic community to provide users with the tools they need to communicate with each other and share files and programs. A network can even help trim costs by allowing several computers to share an expensive piece of equipment, such as a printer, or a costly service, such as a high-speed Internet connection.

If your computer is part of a network, at home or at the office, acquiring a general understanding of how networks function and some basic networking skills can help you fully exploit the power of the network. This chapter provides all the information you need to successfully navigate your network, share files and folders, share a network printer, and take advantage of other network resources.

Networking: An Overview

A *network,* commonly referred to as a *LAN* (*local area network*), is a group of computers that are typically located in the same room or building and that are connected using network cables or wireless devices. These cables or wireless devices make it possible for the computers to communicate with one another and exchange data, just as phone lines enable you to talk with friends and relatives.

Each computer on a network is equipped with a *NIC* (*network interface card*), which enables the computer to send and receive network signals. Cables, similar to telephone cords or TV cables, connect the computers to each other through their NICs. The cables may connect the computers directly to each other or to a central hub, a device containing multiple ports (outlets). Networked computers might also be connected to a central computer called the server. The server manages shared network resources, such as programs, files, e-mail, and printers. Other computers on the network connect to the server to run programs and access shared resources.

 In wireless networks, each computer uses a wireless device instead of a cable to connect to the network.

Networks typically provide the following benefits:

+ **Hardware sharing.** A printer, modem, or backup drive that's connected to one computer on the network is accessible to all computers on the network.

+ **File sharing.** All users on the network have access to shared drives, folders, and files, making it easier for users to collaborate on projects.

✦ **Communications.** Users can communicate via e-mail, network bulletin boards, and chat programs, and can coordinate schedules using personal information management software.

 To learn more about different uses of network systems, go to the CD-ROM segment *Network Uses.*

Domain-based (Client-Server) Networks

Although all networks enable you to enjoy such benefits as hardware sharing, file sharing, and the like, networks commonly are classified into two groups: domain-based, *client-server* networks and workgroup-based, *peer-to-peer* networks (covered in the next section). A client-server network, as shown in Figure 8-1, connects several computers, called *clients,* to a powerful central computer called a *server.* Client-server networks are common in corporations, universities, and large organizations. The server manages shared network resources, such as programs and printers, and enables the other (client) computers to access these resources.

Figure 8-1 A typical client-server network.

A network administrator (the person in charge of managing a network) assigns each computer on the network a unique name to identify it. The administrator also assigns each computer to a *domain,* a group of computers on a network that are managed as a single entity. Domains make it easier for network administrators to manage large numbers of networked computers. For example, if the network administrator wants ten computers in the accounting department to have access to a particular folder, the administrator can create a domain for those ten computers and give the domain access to the folder. Without domains, the administrator would need to assign permission to each of those ten computers individually.

8

Workgroup-based (Peer-to-Peer) Networks

Unlike client-server networks that connect all computers to a central computer, a peer-to-peer network, shown in Figure 8-2, connects the computers directly to each other; each computer acts as both a client and a server. When computer A is using computer B's resources, for example, computer A acts as the client, and computer B acts as the server. When computer B uses computer A's resources, however, computer B is the client, and computer A is the server. Peer-to-peer networks are common in homes and small businesses, where fewer than 20 computers are networked.

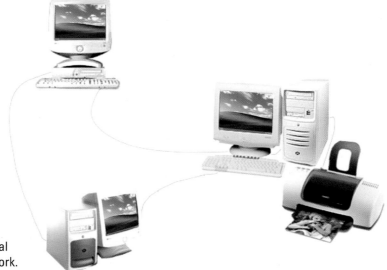

Figure 8-2 A typical peer-to-peer network.

Instead of using domains to group computers on the network, peer-to-peer networks use a simplified way of controlling access to folders and resources: *workgroups*. Each computer on a peer-to-peer network is assigned to a workgroup, which enables each computer to communicate with other computers in the same workgroup. This workgroup arrangement allows each user to control access to resources on his or her computer. For example, a user might designate a folder as shared, so other users in the same workgroup can open files stored in that folder.

If your computer is part of a peer-to-peer network, when you log on to Windows as explained in Chapter 2, Windows automatically logs your computer on to the network. If your computer is on a client-server network, you may need to enter your user name and password to gain access to the network.

To tour a network, go to the CD-ROM segment *Network Components*.

Sharing Files and Folders

In the not-so-distant past, file sharing consisted of swapping floppy disks that held the files you wanted to share. Now, people typically share files by e-mailing them as attachments or by using a network. By default, nothing stored on your computer is available on your network until you decide what to share and whom to share it with.

There are two ways to share files and folders:

✦ By placing files into a default shared folder

✦ By changing an existing folder from private to shared

Placing Files into a Default Shared Folder

Assuming your computer is connected to a network—even a very small one—you use My Network Places to connect to the other computers on your network. *My Network Places* is similar to My Computer, except you can use it to access files and folders on any computer on the network for which you have permission to access, not just your own. My Network Places is where you'll find the default shared folder in which you can place any files or folders you want to share with others on your network.

To view this shared folder, do the following:

❶ Click **start** and click **My Network Places**. The My Network Places window opens.

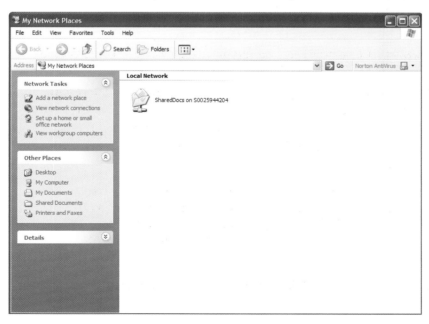

The contents of My Network Places depends on several factors, such as whether your computer is connected to a network, and whether any other computers on that network are sharing items other than the default folder.

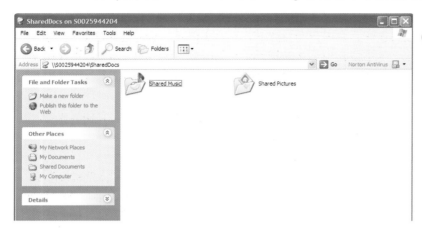

2 Double-click the **SharedDocs** folder listed for your computer. The SharedDocs folder opens, and the two default subfolders are displayed: Shared Music and Shared Pictures.

To add an item to your shared folder, thus enabling others on your network to access the item, do the following (if the SharedDocs window is not open, follow the steps in the preceding numbered list to open it before starting this task):

1 Click the **Minimize** button in the SharedDocs window to minimize the window and reveal the Windows desktop.

2 Locate the file you want to move to the shared folder (in this example, the My First Text Doc file located on the desktop), right-click it, and click **Cut** in the shortcut menu that appears.

3 Click the **SharedDocs** taskbar button to restore the window.

4 Right-click a blank area of the SharedDocs window and click **Paste** in the shortcut menu that appears. The My First Text Doc document is moved to the SharedDocs folder. My First Text Doc is now shared, and is available to others on your network.

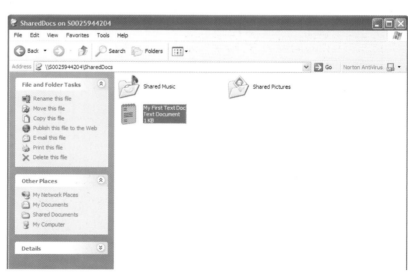

Changing an Existing Folder from Private to Shared

Instead of moving a document to your PC's default shared folder, you can change the folder that houses that document into a shared folder. This is especially useful if you want to share numerous documents on your PC; by turning a private folder into a shared folder, you share all the files that folder contains.

To convert a private folder into a shared folder, first open the SharedDocs folder (follow the steps in the preceding section). Then, do the following:

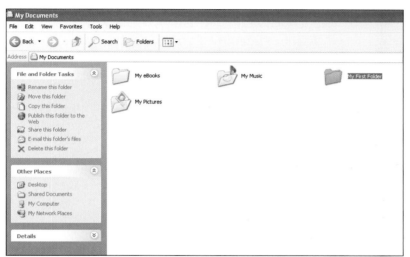

❶ In the SharedDocs window, under Other Places, click **My Documents**. The My Documents window opens.

❷ Click **My First Folder** (or the folder of your choice). The File and Folder Tasks list expands to contain additional options.

❸ Under File and Folder Tasks, click **Share this folder**. The My First Folder Properties dialog box opens.

④ In the Network sharing and security section, click to select the **Share this folder on the network** check box. When you click this check box, the name of the folder (in this case, My First Folder) is automatically added to the Share name field, and the Allow network users to change my files check box is automatically checked.

⑤ Click the **Allow network users to change my files** check box to clear it. With this option disabled, users can open shared files as read-only files, but cannot save files to the shared folder or delete shared files or folders.

⑥ Click **OK**. The Sharing dialog box opens, indicating that users of earlier operating systems have trouble accessing a folder with a name longer than 12 characters, and asking if you want to proceed.

⑦ Click **Yes**. The Sharing and My First Folder Properties dialog boxes close, and you are returned to the My Documents folder. Notice the graphic of the hand holding the My First Folder icon. This graphic indicates that the folder is a shared folder.

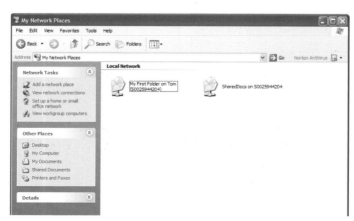

⑧ In the Other Places list, click **My Network Places**. The My Network Places window opens, listing both the SharedDocs folder and My First Folder.

To share folders within a network, go to the Web segment *Folders: Sharing* in the Beyond PC Basics course.

Offline Files

If your computer is frequently disconnected from the network or if you need to take shared files on the road using your notebook computer, you can choose to work with files and folders that reside on the network *offline*. Then, Windows copies the shared files or folders to your computer's hard drive, giving you complete access to them even when you're disconnected from the network. When you reconnect to the network, Windows automatically synchronizes the files on your computer with the ones on the network to ensure that the network files are up to date. This process is called *synchronization*.

 To understand how to work offline from the network, go to the CD-ROM segment *Offline Files*.

Setting Up Your Printer

Printers are commonly used on a network to simplify maintenance costs. You can set up your networked computers to share a single printer or even multiple printers.

First you need to setup the printer itself, and, thankfully, setting up a printer is usually an easy task. In fact, the process is often entirely automatic after you connect the printer's cables to the system unit. Before you connect your printer, it's a good idea to follow the basic setup as defined in the printer's setup manual. This includes installing an ink or toner cartridge and filling the paper tray.

Connecting the Printer

To connect a printer to your PC, follow these steps:

❶ Plug the larger end of the printer cable into the back of the printer.

 Most printers do not include a printer cable; it must be purchased separately.

❷ Plug the other end of the printer cable into the appropriate port—USB or parallel—on the back of your system unit. (Chapter 1 explains the differences between USB and parallel ports and cables.)

❸ Plug one end of the printer's power cable into the printer.

❹ Plug the other end of the printer's power cable into the surge protector.

❺ Turn the printer on.

8

If you have a USB printer, Windows XP may detect it automatically and start the installation process by itself. If so, follow whatever on-screen prompts appear. For example, you may be asked to verify the installation, or to provide a driver disk (often a CD-ROM) if Windows XP doesn't have the necessary drivers pre-loaded. In most cases, the driver disk is included with the printer.

Manually Installing the Printer

If Windows XP does not automatically detect and install your printer after you connect it to your PC, you can install the printer manually. Follow these steps:

❶ Click the **start** button, and then click **Printers and Faxes**.

 If you don't see a Printers and Faxes icon in the start menu, you can access it by clicking **Start**, then **Control Panel**, then **Printers and Other Hardware**, and then **Printers and Faxes**.

❷ The Printers and Faxes window opens. Click the **Add a printer** option in the Printer Tasks area.

❸ The Add Printer wizard starts, displaying the Welcome to the Add Printer Wizard screen. Click **Next**.

❹ The Local or Network Printer screen of the Add Printer wizard appears. Here, you indicate whether the printer is connected directly to your PC (that is, *locally*) or is connected to your machine via a network. These steps assume the printer is connected locally. Click the **Local printer attached to this computer** option button, and under that, select the **Automatically detect and install my Plug and Play printer** check box. Click **Next**.

⑤ The New Printer Detection screen appears as the Add Printer wizard attempts to detect your printer automatically. If the wizard detects your printer, click **Next** and skip to step 13. If not, you'll have to complete the installation manually; click **Next** and continue to step 6.

⑥ In the Select a Printer Port screen, use the selection that appears automatically in the **Use the following port** list or select the port to which your printer is attached. (A parallel port printer is connected to LPT1, whereas a USB printer is connected to a USB port.) Click **Next**.

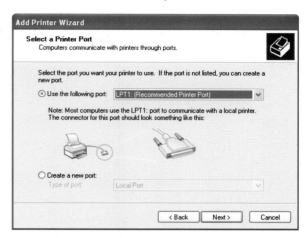

⑦ Select the manufacturer of your printer in the left column of the Install Printer Software screen.

⑧ If your printer is listed in the right column of the Install Printer Software screen, select it, click **Next**, and skip to step 13. If not, click the **Have Disk** button and continue to step 9.

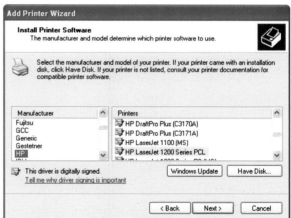

⑨ The Install From Disk dialog box opens. Insert the printer vendor-supplied driver CD or floppy disk into the appropriate drive, and click the **Browse** button in the Install From Disk dialog box.

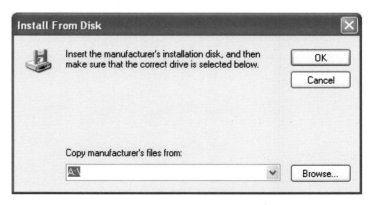

⑩ In the Locate File dialog box, click the **Look in** drop-down arrow and select the drive used in step 9.

⑪ Click **Open**. The setup tool scans the selected drive and displays a list of discovered drivers.

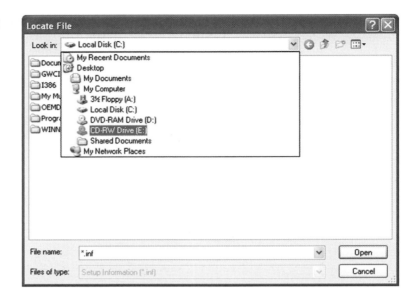

⑫ Select the driver that matches your printer model. Click **OK**.

⑬ The Name Your Printer screen appears. Type a descriptive name for the printer, or accept the suggested name that is provided, and click **Next**.

⑭ The Print Test Page screen appears. Select **Yes** to print a test page, and click **Next**.

⑮ The Completing the Add Printer Wizard screen appears. Click **Finish**.

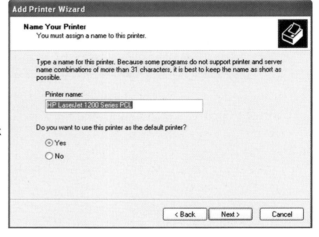

At this point, Windows XP installs the printer driver, configures the printer, and prints a test page. After the test page prints successfully (and it will nine times out of 10), return to your PC and click **OK** when prompted.

To learn more about using the Printer Wizard, go to the Web segment *Add Printer Wizard* in the PC Basics course.

Sharing Printers

Now that you know how to properly setup a printer, this section will walk you through the process of sharing it with other users on a network. The process is easier than you might think.

 Although a printer can be connected to any computer on the network, it's best to connect it to the computer that has the most powerful processor, the most memory, and the most disk space.

To share a printer, you first must designate the printer as a shared resource by taking the following steps:

1 On the computer to which the printer is connected, click the **start** button, and then click **Printers and Faxes**.

 If you don't see a Printers and Faxes icon in the start menu, you can access it by clicking **start**, pointing to **Control Panel**, pointing to **Printers and Other Hardware**, and then clicking **Printers and Faxes**.

2 The Printers and Faxes window opens, displaying icons for any printers or fax machines connected to the computer. Right-click the icon for the printer you want to share and click **Sharing** in the shortcut menu that appears.

3 The printer's Properties dialog box opens with the Sharing tab displayed. Click the **Share this printer** option button.

4 To change the name of this printer as it appears on the network, highlight the printer's name in the **Share name** text box and type the name you want to give this printer.

5 Click **OK**.

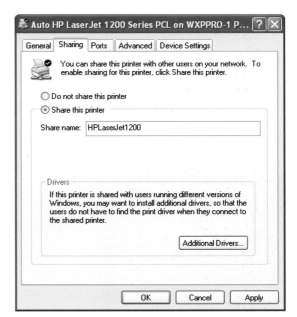

8

Once a computer's printer is flagged as a shared resource, you can install the printer on every other computer on the network. When you install a printer on a networked computer, you copy the printer's driver (software) to the computer and create an icon for the printer in the computer's Printers and Faxes folder. Then, the networked computer can use the printer to print documents,

To install a network printer on a networked computer, do the following (you should follow these steps for each computer on the network that you want to use the shared printer):

1. Click the **start** button, and then click **Printers and Faxes**.
2. The Printers and Faxes window opens. Click **Add Printer**.
3. The Add Printer Wizard starts. Click **Next**.
4. The wizard asks if you want to install a local or network printer. Click **A Network printer or a printer attached to another computer**, and then click **Next**. (A *local printer* is a printer that is directly connected to this computer.)
5. The wizard prompts you to specify the path to the printer. Click **Browse for a printer**, and then click **Next**.

 A *path* is a roadmap to a particular resource, such as a file, folder, or printer. A path to a network printer consists of the name of the computer to which the printer is connected followed by the name of the printer itself.

6. The Add Printer Wizard displays a list of the computers you can access on the network. Double-click the name of the computer to which the printer you want to add is attached.

7. The Add Printer Wizard displays an icon for each printer and fax machine connected to the selected computer. (Some printers double as fax machines.) Click the printer you want to add, and then click **Next**.

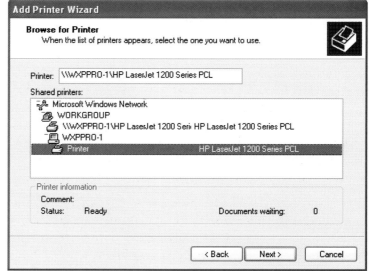

8. The wizard copies the necessary printer driver from the network computer to your computer and asks if you want to make this printer the default printer. If so, make sure **Yes** is selected and then click **Next**.

If you use a local printer for most of your printing and use the network printer only on rare occasions, choose **No** when asked if you want to make the network printer the default printer. The Print command, in most applications, displays the Print dialog box that has a drop-down list of all installed printers. To choose a different printer for a particular print job, open the list and click the name of the desired printer.

If you are adding a printer that is connected to a computer running an older version of Windows, the wizard may display a dialog box indicating that the correct printer driver could not be found. To install the correct printer driver, click **OK**, and then follow the on-screen instructions to install the correct printer driver.

⑨ The final wizard dialog box indicates that you have successfully added the network printer. Click the **Finish** button to close the wizard and return to the Printers and Faxes window, which now displays a new icon for the printer you added.

 To learn more about how to print documents, go to the Web segment *Printing Documents* in the PC Basics course.

 To learn more about the various printer options and how to use them, go to the Web segment *Printer Tasks* in the PC Basics course.

Implementing Computer Security

The Internet empowers your computer by connecting it to millions of other computers all over the world. Unfortunately, this power comes at a price: Not only is your system more vulnerable to viruses, as we will discuss in Chapter 9, it is also more vulnerable to attacks by other users. Someone with the proper know-how can connect to your computer over your Internet connection, access your files, collect any saved passwords, and vandalize your machine. Nobody really knows how frequently these things actually happen, but the fact that they can happen raises some concern.

If you connect to the Internet using a standard modem and disconnect whenever you are done, your computer is in the low-risk category. Because your computer does not stay connected to the Internet, it's tough to track down, let alone break into. If your computer is on a network that has a direct cable connection or if you have a cable or DSL Internet connection, however, your system has a higher risk of attack. These "always on" connections turn your computer into a stationary target, making it much easier for others on the Internet to locate your computer and break in.

One way to protect your computer is to set up a firewall, which acts as a virtual wall around your computer designed to ward off attacks. To supplement your computer's security, you can also encrypt the files on your machine; that way, in the event someone penetrates your firewall, the intruder is unable to read your data.

8

Understanding Firewalls

Although it is impossible to make your computer or network completely impenetrable, you can deter many would-be hackers from attacking your computer or network by building a virtual wall around it, called a *firewall* (see Figure 8-3). Firewalls are hardware devices or software utilities that act as computer security guards. They monitor the data coming into and going out of your computer in an attempt to identify any suspicious activity. If someone attempts to connect to your computer from a remote location, the firewall shuts down the connection, thus preventing a security breach.

There are dozens of firewall programs on the market, including Norton Personal Firewall, Zone Labs ZoneAlarm®, McAfee® Firewall, and Internet Security Systems BlackICE™ Defender. Fortunately, however, you need not rush to your local computer store to buy one. That's because Windows XP includes its own firewall utility, called *Internet Connection Firewall (ICF)*, which you can use to safeguard your system.

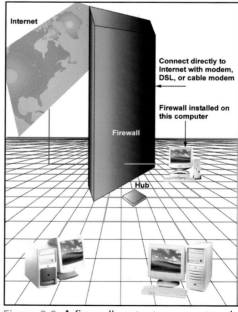

Figure 8-3 A firewall protects your network.

To gain an understanding of firewalls and the role they play in security, go to the CD-ROM segment *Firewall Basics.*

Implementing the Internet Connection Firewall

Windows XP's Internet Connection Firewall keeps track of every request for data your computer makes, and then checks incoming traffic to ensure that your computer initiated the transaction. If an outside source attempts to initiate communications, ICF drops the connection. Unlike many firewalls that display warnings of potential security breaches, ICF works in the background, automatically blocking unauthorized access.

Although ICF was designed to protect always-on Internet connections, such as cable and DSL connections, you can use it to prevent unauthorized access over a modem connection, as well.

To enable ICF on your PC, take the following steps:

❶ Click the **start** button and click **My Network Places**.

❷ The My Network Places window opens. On the left side of the window, below Network Tasks, click **View network connections**.

View network connections ———

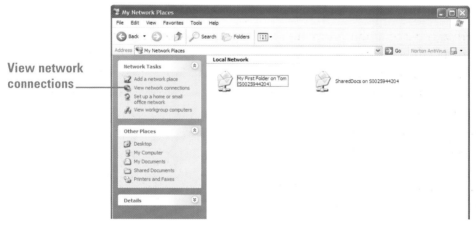

❸ The My Network Places window displays icons for all of your computer's modem and network connections. Right-click the icon for the network card or modem your computer uses to connect to the Internet, and click **Properties** in the shortcut menu that appears.

❹ The Properties dialog box for the selected connection opens. Click the **Advanced** tab.

8

⑤ Click **Protect my computer and network by limiting or preventing access to this computer from the Internet** to place a check in its check box.

⑥ Click **OK**.

 To learn more about how firewalls work to protect your system, go to the Web segment *Firewall Settings* in the Beyond PC Basics course.

Encrypting Files

A firewall is a first line of defense against unauthorized access. If someone gets past the firewall, however, all files on your computer are at that person's disposal. To secure any confidential files, you should store them in an encrypted folder. Files stored in encrypted folders are scrambled, meaning that outside users cannot access the data they contain. When you open an encrypted file on your machine, however, Windows automatically decrypts it, enabling you to access the file's data.

To encrypt a folder, take the following steps:

① Right-click the folder and click **Properties**.

② Click **Advanced**.

③ Click **Encrypt contents to secure data**.

④ Click **OK**.

Network Attributes and Permissions

Network rules come in the form of attributes and permissions. An *attribute* is a setting that controls the way an object behaves for all users. For example, a file's read-only attribute can be turned on to enable users to open the file but not to change its contents. An attribute makes the object behave the same way for all users. *Permissions,* on the other hand, apply to specific users or groups of users. A network administrator, for example, can assign permissions that prevent a user or group of users from creating folders on a particular disk drive. If your computer is not on a network or is a member of a workgroup, Windows XP activates simplified sharing on your computer, so you cannot assign permissions to users or groups. Permissions are treated more like attributes in that you can choose to share a folder or not share a folder, but you cannot choose to share a folder with one user and deny access to another. If your computer is part of a domain, the network administrator typically assigns permissions.

 To practice granting permissions on a network, go to the Web segment *Network Permissions: Granting* in the Beyond PC Basics course.

Go to the CD-ROM and select the segment:

✦ *Network Uses* to learn more about different uses of network systems

✦ *Network Components* to tour a network

✦ *Offline Files* to understand how to work offline from the network

✦ *Firewall Basics* to gain an understanding of firewalls and the role they play in security

Go online to **www.LearnwithGateway.com** and log on to select:

✦ *Add Printer Wizard* in the PC Basics course

✦ *Folders: Sharing* in the Beyond PC Basics course

✦ *Printer Wizard* in the PC Basics course

✦ *Printing Documents* in the PC Basics course

✦ *Printer Options* in the PC Basics course

✦ *Firewall Settings* in the Beyond PC Basics course

✦ *Network Permissions: Granting* in the Beyond PC Basics course

✦ *Internet Links and Resources*

✦ *FAQs*

Gateway offers a hands-on training course that covers many of the topics in this chapter. Additional fees may apply. Call **888-852-4821** to enroll. Please have your customer ID and order number ready when you call.

8

Caring for Your Computer

Performing Maintenance Tasks

As you use your computer, dust blankets the keyboard and coats the inside of your mouse. Likewise, as you create documents, browse the Web, and correspond via e-mail, your computer's hard disk becomes cluttered with data. And as time passes, your programs become old and outdated. The following sections act as your computer maintenance manual and show you how to perform each one properly.

Creating an Emergency Disk

Previous versions of Windows (Windows 95, 98, and Me) included a utility you could use to create a disk for *booting* (starting) your computer. You could use the disk to start your computer if a Windows system file became corrupted and prevented Windows from starting properly. Using this *emergency disk* or *recovery disk*, you could safely start your computer and restore earlier settings to get your computer up and running. To create a bootable disk, take the following steps:

1. Insert a blank disk (or one that has files you no longer need) into your computer's floppy disk drive. (Any files on the disk will be erased permanently.)
2. Click the **start** button and click **My Computer**.
3. My Computer opens, displaying an icon for each of your computer's disk drives. Right-click the **3½ Floppy** (A:) icon and click **Format**.
4. The Format 3½ Floppy (A:) dialog box opens. Click **Create an MS-DOS startup disk**.
5. Click **Start**.
6. Windows displays a warning that all data on the disk will be erased. To proceed with the formatting, click **OK**. Windows formats the disk.
7. Windows displays a dialog box to notify you when the formatting process is complete. Click **OK**.
8. Windows returns you to the Format 3½ Floppy (A:) dialog box. Click **Close**.
9. Windows returns you to My Computer. Insert your Windows XP Operating System Installation CD in your computer's CD drive.
10. In My Computer, right-click the icon for your CD drive and click **Explore**.

 To learn about the importance of cleaning up space and maintaining your hard disk, go to the CD-ROM segment: *Caring for Your Computer*

⑪ Windows Explorer displays the contents of the Windows XP Operating System Installation CD. Double-click the **I386** folder.

⑫ Windows Explorer displays the contents of the I386 folder. Scroll down the file list to display the NTDETECT.COM file.

⑬ Right-click **NTDETECT.COM**, point to **Send To**, and click **3½ Floppy (A:)**.

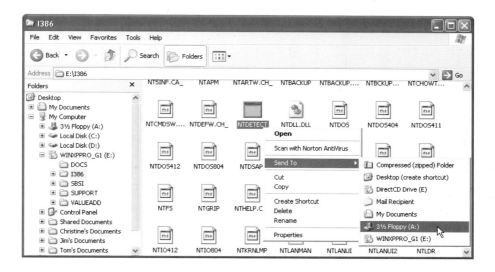

⑭ Scroll down to display the NTLDR file.

⑮ Right-click **NTLDR**, point to **Send To**, and click **3½ Floppy (A:)**.

⑯ Click the **start** button and click **Search** to track down one last file for your disk.

⑰ The Search Results window opens. Click **All files and folders**.

⑱ Windows prompts you to type the name of the file you're looking for. Type **boot.ini** and click **Search**.

⑲ Windows displays the names of any files it finds that have "boot.ini" in their names. Right-click the file named **boot.ini**, point to **Send To**, and click **3½ Floppy (A:)**.

 If no file named **boot.ini** appears, but you see a file with a similar name, such as boot.ini.backup, right-click that file, point to **Send To**, and click **3½ Floppy (A:)**. Then, using My Computer, display the contents of the disk in drive A and rename the file boot.ini.

⑳ Eject the disk from drive A and store it in a safe location.

 To learn about saving your files to disc, go to the CD-ROM segment: *File Backup*

9

Understanding Disk Management

Newer hard disks have sufficient storage to accommodate a great deal of careless dumping, but sooner or later, your computer's hard disk will start to strain under the weight of excessive cyber trash. As the disk becomes more and more cluttered, it becomes slower, less efficient, and more prone to errors.

Before your hard disk starts to experience problems, it's a good idea to give it a thorough cleaning and tune-up. The following sections show you just what to do.

Compressing Drives, Folders, and Files

The Windows compression utility can help you reclaim a significant amount of used disk space by reducing the size of the files occupying the disk. Windows automatically compresses the files when they're not in use and decompresses them to open them. This slows your system slightly, because it takes time to compress and decompress files, but on most systems, you won't notice the difference. Windows allows you to compress all the files in an entire drive or in selected folders.

Before you take any drastic action, check out how much free space is remaining on your hard disk by performing the following steps:

❶ Click the **start** button and click **My Computer**.

❷ My Computer opens, displaying an icon for each drive on your computer. Right-click the icon for your computer's hard disk drive and click **Properties**.

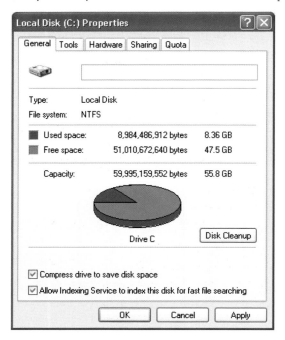

❸ The hard disk drive's Properties dialog box opens with the General tab selected. This tab displays a pie chart that shows the amount of free and used space on the hard disk.

❹ Click **Compress drive to save disk space**.

❺ Click **OK**.

⑥ The Confirm Attribute Changes dialog box opens, asking you to confirm the change. You are also asked whether you want to compress only the selected drive or the drive and its folders and files. To reclaim the most disk space, click **Apply changes to C:\, subfolders and files** (where C is the letter of the selected drive). To keep the subfolders and files uncompressed, click **Apply changes to C:\ only**.

⑦ Click **OK**. Windows compresses the drive and any subfolders or files as instructed.

To compress a single folder, do the following:

① Click the **start** button and click **My Computer**.

② My Computer opens. Double-click **Local Disk (C:)**, double-click **Document and Settings**, and then double-click the **Tom** folder (or any other user's folder).

③ Right-click the **My Documents** folder and click **Properties**.

④ The Properties dialog box for the selected folder opens. Click the **Advanced** button.

⑤ The Advanced Attributes dialog box opens. Below Compress or Encrypt attributes, click **Compress contents to save disk space**. (A check mark next to this option indicates that the folder will be compressed.)

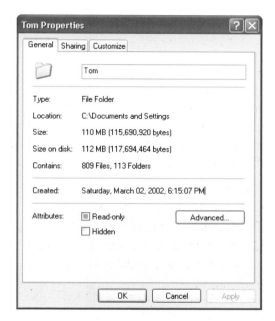

 You can choose to either compress a folder or encrypt it, but you cannot choose to both compress and encrypt a folder. (Encryption typically increases the size of a file.)

⑥ Click **OK**.

⑦ Windows returns you to the Properties dialog box for the selected folder. Click **OK**.

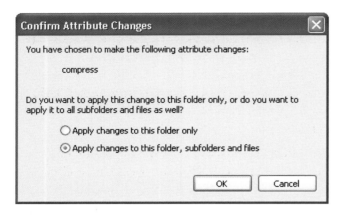

8 The Confirm Attribute Changes dialog box opens, asking you to confirm the change. You are also asked whether you want to compress only the selected folder or the folder and its subfolders and files. Click the desired option: **Apply changes to this folder only** or **Apply changes to this folder, subfolders and files**.

 If you choose Apply changes to this folder only, Windows compresses only the files in the selected folders. Files in any of this folder's subfolders remain uncompressed.

9 Click **OK**. Windows compresses the folder and any of its subfolders or files as instructed.

To decompress the folder, repeat the steps. In step 5, click **Compress contents to save disk space** to remove the check mark next to it. Then proceed with steps 6 through 9.

Cleaning Up Your Hard Disk

As you install programs, browse the Web, send and receive e-mail, record audio clips, create documents, and perform other computer-related tasks, your hard disk becomes littered with temporary files, downloaded program files, copies of deleted items, backup files, and other useless data. To reclaim additional disk space, use the Disk Cleanup utility to take out this trash:

1 Click **start**, point to **All Programs**, point to **Accessories**, point to **System Tools**, and click **Disk Cleanup**.

2 Disk Cleanup starts and scans your hard disk to find candidates for deletion. When scanning is complete, Disk Cleanup displays a list of file groups you can choose to delete. To view a brief description of any of the file groups, click its name. Disk Cleanup displays a description of the group in the Description area.

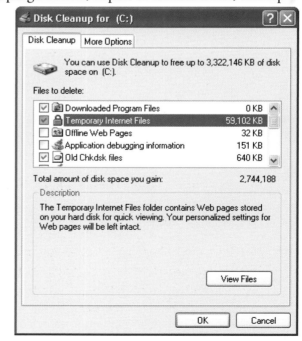

❸ If the check box next to a group of files you want to delete is blank, click the check box to flag the group for deletion. (To prevent Disk Cleanup from deleting a group of files, click the check box to remove the check mark.)

❹ Click **OK**.

❺ A Disk Cleanup dialog box opens asking if you're sure you want to perform the actions. Click **Yes** to delete the files.

❻ Disk Cleanup erases the selected files and closes.

If your computer starts to run low on disk space, consider removing any Windows components you never use and programs you never run to free up space. Using Disk Cleanup, here's how:

❶ Click **start**, point to **All Programs**, point to **Accessories**, point to **System Tools**, and click **Disk Cleanup**.

❷ In the Disk Cleanup dialog box, click the **More Options** tab. You have three options:

+ **Windows Components.** Clicking **Clean up** under Windows Components runs Windows XP Setup, which allows you to uninstall Windows components you never use.

+ **Installed Programs.** Clicking **Clean up** under Installed Programs runs Add/Remove Programs, which displays a list of applications installed on your computer. To remove a program, click its name and click the **Change/Remove** button.

9

◆ **System Restore.** Clicking **Clean up** under System Restore displays a confirmation dialog box asking whether you're sure you want to remove all but the most recent restore points from your system.

❸ If desired, click any of the Clean Up buttons and use the resulting utility to reclaim additional disk space. Click **OK** to perfom any actions and close Disk Cleanup.

 To learn about the importance of cleaning up space and maintaining your hard disk, go to the CD-ROM segment *Disk Cleanup*.

Scanning Your Hard Disk for Errors

Windows XP is equipped with a Check Disk utility that can test a disk (hard or floppy) for errors and repair most problems. Check Disk can also find defective areas on a disk and block them to prevent your computer from using defective storage areas in the future. In addition, Check Disk can find and delete misplaced (usually useless) file fragments that might be causing your computer to crash.

You should run Check Disk at least once every month and whenever your computer seems sluggish or unstable. To run Check Disk and scan a disk for errors, take the following steps:

 Check Disk can take an hour or more to complete a scan of a large hard disk. Start the operation when you won't be needing your computer for some time.

❶ Click the **start** button and click **My Computer**.

❷ My Computer opens and displays an icon for each of your computer's disk drives. Right-click the icon for your hard disk drive (typically the C: drive) and click **Properties** in the shortcut menu that appears.

❸ The Properties dialog box for the selected disk opens. Click the **Tools** tab.

❹ The Tools tab displays buttons for several disk-maintenance utilities. In the Error-checking area, click the **Check Now** button.

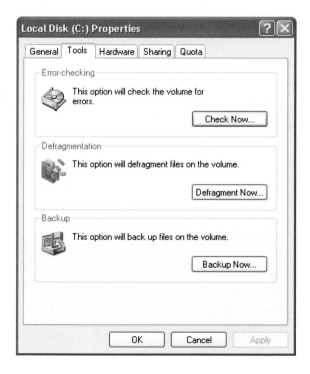

⑤ The Check Disk dialog box opens. Click **Automatically fix file system errors** to select it; doing so enables Check Disk to complete the task without prompting you for confirmation when it detects errors.

⑥ Click **Scan for and attempt recovery of bad sectors** to select it. If Check Disk detects a defective storage area on the disk that contains data, Check Disk attempts to move the data to a reliable storage area.

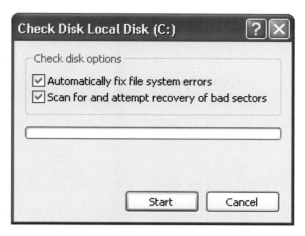

⑦ Click the **Start** button. The Checking Disk dialog box opens, indicating that the disk cannot be scanned because Check Disk needs exclusive access to the files on the disk. To schedule Check Disk to scan this disk the next time you start your computer, click **Yes**.

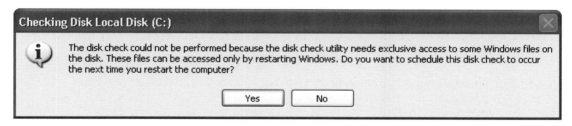

⑧ Save any documents that are currently open, and exit any programs that are running.

⑨ Click the **start** button and click **Turn Off Computer**.

⑩ The Turn off computer dialog box opens. Click **Restart**.

⑪ Windows shuts down your computer, restarts it, and runs Check Disk. As it runs, Check Disk displays its progress. When error checking is complete, Check Disk displays the results for a few seconds and then Windows displays the log on screen. Log on as you normally do.

 If you have a floppy disk that your computer cannot read, the Check Disk utility might be able to repair the disk and recover any data from it. The steps you take to run Check Disk on a floppy disk are almost identical to those taken to run this utility on your hard disk; simply right-click the floppy drive icon in My Computer instead of right-clicking the icon for your hard disk drive.

Defragmenting Your Hard Disk

When you delete files on your hard disk, you create gaps where other files can be stored. The next time you save a file, your computer stores as much of the file as will fit in one of the gaps, and the rest of the file in other empty spaces on the disk. The file is called *fragmented,* because its parts are scattered. This slows down your disk drive, because it must first locate all its parts. Further, the odds of your computer losing track of a portion of the file (or the entire file) increase.

Defragmenting rearranges the data on a disk to store each file in its own discrete location. In addition to making each fragmented file whole again, defragmenting creates a wide-open area on the disk for saving new files, thus reducing future fragmentation.

Windows is equipped with a utility called Disk Defragmenter that you can use to defragment your disks. Disk Defragmenter can take over an hour to defragment a hard disk, depending on the size of the disk, how fragmented the files are, and how fast your system is.

 If an anti-virus program is running in the background, disable it before running Disk Defragmenter. If you're using Norton AntiVirus, right-click its icon (on the right end of the Windows taskbar) and click **Disable Auto-Protect**. If you have a screen saver enabled, you'll need to disable that also to ensure that Disk Defragmenter runs properly. Right-click a blank area on the desktop, click **Properties** from the shortcut menu, click the Screen Saver tab, open the **Screen saver** list, and click (**None**).

To run Disk Defragmenter, take the following steps:

1 Click the **start** button, point to **All Programs**, point to **Accessories**, point to **System Tools**, and click **Disk Defragmenter**.

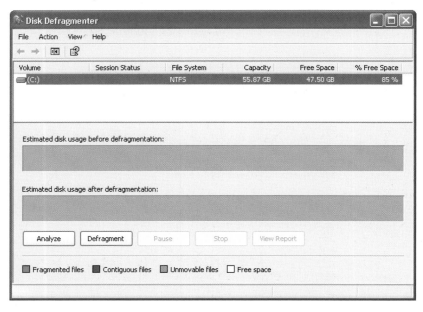

2 Disk Defragmenter opens and displays an icon for each drive on your machine that can be defragmented. Click the icon for the drive you want to defragment.

3 Click the **Analyze** button.

④ Disk Defragmenter scans the hard disk and displays graphs to illustrate the extent to which the drive's performance can be improved. In addition, Disk Defragmenter displays a dialog box indicating whether you should defragment the disk. To defragment the selected disk, click the **Defragment** button.

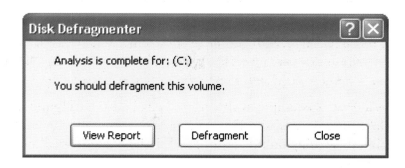

Disk Defragmenter

Analysis is complete for: (C:)

You should defragment this volume.

[View Report] [Defragment] [Close]

⑤ Disk Defragmenter starts defragmenting the selected disk and displays its progress. When defragmentation is complete, you are returned to the Disk Defragmenter window; click the window's **Close** button to close it.

 Enable the anti-virus program and screen saver, if you disabled them before running Disk Defragmenter. To enable Norton AntiVirus, right-click its icon on the right end of the Windows taskbar and click **Enable Auto-Protect**. To enable your screen saver, right-click a blank area on the desktop, click **Properties** from the shortcut menu, click the **Screen Saver** tab, open the Screen saver list, and click **Windows XP** (or the screen saver of your choice)

 To practice saving space and cleaning up your hard drive, go to the Web segment *Defragmenting Hard Drives* in the Beyond PC Basics course.

Protecting Your System from Viruses

Computer viruses, which are simply lines of computer code designed to be mischievous or downright destructive, can be avoided by practicing some safe-computing strategies. In the following sections, you learn about some great software and strategies you can implement to keep your computer free from viruses.

9

 Most anti-virus programs feature automatic updates over the Internet, and should be kept updated.

Discovering Anti-Virus Software

Anti-virus programs work like computerized antibodies to identify, attack, and destroy computer viruses before they do any serious damage to your computer. To protect your computer against viruses, you should install an anti-virus program and use it to perform the following tasks:

✦ Scan your entire system for viruses at least once every week.

✦ Scan for viruses in the background (in your computer's memory, without displaying a window) to identify risks posed by files you receive via the Internet or your network connection. The anti-virus program scans any incoming Web page, e-mail messages, and other data for known viruses and informs you of possible infections.

✦ Scan any disks or CDs you load into your computer before opening files or programs on the disks or CDs.

✦ Scan any files you receive as attachments to e-mail messages.

 Several different companies manufacture anti-virus software; a few of the more popular programs include The Norton AntiVirus®, McAfee VirusScan®, and Trend Micro PC-cillin®.

One of the best ways to protect your system is to enable any auto-protect features that your anti-virus program offers. Auto-protection typically consists of scanning for incoming viruses and keeping track of suspicious activity that might signal the presence of a virus; for example, if a program is trying to reformat your computer's hard drive. With auto-protection, instead of running the anti-virus program and choosing to scan your computer for viruses, the anti-virus program remains on alert at all times.

The instructions for enabling auto-protect features differ from product to product. To give you an idea of how the process works, we'll demonstrate how to enable the auto-protect features in Norton AntiVirus, which comes pre-loaded on a wide variety of computers:

① Click the **start** button, point to **All Programs**, point to **Norton AntiVirus**, and then click **Norton AntiVirus 2002**.

② The Norton AntiVirus window opens. Click the **Options** button.

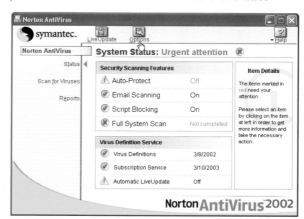

③ The Norton AntiVirus Options window opens. Make sure the following three options are selected in the How to stay protected section: **Enable Auto-Protect, Start Auto-Protect when Windows starts up**, and **Show the Auto-Protect icon in the tray**.

④ Click **OK**.

⑤ Click the **Close** button to close the Norton AntiVirus window. The Norton AntiVirus icon appears in the taskbar's notification

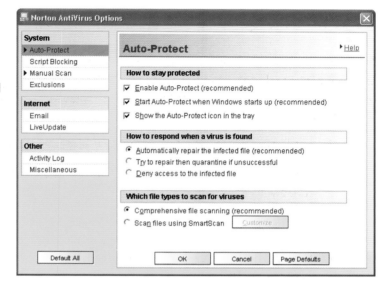

area, indicating that the program is running in the background.

⑥ Rest your mouse pointer on the icon. The message "Norton AntiVirus Auto-Protect Enabled" appears.

Safety Guidelines

Isolating your computer is not a viable solution for preventing virus infections. You can, however, reduce your risk by following a handful of safe-computing practices:

✦ **Install and run programs only from the manufacturer's disks or CDs.** Viruses most frequently travel in infected programs.

✦ **Avoid running any programs you receive via e-mail.** Although the original program file may not have been infected, the program could have picked up a virus on the computer of the person who sent you the file.

✦ **Avoid opening files or running programs posted in newsgroups.** In any newsgroup, users can post files to share with other users. Don't download any files or programs unless you have an anti-virus program running and actively scanning for viruses.

✦ **Download programs and files only from reputable sites.** Most Web sites that legally distribute commercial software and shareware (try-before-you-buy programs) scan their systems regularly to ensure their programs are virus-free.

✦ **Use your anti-virus program every week or two to do a full scan of all files on your computer.** Anti-virus programs typically feature a Full Scan option, which scans your computer's memory and all the files on your computer for known viruses.

+ **Set up your computer to scan for viruses in the background.** Most anti-virus programs can scan files as they are downloaded or received via e-mail, and can notify you immediately of any risks.

+ **Keep your anti-virus software up to date.** Your anti-virus program uses a list of virus definitions to identify known viruses. This list quickly becomes outdated, so it's important to download available updates regularly.

+ **Keep Windows XP, Outlook Express, and Internet Explorer up to date.** Run Windows XP's Update utility to download and install the latest updates and security improvements, as explained later in this chapter.

+ **Make sure Internet Explorer's security level is set to Medium or higher.** In Internet Explorer, open the **Tools** menu and click **Internet Options**. Click the **Security** tab and then click the **Default Level** button. If the Default Level button is dimmed (appears light gray), Default Level is already enabled.

 To know guidelines for using software to protect against computer viruses, go to the Web segment *Anti-Virus Software* in the Beyond PC Basics course.

Updating Your System

Windows XP is designed to be a stable and robust operating system for both home and network users. Even so, software released by even the most cautious manufacturer may contain imperfections (which may include errors, also known as *software bugs,* or potential security compromises, also known as *security holes*), which are discovered only after customers put a product to the test. In response, software vendors typically release code corrections known as *patches* or *security fixes* to repair such problems.

Microsoft is concerned about keeping your PC as secure and up-to-date as possible, and distributes update files for Windows XP via the Internet. You can configure your PC to download and install such update files for you using Automatic Update, or you can handle them manually by running Windows Update.

Using Automatic Updates

Soon after you install or configure Windows XP, you'll notice an icon in the notification area that looks like a globe bearing the Windows XP logo. Click this icon, called the Dynamic Update icon, to open the Automatic Updates tab in the System Properties dialog box, shown in Figure 9-1.

The Notifications area of this tab includes three options:

✦ Download the updates automatically and notify me when they are ready to be installed.

✦ Notify me before downloading any updates and notify me again before installing them on my computer.

✦ Turn off automatic updating. I want to update my computer manually.

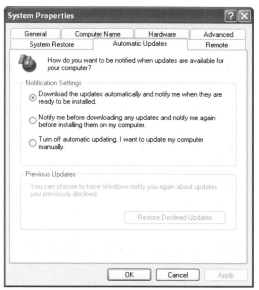

To proceed, make a selection and click **OK**.

To change the settings in the Automatic Updates tab, follow these steps:

❶ Click the **start** button, and then click **Control Panel**.

Figure 9-1 The Automatic Updates tab in the System Properties dialog box.

❷ The Control Panel window opens displaying the Category view mode by default. Click the **Performance and Maintenance** category.

9

③ The Performance and Maintenance category window opens. Click the **System** icon.

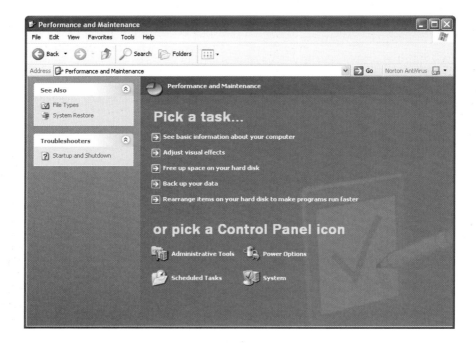

④ The System Properties dialog box opens. Click the Automatic Updates tab. Notice that this screen looks like the Automatic Updates dialog box (see Figure 9-1).

⑤ Select the preferred option, and click **OK** to close the System **Properties** dialog box.

⑥ Click the **Close** button to close the Performance and Maintenance window.

Manually Updating Windows

If you prefer to manage your system manually and control which updates are installed, Microsoft's Windows Update Web site enables you to download and install patches and other software yourself. Be sure to check the Windows Update Web site for critical updates on a weekly basis. *Critical updates* are patches for your PC that fix or prevent potentially serious problems, such as security holes or operational failures.

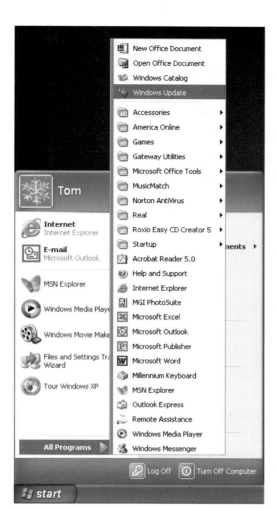

To access the Windows Update Web site, do one of the following:

✦ Click the **start** button, point to **All Programs**, and then click **Windows Update**.

✦ Start Internet Explorer, open the **Tools** menu, and select the **Windows Update** command.

✦ Open the Control Panel (start, Control Panel), then click **Add and Remove Programs**, click **Add New Programs**, and then click **Windows Update**.

The first time you visit the Windows Update Web site, you see a dialog box asking whether to trust content from Microsoft. Select the **Always Trust Microsoft** check box and click **OK**. The Windows Update site, shown in Figure 9-2, appears.

More About . . . Always Trust

Internet Explorer has a built-in security feature that prevents software from being downloaded from un-trusted Web sites and companies. All Web sites and companies are un-trusted by default, including Microsoft. As you attempt to download software, Internet Explorer will prompt you whether to trust the source of the software this time only, always, or never. If you are reasonably confident about a company or a Web site, go ahead and select to trust them always. Doing so will prevent you from having to see this dialog box again for this Web site or company. If you have doubts about a Web site or company, only trust them for the current download.

9

To use the Windows Update Web site, perform the following steps:

1 Click **Scan for updates**. The Windows Update Web site determines what updates your PC requires.

2 Click **Critical Updates**. A list of critical updates is displayed.

3 Click **Add** beside each update. You may need to scroll to see all the updates.

4 Click **Windows XP**. A list of recommended but not critical updates is displayed.

5 Click **Add** beside each update you want to apply to your PC. You may need to scroll to see all the updates.

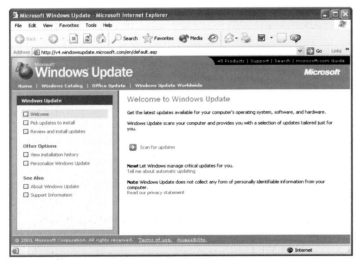

Figure 9-2 The Windows Update Web site.

6 Click **Driver Updates**. A list of updates related to device drivers and hardware on your PC is displayed.

7 Click **Add** beside each update. You may need to scroll to see all the updates.

8 Click **Review and install updates**. A list of all selected updates is displayed.

9 Click **Install Now**.

10 A dialog box opens, asking whether you accept the terms of the license agreement for the updates. Click **Accept**.

11 The updates are downloaded to your PC and are automatically installed.

12 If additional dialog boxes open, read them carefully and follow any instructions provided. You are often required to accept a Microsoft license agreement so the update can proceed. Sometimes, you may be asked to approve a backup directory for previous file versions when an update includes an "uninstall" feature (so you can remove it from your PC and restore it to its former state, should the fix itself cause any problems).

13 In some cases, you will be prompted to restart your system. If prompted, click **Yes** to allow the update process to restart your PC.

 It's a good idea to restart your system even if the update process doesn't prompt you to do so. Also, consider repeating the Windows Update process twice. That way, you can catch any additional updates that may now be required based on what you just installed.

Go to the CD-ROM and select the segment:

✦ *Caring for Your Computer* to learn the importance of cleaning up space and maintaining your hard disk.

✦ *File Backup* to learn about saving your files to disc.

✦ *Desktop Cleanup* to learn the importance of cleaning up space and maintaining your hard drive.

Go online to **www.LearnwithGateway.com** and log on to select:

✦ *Defragmenting Hard Disks* in the Beyond PC Basics course

✦ *Anti-Virus Software* in the Beyond PC Basics course

✦ *Internet Links and Resources*

✦ *FAQs*

With Gateway and the *Survive & Thrive* series, refer to *Use and Care for Your PC* for more information on:

✦ *Caring for your computer*

Gateway offers hands-on training courses that cover many of the topics in this chapter. Additional fees may apply. Call **888-852-4821** to enroll. Please have your customer ID and order number ready when you call.

9

Tips and Troubleshooting

M odern computers and Windows XP are both remarkably stable, but they're not perfect. Sometimes things go wrong: the computer freezes, the printer won't print, or the speakers are silent for no obvious reason. The good news is that these and other common computer problems are often easier to solve than you might think.

This chapter focuses on teaching you how to troubleshoot common computer ailments and administer proper remedies. You'll learn some general troubleshooting tips and techniques and how to get assistance elsewhere when all else has failed.

Exiting Frozen Programs

Now and then, you may encounter a problem when running various software programs on your PC. For example, a program might *freeze* or *hang*—that is, it might stop responding to the mouse or the keyboard, or it might not display properly on the monitor screen. Sometimes, the operating system might present an error message to tell you that something is wrong. When a program freezes, or error messages appear, that failure may stem from a problem with the program itself, a problem with the operating system, or a problem arising from interaction among other active programs. Alternatively, the problem could just be a fluke.

When you encounter such a problem, it may take one or more of the following actions to resolve the issue: wait it out, exit the frozen program, log off, or as a last resort restart your PC.

More About . . . Preventing Problems

Once you get your system up and running again, you might want to look for an update or patch for the program to prevent it from happening again. You can typically find program updates on the Web site of the company that makes the program in question; check the site's Support or Download section for details. If you can't find what you need, call the company's technical support line.

You may also need to update Windows XP to prevent your system from hanging again. Refer to the section "Updating Your System" earlier in this chapter for more information.

Wait It Out

In some cases, your system may appear to be frozen when, in fact, it is simply in the process of performing an intense calculation or some other resource intensive task. If you suspect this is the case, or if you haven't saved your document for a long time and want to avoid losing information it contains, then your best bet is to wait. The system may restore itself after it completes the task. If the system responds within 10 minutes or so, save your document, exit the program, and restart your system. If after 10 minutes the system is still frozen, however, it's unlikely that the program will return to normal. If so, it's best to move on to the next option: exiting the frozen program.

 From this point on, any of the actions you perform as you attempt to unfreeze your system will result in the loss of any information you have not yet saved. Let this be a warning to you: Make a habit of saving your documents regularly to prevent data loss. Saving every five to 10 minutes is a good idea.

Exit the Program

If you've waited for your system to restore itself to no avail, it's best to attempt to exit the frozen program while allowing other programs and the operating system to keep working. There are two ways to accomplish this; be sure to try both before moving on to the next procedure:

+ Use the taskbar button's shortcut menu

+ Use the Task Manager

If after you attempt to exit a program, it remains open but is still frozen, it's best to move on to the next option: logging off your system.

Exit Using the Program's Taskbar Button

To exit a frozen program using its taskbar button, perform the following steps:

1. Right-click the program's button in the taskbar. A shortcut menu appears.
2. Click the **Close** command.
3. Wait for the **End Program** dialog box to open. If it opens, continue to step 4. If the program exits without displaying the End Program dialog box, however, you are finished; you need not perform additional steps.

 If the program fails to close, but the End Program dialog box does not open in two minutes or so, repeat steps 1 through 3 again.

4. In the End Program dialog box, click **OK**, **Yes**, or **End** to terminate the program.

Exit Using Task Manager

Another way to exit a frozen program while allowing other programs and the operating system to keep working is to use the Task Manager. To launch the Task Manager and access its Applications tab (shown in Figure 10-1), do one of the following:

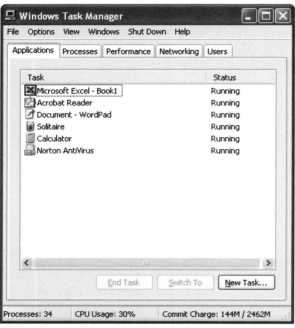

Figure 10-1 The Applications tab in Windows Task Manager.

- ✦ Press the **CTRL+SHIFT+ESC** key combination.

- ✦ If your Windows XP Professional or Windows XP Home system is a stand-alone system or a member of a workgroup, you can use the **CTRL+ALT+DEL** key combination. However, on other systems, especially network clients, the **CTRL+ALT+DEL** key combination opens the Windows Security dialog box. In the Windows Security dialog box, you can click the **Task Manager** button.

- ✦ Right-click an empty area of the taskbar, click the **Task Manager** command in the shortcut menu that appears, and then click the **Applications** tab, if necessary.

The Task Manager's Applications tab names every active program. To the right of this list is a column stating the status of each program. If a program is working properly, its status appears as "Running." If a program is frozen, however, its status appears as "Not Responding."

To use the Task Manager to close or terminate a program that is not responding, perform the following steps:

❶ In the Task Manager's Applications tab, click the name of the program whose status is listed as "Not Responding."

❷ Click the **End Task** button.

❸ Wait for the **End Program** dialog box to open. If it opens, continue to step 4. If the program exits without displaying the End Program dialog box, however, you are finished; you need not perform additional steps.

 As in the preceding section, if the program fails to close, but the End Program dialog box doesn't open in two minutes, repeat steps 1 through 3 again.

❹ In the End program dialog box, click **OK**, **Yes**, or **End** to terminate the program.

10

Log Off

If you've attempted to close the frozen program, but your system is still not responding, your best bet is to log off and then log back in. This stops all programs currently running on your desktop. To accomplish this, do the following:

❶ Click the **start** button, and then click **Log Off**.

❷ In the Log Off Windows dialog box, click **Log Off**.

❸ If an End Program dialog box opens, click **OK**, **Yes**, or **End** to terminate the program. If no such dialog box opens, continue to step 4.

 As noted previously, if a program fails to close, but the End Program dialog box doesn't open in two minutes, repeat steps 1 through 3.

❹ When you see the Windows Welcome logon screen, log back on.

If the program remains frozen even after you've taken all steps outlined in the preceding paragraphs, there's only one option left: You must restart your PC. Hopefully, you can force a shutdown and restart. To do so, try the following:

❶ Click the **start** button, and then click **Turn Off Computer**.

❷ In the Turn off computer dialog box, click the **Restart** button.

3 If an End Program dialog box opens, click **OK**, **Yes**, or **End** to terminate the program. If no such dialog box opens, continue to step 4.

4 After the computer shuts down and restarts, the Windows Welcome logon screen appears. Log back on.

 Again, if the program fails to close, but the End Program dialog box does not appear in two minutes, repeat steps 1 through 3 again.

If this restart process fails, you must resort to powering down your PC manually using its power button, then switch it back on to restart. See Chapter 3 for information on starting your PC; logging on is covered in Chapter 5.

Troubleshooting Your PC

Although troubleshooting your PC may seem mysterious now, over time you'll develop the skills you need to diagnose and resolve problems with your computer. As you gain experience using your PC and work through issues as they arise, your ability to troubleshoot will improve. Here are several important tips to help you better troubleshoot your system:

✦ Stay calm and be patient. Getting angry or trying to rush won't make troubleshooting any easier. Take your time and keep a clear head.

✦ Because many problems revolve around loose connections or cables, it's a good idea to check these first. Make sure all cables are securely attached both to your PC and to the connected device, such as your printer, modem, speakers, etc.

✦ If a device fails to turn on, check their power supplies. If they show a green indicator light (for those that have them), or are slightly warm to the touch (for those that lack indicator lights), chances are good they're working properly. If they're showing red indicators or are room temperature, they probably aren't working properly (and may need to be replaced).

✦ As you attempt to fix your PC, take things one step at a time, eliminating possible problems with your machine methodically. Make one change to your system, such as updating the driver, changing a single configuration setting, etc. Then test your PC to see if that change helped. If not, reverse or undo that change, then make another change, and test again. Continue making changes one at a time until the problem is resolved. That way, you'll know exactly which change resolved the issue, and you'll be able to fix the problem easily should it occur again in the future.

+ Take notes on the problems you encounter with your PC and what steps you take to resolve them. Include both successful and failed actions. This information will be useful if a problem ever repeats itself. Additionally, if you ever need to call tech support or take your PC in for repairs, you'll be able to tell them exactly what kinds of problems your PC has had and what you tried to do to fix them.

+ Never be afraid to ask for help. If you can't resolve your computer's problem in a reasonable amount of time, call someone, be it your PC manufacturer or reseller, a custom computer shop, or a PC service center. Chances are, they'll be able to help.

In the next few sections, you'll learn about at a few common problems that crop up from time to time and what actions you can take to try to resolve each issue.

The Printer Won't Print

Printer problems can be frustrating, but there is good news: Some printing problems are simple to resolve. If the problem is with the printer hardware, however, you may be in for an repair job or a new printer.

When you experience printer problems, perform the following steps. After each step, try to print to see if the problem is resolved.

1. Verify that the printer is turned on.
2. Make sure there is paper in the paper tray. If the paper tray is removable, ensure that it is inserted properly. Also, while inspecting the paper tray, make sure the paper is not creased or torn, as this could cause paper jams.
3. Check that there is ink or toner in the printer. If not, replace the ink or toner cartridge (check your printer's documentation for instructions).
4. Ensure that all covers, lids, doors, and other components are closed on the printer.
5. Make sure the printer's power supply is, in fact, supplying power. Plug something else into the outlet, such as a lamp, to see if it is working properly.
6. Disconnect and reconnect every cable connected to your printer. Be sure to disconnect and reconnect the cable connecting your printer to your PC on both ends.
7. Turn your printer off then back on three times. Wait about 15 seconds between each on and off switch. Cycling the power is intended to clear the printer's memory; this may take three cycles to accomplish.

10

⑧ Restart your PC.

⑨ Perform a Windows Update. Look for any device-driver updates related to your printer. If you find any, download them to your PC. (For more information about Windows Update, refer to the section "Updating Your System" earlier in this chapter.)

⑩ Click **start**, and then click **Printers and Faxes**. In that window, right-click on the icon, then select **Delete** from the menu to delete the icon for the problem printer. Reinstall that printer, following the steps outlined in Chapter 3.

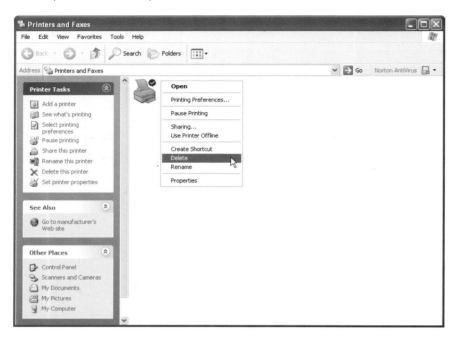

⑪ Check your printer manufacturer's Web site for an updated driver. If one exists, download and install it on your PC using the instructions provided by the manufacturer.

If your printer still doesn't work, call for help. You can try the printer manufacturer, or contact the store or outlet where you bought it. Check your paperwork (or the manufacturer's Web page) for technical support contacts.

The Monitor Is Blank

As with printers, many problems related to monitors are easy to resolve. If your troubleshooting actions fail to resolve the problem, however, your monitor might need to be repaired or replaced.

When you experience monitor problems, perform the following steps:

❶ Verify that the monitor is turned on.

❷ Verify that the monitor's power outlet is, in fact, supplying power. Plug something else into that outlet, such as a lamp, to see if it's working properly.

❸ Turn off your system and all components. Disconnect and reconnect every cable connected to your monitor. (While the monitor cable is disconnected, check the male end to ensure that all the pins are straight.)

❹ Restart your PC.

If the monitor remains unavailable, seek professional help from a qualified computer repair technician.

The Keyboard or Mouse Doesn't Work

Your keyboard and mouse get the most use of any device connected to your PC. Even though they're designed for intense daily use, they are still complex electronic devices, susceptible to occasional problems. If your keyboard or mouse stops working, perform the following:

❶ Unplug and re-connect the cables to the PC.

Keyboard port

Mouse port

❷ Restart the PC.

10

If the keyboard or mouse still doesn't work, there are two possible causes:

✦ The keyboard or mouse is damaged. This is the most likely possibility. The solution to this is to replace the failed device.

✦ The keyboard or mouse port on your PC is damaged. If you try a brand-new replacement and it still doesn't work, your next step should be to seek help from a qualified computer technician.

The Speakers Are Silent

If your speakers suddenly don't work, the first step is to verify that the volume setting on your PC is turned up and not muted. To do so, follow these steps:

1 Click the **start** button, and then **Control Panel**.

2 In Control Panel, click **Sounds, Speech, and Audio Devices**.

3 Click **Adjust the system volume**.

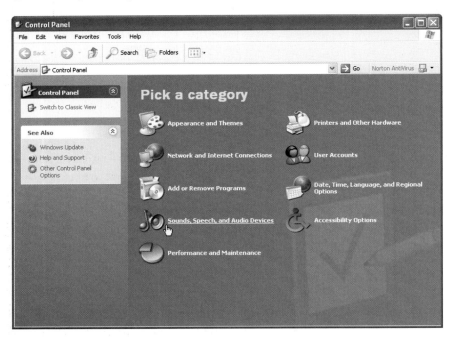

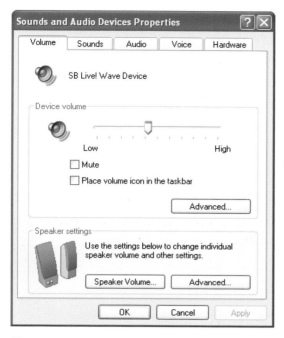

4 In the Sounds and Audio Devices Properties dialog box, drag the **Device volume** slider to the middle of the Low-High range.

5 Click sure the **Mute** check box is not checked.

6 Click the **OK** button.

If following these steps fails to resolve the problem, do the following:

1 If your speakers have volume knobs or other controls, ensure that they are turned up.

2 Some speaker sets have power switches on each speaker, some only have a single switch on one speaker; make sure all such switches are turned on.

3 Make sure the speakers' power cable is plugged into a surge protector or power strip and that the speakers are in fact receiving power. Plug something else into the surge protector or power strip, such as a lamp, to see if it is working properly.

4 Check the connections between each speaker and the PC (they usually plug into a sound card) by unplugging and re-connecting each connector. If the speakers connect to each other, unplug then re-connect those cables as well.

Microphone port   Speaker ports

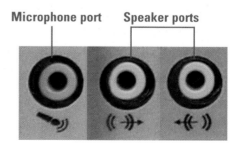

5 Ensure that all speaker cables are properly plugged into the correct ports. Check your speaker manuals to make sure all connections are correct.

10

6 Plug your speakers into a portable radio or CD player. If you hear sound, you probably have a problem with your sound card or with your PC in general. If not, you may need to replace your speakers.

7 Plug a set of working headphones into the speaker out port on your PC. If you hear sound, your problem lies with your speakers; your best bet is to replace them. If not, you may have a problem with your sound card or your PC.

The PC Won't Boot

The most frustrating problem you may encounter with your PC is if you can't get it to power on and start. Although there are a few easy ways to resolve this issue in the short term, it can be a sign of bigger problems. To address this problem, perform the following steps. After each step, try to start the PC to see if the problem is resolved.

1 Make sure the PC's power outlet is working. Plug something else into that outlet, such as a lamp, to check.

2 Firmly press the power button on the front of your PC once or twice; be sure you press it all the way in. If that doesn't work, try pressing the button in for 10 seconds or so.

3 Disconnect and reconnect every cable attached to the PC, and then try to turn the power on again.

4 A damaged keyboard or mouse can cause a short circuit that prevents the PC from booting. This is a safety feature to prevent further damage to other PC components. To determine whether this is the case, disconnect the keyboard and mouse and then try powering on your machine.

If these efforts are unsuccessful, consider the following:

✦ If the fan next to the power-cord plug on the back of the system unit case turns on, that indicates your PC's internal power supply is working, but that the PC's motherboard may be damaged or that the on/off switch on the front of the system unit case is not working.

✦ If the fan does not turn on, it could indicate that your PC's internal power supply has failed. In some cases, a power supply that doesn't power on simply indicates a blown fuse or breaker. (The fuse or breaker prevents electrical surges from reaching the delicate internal components of the PC.) In many cases, that fuse or breaker can be reset. In some instances, however, once the fuse or breaker is tripped, the power supply must be replaced.

✦ If the on/off switch on the front of the system unit case doesn't click or work, it is broken and must be replaced.

✦ If the power indicator(s) light up on the front of the case but nothing else happens, the hard drive(s) or the motherboard could be damaged.

If the PC powers up but still doesn't boot, it could require a system restoration. This can be accomplished by using system restoration CDs that may have shipped with your PC or by calling upon the services of a professional computer technician.

Troubleshooting: General Advice

When faced with a computer problem, keep in mind that the solution might be a simple fix that you can perform yourself. If you find that you require assistance, it's best to have as much information available as possible before calling for help. The next time your PC causes trouble, start with these troubleshooting tips:

✦ **Quit all programs and restart your computer.** Quitting all programs and restarting your computer gives it the opportunity to clear and refresh its cluttered memory.

✦ **Check for obvious problems.** When a device is not working, make sure it's plugged in and turned on before changing any of its settings.

✦ **Read the screen.** When a problem occurs, a message usually pops up on the screen. Write down the message exactly as it appears, so you can relay the message to a technical support person if necessary.

✦ **Focus on software issues.** Most hardware problems are software-related. The device might require an updated driver or some setting modifications in order to work properly.

✦ **Ask yourself the right questions.** When did the problem start? Is the problem always present or only when you enter certain commands? Asking the right questions can help you zero in on the cause of the problem.

✦ **Change one setting at a time.** To determine whether a particular setting is causing a problem, change only that setting, and then try to reproduce the problem. If the problem persists, return the setting to its original state and try something else.

✦ **Read the documentation.** An owner's manual is included with most devices and programs; check this manual for a troubleshooting table or list of common questions and issues.

✦ **Check the manufacturer's Web site.** Most manufacturers have a support area where you can view a *FAQ (Frequently Asked Questions)* list, search a database for help, and download software updates.

 To learn more about troubleshooting your PC, go to the Web segment *Troubleshooting Problems* in the Beyond PC Basics course.

10

If the PC powers up but still doesn't boot, it could require a system restoration. This can be accomplished by using system restoration CDs that may have shipped with your PC or by calling upon the services of a professional computer technician.

Utilizing Remote Assistance

Most people have a knowledgeable friend or relative whom they can consult when a computer problem has them stumped, but it's not always convenient for that friend or relative to offer assistance in person. Windows XP includes a feature called Remote Assistance that allows users to help one another over the Internet. Be sure the person you give access to fix your machine is someone you trust. Anyone who connects to your computer will be able to delete files and cause other acts of destruction just as if they were typing away at your keyboard. To learn how to use Remote Assistance, refer to the following CD-ROM and Web tutorials.

 To learn more about remote assistance for user accounts, go the CD-ROM segment *Remote Assistance: Features*.

 To practice requesting remote assistance for user accounts, go to the Web segment *Remote Assistance: Requesting* in the Beyond PC Basics course.

Getting Professional Help

Professional help is aid from any computer technician. That technician can be from your point of purchase, the manufacturer of your PC, individual hardware device or specific software, a custom local repair shop, or a dedicated technical support service. Be sure to have your sales paperwork handy (this includes the receipt and any technical description of the PC or peripheral device). You can refer to this paperwork to look up make and model information or verify warranty coverage. If you need a technician to service your PC, be sure to give them a copy of that paperwork. This saves time and effort answering many questions they might otherwise need to ask you.

You'll usually find technical support contact information either on the company's Web site or in the user manual that accompanied their product. If you are unable to locate proper technical support access information, contact your point-of-sale and inquire how to obtain technical support. As a last resort, you can find local computer repair and technical support centers listed in the phone book under "Computers."

 To get more help, go to the Web segment *Help and Support Features* in the PC Basics course.

Go to the CD-ROM and select the segment:

♦ *Remote Assistance: Features* to learn more about remote assistance for user accounts

 Go online to **www.LearnwithGateway.com** and log on to select:

♦ *Troubleshooting Problems* in the Beyond PC Basics course

♦ *Remote Assistance: Requesting* in the Beyond PC Basics course

♦ *Help and Support Features* in the PC Basics course

♦ *Internet Links and Resources*

♦ *FAQs*

 Gateway offers hands-on training courses that cover many of the topics in this chapter. Additional fees may apply. Call **888-852-4821** to enroll. Please have your customer ID and order number ready when you call.

Glossary

.NET Pronounced dot-Net, an operating system design intended to erase the boundaries between personal computers and the Internet.

activation A security measure enacted by Microsoft to guard against software piracy. When Windows XP asks you to activate your copy, you must do so within 30 days by phone or on the Internet, or the software stops working.

active program The program whose window has a dark title bar; title bars for inactive program windows are subdued in color. In addition, an active program's taskbar button appears depressed, while taskbar buttons of inactive programs do not.

address field In a Web browser, shows a URL for the Web site currently on display in the workspace area of the application window.

AGP (Accelerated Graphics Port) A type of motherboard connection used to connect to high-speed video cards. Most motherboards have only one AGP port.

anti-virus software A special type of program that scans your PC for viruses and removes them before they can do any harm. It can also actively monitor PC memory and scan all downloaded files and incoming e-mail messages to stop infections before they occur.

ATA (Advanced Technology Attachment) Enables connections for Integrated Drive Electronics (IDE) hard drives and CD and DVD drives. An ATA ribbon cable connects one or two IDE drives to each ATA port. Most motherboards include two ATA ports.

Auto-hide A display property that causes the taskbar to vanish when not in use.

autorun A program that automatically opens a file or begins an installation routine when a CD is placed in a computer's CD-ROM drive.

booting The sequence of steps that activates a PC. The start-up process includes powering up, testing hardware, launching the operating system, and establishing an account in which to operate. Generally called *starting*.

browse (your computer) To look through a display or listing in search of something of interest, perhaps a specific document or program.

burner A device that records data to recordable CD and DVD discs.

burning a CD The process of writing data to a CD-R or CD-RW.

buttons Common dialog controls; you click buttons to execute commands or to apply whatever settings you've selected in a dialog box. Common buttons include Close, Cancel, Apply, Print, Open, and Save; usually, the name on a button defines its function.

central processing unit (CPU) The main processor chip on a PC's motherboard—not the whole system unit (a common, but mistaken, use of the term).

CD-R (compact disc-recordable) A CD storage medium that can be recorded only once, but can be played or read many times.

CD-ROM drive A device that reads CDs. CD-ROM is a read-only medium; the "ROM" in its name stands for Read-Only Memory.

CD-ROM (compact disc-read only memory) A CD storage medium that uses the same type of discs you play in your audio CD player to store computer programs and files; you can read from CD-ROM discs but you cannot write to them.

CD-RW (compact disc-rewritable) A CD storage medium on which data can be stored and then erased as needed; thus, CD-RW discs are reusable.

check boxes   Controls, found in a dialog box, used in lists of options when more than one option can be selected, or when a single option can be turned on or off.

click   The most common mouse action; to click, position the pointer over an object on your screen. Then press and release the primary mouse button.

client   A program that runs on your computer and calls on a server to deliver information or perform a task. An e-mail program, for example, is a client.

client-server   A type of network on which workstation computers connect to a powerful central computer to run programs, access files, and share resources.

color quality   A value set by a PC's video card or graphics adapter that controls the number of colors on display (settings are: medium, high, and highest). More colors produces a higher-quality image.

communication devices   Various types of hardware that allow two or more PCs to communicate. Such devices normally connect to expansion cards inside the system unit, or to external serial, USB, FireWire, PC Card, or NIC connections.

computer administrator user account   A privileged Windows XP account that can create, manage, and delete user accounts; change PC and user configurations; install programs; and access all files on a PC.

connections   The cables, plugs, connectors and ports needed to add devices to your system unit.

container   A named folder or location on a Windows PC, which may be a default folder such as My Documents, local hard drives, My Computer, or other icons.

Control Panel   A Windows icon that provides access to all the utilities needed to configure your PC and install new hardware reside within the Control Panel.

CPU (central processing unit)   The "brain" of a computer. Its role is to interpret and carry out instructions, perform computations, and control devices connected to the PC. A dual processor PC has two CPUs, for more computing power.

critical updates   Patches for your Windows-based PC that fix or prevent potentially serious problems, such as security holes or bugs.

desktop   The main work area or computing environment in the Windows environment that appears once you start up and log on to your PC.

details pane   The right side of the window in My Computer or Windows Explorer that displays the contents of a folder or drive.

device driver   A special type of software that allows a specific hardware device to communicate with a PC. Without a device driver, hardware devices won't work.

dialog box   Used by Windows XP to solicit user input, they often appear as a result of selecting certain menu commands or performing other actions.

digital versatile disc (DVD)   A high-capacity optical storage medium, a DVD looks the same as a CD, but can store between 4.7 and 17 GB of data which may be audio, video (it's a preferred format for movies), or other information.

double-click   An action performed with the primary mouse button to initiate some activity; similar to clicking, except you click twice, quickly, without moving the mouse.

domain   A group of computers on a network managed as a single entity. Domains make it easier for network administrators to handle large numbers of networked computers.

dragging   A technique that enables you to move text, graphics, files, and objects of any kind on your screen. Simply position your mouse pointer on the object to be moved, press and hold down the primary mouse button, and slide the mouse. Also called *clicking and dragging*.

DSL (digital subscriber line) modem   A digital telephone service used to provide high-speed Internet access. It requires specific hardware.

DVD-R (digital versatile disc-recordable)   A DVD storage medium that can be written to only once. DVD recorders and discs use much narrower tracks than those used on CDs, allowing them to store up to seven times more data than CDs.

DVD-RAM (digital versatile disc-random access memory)   A storage technology for computers that uses a type of disc similar to those used in a TV's DVD player. DVD-RAM discs can be read and written many times, so they may be used like a computer's hard disk drive.

e-mail   Any of a number of messaging systems used on the Internet. E-mail may be plain text, but messages can include pictures, formatting, and animation. You can also attach just about any kind of file to an e-mail message.

e-mail account   A service you get from an ISP, online service, or an independent Internet company such as Yahoo or Hotmail.

e-mail address   Represents the person and their location to which to send e-mail on the Internet, similar to how the address of your home allows people and companies to send mail to you. An e-mail address includes a user name separated from an ISP, online service, or company name by an @ sign.

e-mail client   A program used to read and send e-mail messages.

emergency disk   Also called a recovery disk; a special disk from which you can start a PC that might not be able to start up completely otherwise; most versions of Windows include utilities to create such disks for emergency use.

FAQ (Frequently Asked Questions)   A list of common questions with their answers, normally compiled by technical support operations to provide ready access to information and answers in high demand (or of high interest).

file name extension   Groups of three or more characters that appear to the right of the rightmost period in a file name; Windows uses this data to associate programs with files.

file   A container for text, programs, documents, images and other stored items on a PC; also, objects in a PC file system where actual documents and data reside.

Files and Settings Transfer Wizard   A Windows wizard you can use to move your personal data files and desktop settings from one PC to another.

folder   A named container in a PC file system that contains other objects (either files or other folders, called subfolders); used to organize files and containers into a recognizable and navigable folder structure.

fragmented   When you delete files on your hard disk, you create gaps where other files can be stored. The next time you save a file, your computer stores as much of the file as will fit in those gaps, and the rest of the file in other empty spaces on the disk. Such a file is said to be *fragmented,* because its parts are scattered.

floppy drive   A storage device reads and writes to 3.5" diskettes (also known as floppy disks), a common removable storage medium. Typical floppy disks hold up to 1.44 MB.

freeze   What programs are said to do when they stop responding to the mouse, keyboard, or fail to display properly on the monitor screen. Sometimes the operating system might present an error message to tell you that something is wrong.

full backup A copy of all files in your My Documents folder, your list of Internet Explorer Favorites, your desktop settings, your e-mail correspondence and address book (assuming you use Outlook Express), plus all other files on your PC's hard disks. Usually recorded with a back-up program, this copy is meant to be restored should anything happen to your PC that affects the original.

graphical user interface (GUI) The use of graphics, windows, and icons instead of text to interact with PC users.

guest account A pre-defined Windows user account that allows anyone to log on and use the computer without entering a password.

hard drive A storage device typically located inside the computer. A hard drive stores both the instructions a computer needs to run and any data a user types in and saves.

hardware All physical objects or devices attached to a PC, including the monitor, keyboard, mouse, printer, and the system unit itself qualify as hardware.

Help and Support A Windows icon that provides access to a Help and Support Center; the first, best place to go when you need help with Windows XP.

home page Identifies a predefined URL that your Web browser loads when it opens.

hyperlink Text or graphical elements on a Web page that you click to jump to another Web page. A hyperlink can appear underlined and as a different color than surrounding text. Also called link.

hub A device containing multiple ports to interconnect two or more computers or devices; commonly used to interconnect networked computers.

ICF (Internet Connection Firewall) A Windows XP utility that prevents unauthorized access to your PC over a modem connection or always-on Internet connection, such as cable or DSL.

icon A small graphic with a text label; it represents an object or a shortcut to an object stored in another location.

IEEE 1394 (FireWire) A high-speed peripheral interface that is much faster than USB 1.1 and supports as many as 127 devices (the same as USB). PCs with built-in FireWire support usually have two such ports: one in the back and one in the front.

inkjet printer A printer that produces output by spraying microscopic drops of ink onto the paper as it passes through the printer. Most inkjet printers can print both color and black images.

input hardware Any device used to enter information (text, sound, or images) into a PC. Examples of input hardware include keyboards, mice, scanners, digital cameras, and microphones. Also known as *input devices.*

insertion point A blinking vertical bar that appears in the upper-left corner of a program's workspace to indicate where text will appear when you start typing.

Internet Explorer A Web browser you can use to surf Web sites located on the Internet throughout the world.

ISP (Internet Service Provider) or Online Service A company that provides online access. ISPs typically offer Internet access and other services such as e-mail, while online services also offer their members specialized private "communities."

keyboard A PC input device, used to enter numbers, letters, symbols, and even control commands in your PC, typically connected to a PC through a PS/2 or USB connection.

LAN (local area network)   A group of connected computers typically located in a single room or building, connected to a single hub.

laser printer   A printer that produces output by using lasers to adhere and bond a powdered (black) toner onto paper. Laser printers produce detailed high-quality images.

limited user account   An unprivileged Windows XP account for regular users that can only create or delete its own password, change its own picture, theme, and desktop settings, access files it creates, and access files in the Shared Documents folder.

local printer   A printer that is connected to a computer is *local* to that computer.

log off   In the Windows environment, to close your desktop and return to the logon screen. This gives the next user quick access to the logon screen.

log on   In the Windows environment, to select a user account and provide a password, if one is required, to gain access to the PC.

Maximize button   The middle button in the group of three Windows controls at the top right of every window. It looks like a single Window icon and causes the window to fill the entire display when clicked.

media   Individual items, such as floppy disks, CD-Rs, CD-RWs, tapes, or Zip/Jaz cartridges, that you can insert into or remove from a removable storage device.

menu bar   A list of words or names appearing below the title bar and above the first toolbar in a window.

Minimize button   The minus-sign-shaped button leftmost in the group of three Windows controls at the top right of every window. Use this button to hide its program window, thus freeing up space on your desktop, without shutting down the program.

modem   A device that allows a PC to communicate with other PCs using a standard phone line. A modem can be an expansion card installed inside the system unit or an external device connected via a USB or serial cable.

monitor   A device that displays visual output for a PC. A tube monitor looks like a television set—heavy, large, and boxy. A flat-panel monitor is narrow in profile and provides crisp, clean images that are more vibrant and brilliant than some tube monitors.

motherboard   The foundation of a modern PC; it provides numerous sockets or ports to accommodate and interact with other devices, such as CPU, memory and expansion cards, with cables to link to hard drives and CD-ROM/DVD drives. Any motherboard accepts only specific CPU and memory types. Also called a *mainboard.*

mouse   A small device that you use to move the mouse pointer on a PC screen; designed to help control graphical user interfaces of all kinds; connects to a PC using serial, PS/2, or USB connections.

mouse pointer   A small, white, left-pointing arrow that appears somewhere on your screen that the mouse can direct to select objects, buttons, menus, or other screen items.

MP3 player   A portable device that plays back digitally recorded music. MP3 players have either a large amount of memory or a hard drive on which digital music is stored.

MSN Explorer   A version of Internet Explorer specifically configured for the MSN Internet access service.

multi-window taskbar button A special kind of button that appears when there are two or more windows open in a single program, and the taskbar holds six or more taskbar buttons: same-program windows collapse into this single taskbar button. Such buttons are indicated by the presence of a number between the icon and the program name.

My Computer A Windows icon that opens a window showing all hard drives, folder shares, and removable storage devices available on your PC.

My Network Places A Windows icon that becomes useful when your PC is connected to a network. Its window displays all shared data accessible from the network, with links to common tasks and other network locations.

network Two or more computers connected so they can share resources and exchange data.

network interface card (NIC) A special type of PC adapter that connects the PC to some type of network medium and facilitates network communications.

network printer A printer that is accessible by a network user, even though the printer is not attached directly to his or her computer.

notebook computer A fully functional computer that's about the size of a college textbook (or even smaller) with a built-in screen, keyboard, and pointing device. Also called a *laptop*.

notification area An area located on the far right side of the taskbar that displays small icons to represent running programs that do not appear on your desktop.

object A named Windows element, which may be a file, folder, printer, or some other kind of Windows resource, that uses a unique "address" to identify it among all other resources on your PC.

object path The location information that identifies any object's exact location on a Windows PC as a prefix to the object's name. See also *path*.

object-selection field An area that lists one or more options. In most cases, you can select only a single item at a time; the selected item is highlighted.

operating system (OS) The fundamental software that runs on a PC (or other computer) to create a working computing environment that supports access to the hardware, and permits other programs (word processing, Web browser, e-mail client, and so forth) to run.

option buttons Windows controls used to select only one item from a list of options. To select an option button, click it; when selected, a dot appears inside the button.

Outlook Express A Microsoft e-mail program that enables you to read and send e-mail to anyone with an address on the Internet

output hardware Any device that produces information from a PC system. Examples of output hardware include the monitor, printers, loudspeakers, and those storage devices that can create or update files, media, and much more. Also known as *output device(s)*.

pane A subsection of an application window, a dialog box, or a subsection of the workspace within an application window, that is usually outlined and named.

parallel port Normally used to attach printers to a PC, the parallel port on a system unit is always female. Usually, only a single external device can connect to a parallel port.

passport An electronic identification badge that provides access to sites and services on the Internet through a single log on or account.

patches   Program or Windows updates that include bug fixes (corrections provided to repair known problems), security updates (to prevent unauthorized access to your data), or database updates (to give a program the latest data it needs to perform its job).

path   A roadmap to a particular resource or object, such as a file, folder, or printer. A path to a network printer, for example, consists of the name of the computer to which the printer is connected followed by the name of the printer itself.

PC Card   A common connection type used mainly on notebooks, where PC card devices plug into PC card slots.

PCI (Peripheral Component Interconnect)   The most widely used type of connection points on a motherboard. Some PCs have only two PCI slots, others have as many as six.

peer-to-peer   A type of network in which computers connect directly to one another, rather than to a common central computer.

peripherals   Hardware devices that connect to a PC. Some peripherals are required, such as a monitor; others are optional, such as a scanner. Also known as *add-on devices* or *external devices*.

personal computer (PC)   A device that processes information. A PC can deliver education and entertainment, manage personal information and records, and support essential business activities. You can also use a PC to type letters, send messages, interact with others, listen to music, play games, learn new skills, and more.

personal data assistant (PDA)   A portable computer designed to act as an organizer, note taker, communication device, and so forth. PDAs are fast, functional, and include various user-friendly applications to help you organize business and personal activities.

pinned   Programs that appear on the top left portion of the start menu, and are always available for you to choose.

pointer images   Specific shapes such as I-beams, pointing fingers, and so forth that Windows uses to indicate the current function or status of the mouse pointer.

ports   See *connections*.

printer   A device that prints text or graphical images from a computer. A printer can produce black or color output on paper and typically connects to a PC using a parallel or USB port.

program   A piece of software designed to work with your PC's operating system to perform one or more tasks and to manage various types of information (such as text, numbers, and images). Also called an *application*.

PS/2   A common type of serial port on PCs. Two female PS/2 ports occur on most desktop PCs: one for the mouse, the other for the keyboard. Most notebooks have only a single PS/2 port, which can be used to attach either an external mouse or keyboard.

random access memory (RAM)   Temporarily stores data, software, and the operating system while a PC is operating; everything in RAM is temporary.

Recycle Bin   A temporary storage location for recently deleted files; use it like a wastebasket.

removable storage   Any storage device that uses readable and writable media that can be removed from the drive. They include floppy drives, CD and DVD drives, tape drives, and Zip/Jaz drives.

restore point   A method of capturing a snapshot of Windows desktop settings and preferences to which you can return in the future.

right-click   Click the secondary button once over an object to cause a related shortcut menu to appear.

root directory   The topmost container in a folder list, it contains files and folders that appear in the details pane when you select a drive icon in the folder pane in My Computer or Windows Explorer.

Run   A Windows icon that permits you to launch any program on your Windows PC.

screen resolution   The number of individual bits of information (called *picture elements*, or *pixels*) that a PC display shows. The first number counts horizontal pixels (width) and the second vertical pixels (height).

screen saver   A utility available in many operating systems that displays a picture on the screen after a specified period of inactivity has lapsed to prevent an unchanged image from being burned onto your monitor screen. You have a wide-range of images to choose from and can include your own preferred picture.

scroll bars   Special window positioning controls that appear when a window isn't big enough to display the entire contents of a document or page. These allow you to scroll up and down or left and right through the page or document so you can view all its contents.

Search   A Windows icon that provides access to a Search tool; use this tool to locate files and folders on your local system or the network. You can also use this tool to search for pictures, music, video, documents, computers, and network users.

server   A central computer that manages shared network resources, such as programs, files, e-mail, and printers, that allows other computers to connect.

shared network resources   Anything on a network that is accessible by users, such as drives (files and folders), printers, and scanners.

shortcut   An object that enables you to associate an icon on the desktop or in some other convenient location with a specific resource.

shortcut menu   A menu that is context- or content-sensitive; here, the object or objects under the mouse pointer determine what commands appear in such a menu.

shutdown   The process whereby Windows XP saves important data still resident in memory, closes the desktop and the operating system, then powers off the PC.

software   All programs, tools, or utilities that permit PCs to perform all kinds of tasks, and handle data and services for users. Software is intangible, but still quite real.

software bugs   Imperfections sometimes found in software released by even the most cautious manufacturer.

speakers   Devices that produce audio output from a PC. Through speakers or a set of headphones, you can hear operating-system sounds, music, sound effects and so forth.

stand-alone PC   A PC that is not part of a network.

start button   A taskbar button labeled "start" that opens the *start menu*, where you can start programs, find documents, configure your computer, and more.

start menu   To launch this menu, click the start button on the task bar. From here, you can start programs, find documents, configure your computer, and more.

status bar   An area located along a window's bottom edge that displays program-specific information and messages.

subfolder   Folders that reside inside other folders, designed to help you locate documents, programs, and data more easily.

submenu   If a submenu is present, an arrow appears beside a command in a menu. Select and execute submenu commands just as you do commands on main menus.

surge protector   A power-outlet multiplier and an electric-spike protector; includes a fuse or built-in circuit breaker that disconnects power if a spike occurs.

SVGA/VGA (Super Video Graphics Array/Video Graphics Array)   An enhanced version of VGA capable of improved display resolution and color depth. An SVGA/VGA port is the same size and shape as the small serial port, but has 15 pins instead of 9.

system unit   A box or enclosure that contains many smaller electronic components, such as a motherboard, processor, memory cards, video card, one or more hard drives, floppy drive, CD-ROM drive, and power supply. A system unit may be called a case or a tower.

taskbar   The long bar at the bottom of your Windows screen, this visual element reports on open applications, provides access to the start menu, and includes a notification area.

text box   A text field in a dialog box in which you can enter data using your keyboard.

theme   A set of appearance options that work as a named group, and that create a quick and easy way for you to personalize Windows XP.

third-party program   Any program that is not included with the operating system. This includes programs from Microsoft as well as any other software company.

throughput   A rating of how much data can be sent or received by a device within a specific amount of time; normally measured in Kbps, Mbps, or Gbps.

Tiles   The default view for files and folders in My Computer and Windows Explorer (a bright yellow file folder and a picture of a hard disk) is called *Tiles*. There are four other *views*.

title bar   A Windows element (at the top of the window frame) that displays the name of the program or function underway. When a window contains an open document, the title bar also displays that document's file name.

toolbar   The icons that appear below the menu bar but above the workspace. Click buttons on a toolbar to access common functions or perform common tasks.

Tour Windows XP   An audiovisual tour of Windows XP's features and functions.

uninterruptible power supply (UPS)   A battery and power conditioner; connects between the wall outlet and your PC. If power fails, a UPS can supply a PC with power from its battery, where uptime depends on battery size how much power attached devices draw.

URL (Universal Resource Locator)   A special kind of Internet address that you must supply to access a Web site.

USB (Universal Serial Bus)   A newer, faster type of peripheral port on PCs that supports up to 127 devices per port. USB is available in two versions: 1.1 and 2.0. The 2.0 version offers throughput speeds greater than FireWire.

user account   A Windows feature that enables a computer to be set up for use by two or more people, where each one can personalize the desktop and keep documents and e-mail private.

user profile   In Windows operating systems, this refers to the collection of settings that defines how your desktop looks, sounds, and operates. As you use your PC and change its look and feel, your user profile becomes unique.

views Ways to view information displayed in My Computer and Windows Explorer. Click the Views button (far right of the button bar) to see all five views.

Web browser A software utility used to access the World Wide Web.

Web page A basic container for text and other content; it's what you see on the Internet through a browser. A Web page often includes links to other Web pages or Web sites.

Web server A computer on the Internet that houses one or more Web sites; Web browsers communicate with Web servers to access Web pages.

Web site A collection of online documents maintained by a group or an individual that addresses one or more topics.

window corner Either the bottom left or right corner of a program window, this control enables you to alter the height and width of a window at the same time.

window A rectangular area displayed on your desktop that contains numerous common elements, such as a workspace, toolbars, a menu bar, and other standard controls. Almost every Windows-based program uses a window as its primary interface.

Windows Media Player A utility that can play back many types of music and video files, Internet radio, Internet TV, and CDs.

Windows Movie Maker A video-editing tool. If you have a video input card or a digital video camera with USB or fire-wire connections, you can use Windows Movie Maker to create your own customized home videos.

wizard A window similar to a dialog box, in that it presents a series of options from which you must choose. Unlike a dialog box, which presents all available controls, options, and selections, a wizard presents controls one at a time, in a specific order.

workgroup A group of computers on a network that can connect to one another and share resources. For any two computers to communicate, they must belong to the same workgroup.

workspace The area in a window between the toolbars and the status bar. In some programs, the workspace acts like a piece of paper in the real world, and uses the keyboard to enter input; in others, it acts more like an interface. You interact with it by clicking buttons, choosing options from drop-down lists, and so on.

World Wide Web A vast collection of interconnected graphical or textual information available to those with Web browsers and network (or Internet) access.

Index

E

Easy CD Creator 5 (software), 171–74
Edit commands, 143
Effects button, 191
electrical surges, protection from, 33
E-mail button, 66
emergency disks, 234–35
emergency shutdown, 72
emptying Recycle Bin, 148
END key, 64, 66
ENTER key, 64, 65
ergonomic keyboards, 24
ESC key, 64, 65
expansion-card modem, 30
external devices, 17. *See also* connection types

F

fast user switching, 47, 73
File name list, Save as Dialog Box, 110–11
files
   See also folders
   compressing, 236–38
   creating shortcut to, 134–35
   deleting, 145–46
   details view, sorting, 125–26
   learning more about, 127, 153
   managing associations, 119–21
   name extensions for, 119
   offline, 221
   opening, 114–15, 159
   revising, 113–16
   saving, 108–13
      save as and save commands, 109–10
      Save As dialog box, 110–11
      with shortcut menu, 112–13
      using a program, 108–9
   sharing, 214, 217–21. *See also* networking

storing with CD drives, 171–76
copying files to CD-RWs, 174–75
ejecting and closing disk, 175–76
Finances folder, 121
firewalls, 228, 231
FireWire (IEEE 1394) technology, 23
flat panel monitors, 27
floppy disks, 14, 117–19
folders
   See also files; *names of specific folders*
   browsing, 68–69
   changing view, 123–25
   compressing, 236–38
   creating, 106–7
   creating shortcut to, 133–34
   deleting, 145–46
   learning more about, 127, 153
   sharing, 217–21, 231
   structures, 121–23
Forward button, on MusicMatch Jukebox, 166
Forward button, on Windows Media Player, 164, 165
fragmented drives, 241–43
function keys, 64, 65

G

Gateway Box, 48
GB (gigabyte), 14
gbps (gigabits per second), 31
GHz (gigahertz), 12
gigabits per second (gbps), 31
gigabyte (GB), 14
gigahertz (GHz), 12
GUIs (graphical user interfaces), 25

H

hard drives, 14–15, 121
   cleaning, 238–40
   defragmenting, 241–43

managing, 236
ports for, 18
replacing, 15
scanning for errors, 240–41
storage capacity, 14
Hardware category, 209–10
hardware sharing, 214
Help button, 66
hertz, 12
Hibernate button, 71
Hide inactive icons check box, 51
history of computers, 2–5
HOME key, 64, 66
hubs, USB, 22

I

ICF(Internet Connection Firewall), 229
IDE (Integrated Drive Electronics), 19, 19
Identify button, 194
IEEE 1394 (FireWire) technology, 23
inkjet printers, 28
input devices, 7, 24–26
INSERT key, 64, 65
install path, 171
installing
   printers, 222–24
   software, 168–71
Integrated Drive Electronics (IDE), 19, 19
Intel processors, 11
internal connections, 18
Internet
   beginning of, 4
   learning more about terminology, 35
Internet button, 66
Internet Connection Firewall (ICF), 229
Internet Explorer (Web browser), 76, 187–88
Item list, 192

GATEWAY, INC. END-USER LICENSE AGREEMENT

IMPORTANT - READ CAREFULLY: This End-User License Agreement (EULA) is a legal agreement between you (either an individual or an entity), the End-User, and Gateway, Inc. ("Gateway") governing your use of any non-Microsoft software you acquired from Gateway collectively, the "SOFTWARE PRODUCT".

The **SOFTWARE PRODUCT** includes computer software, the associated media, any printed materials, and any "online" or electronic documentation. By turning on the system, opening the shrinkwrapped packaging, copying or otherwise using the SOFTWARE PRODUCT, you agree to be bound by the terms of this EULA. If you do not agree to the terms of this EULA, Gateway is unwilling to license the SOFTWARE PRODUCT to you. In such event, you may not use or copy the SOFTWARE PRODUCT, and you should promptly contact Gateway for instructions on returning it.

SOFTWARE PRODUCT LICENSE

The SOFTWARE PRODUCT is protected by copyright laws and international copyright treaties, as well as other intellectual property laws and treaties. The SOFTWARE PRODUCT is licensed, not sold.

1. **GRANT OF LICENSE.** This EULA grants you the following rights:
   - **Software**. If not already pre-installed, you may install and use one copy of the SOFTWARE PRODUCT on one Gateway COMPUTER, ("COMPUTER").
   - **Storage/Network Use**. You may also store or install a copy of the computer software portion of the SOFTWARE PRODUCT on the COMPUTER to allow your other computers to use the SOFTWARE PRODUCT over an internal network, and distribute the SOFTWARE PRODUCT to your other computers over an internal network. However, you must acquire and dedicate a license for the SOFTWARE PRODUCT for each computer on which the SOFTWARE PRODUCT is used or to which it is distributed. A license for the SOFTWARE PRODUCT may not be shared or used concurrently on different computers.
   - **Back-up Copy.** If Gateway has not included a back-up copy of the SOFTWARE PRODUCT with the COMPUTER, you may make a single back-up copy of the SOFTWARE PRODUCT. You may use the back-up copy solely for archival purposes.

2. **DESCRIPTION OF OTHER RIGHTS AND LIMITATIONS.**
   - **Limitations on Reverse Engineering, Decompilation and Disassembly**. You may not reverse engineer, decompile, or disassemble the SOFTWARE PRODUCT, except and only to the extent that such activity is expressly permitted by applicable law notwithstanding this limitation.
   - **Separation of Components.** The SOFTWARE PRODUCT is licensed as a single product. Its component parts and any upgrades may not be separated for use on more than one computer.
   - **Single COMPUTER.** The SOFTWARE PRODUCT is licensed with the COMPUTER as a single integrated product. The SOFTWARE PRODUCT may only be used with the COMPUTER.
   - **Rental.** You may not rent or lease the SOFTWARE PRODUCT.
   - **Software Transfer.** You may permanently transfer all of your rights under this EULA only as part of a sale or transfer of the COMPUTER, provided you retain no copies, you transfer all of the SOFTWARE PRODUCT (including all component parts, the media and printed materials, any upgrades, this EULA, and the Certificate(s) of Authenticity), if applicable, and the recipient agrees to the terms of this EULA. If the SOFTWARE PRODUCT is an upgrade, any transfer must include all prior versions of the SOFTWARE PRODUCT.
   - **Termination**. Without prejudice to any other rights, Gateway may terminate this EULA if you fail to comply with the terms and conditions of this EULA. In such event, you must destroy all copies of the SOFTWARE PRODUCT and all of its component parts.
   - **Language Version Selection.** Gateway may have elected to provide you with a selection of language versions for one or more of the Gateway software products licensed under this EULA. If the SOFTWARE PRODUCT is included in more than one language version, you are licensed to use only one of the language versions provided. As part of the setup process for the SOFTWARE PRODUCT you will be given a one-time option to select a language version. Upon selection, the language version selected by you will be set up on the COMPUTER, and the language version(s) not selected by you will be automatically and permanently deleted from the hard disk of the COMPUTER.

3. **COPYRIGHT.** All title and copyrights in and to the SOFTWARE PRODUCT (including but not limited to any images, photographs, animations, video, audio, music, text and "applets," incorporated into the SOFTWARE PRODUCT), the accompanying printed materials, and any copies of the SOFTWARE PRODUCT, are owned by Gateway or its licensors or suppliers. You may not copy the printed materials accompanying the SOFTWARE PRODUCT. All rights not specifically granted under this EULA are reserved by Gateway and its licensors or suppliers.

4. **DUAL-MEDIA SOFTWARE.** You may receive the SOFTWARE PRODUCT in more than one medium. Regardless of the type or size of medium you receive, you may use only one medium that is appropriate for the COMPUTER. You may not use or install the other medium on another COMPUTER. You may not loan, rent, lease, or otherwise transfer the other medium to another user, except as part of the permanent transfer (as provided above) of the SOFTWARE PRODUCT.

5. **PRODUCT SUPPORT.** Refer to the particular product's documentation for product support. Should you have any questions concerning this EULA, or if you desire to contact Gateway for any other reason, please refer to the address provided in the documentation for the COMPUTER.

6. **U.S. GOVERNMENT RESTRICTED RIGHTS.** The SOFTWARE PRODUCT and any accompanying documentation are and shall be deemed to be "commercial computer software" and "commercial computer software documentation," respectively, as defined in DFAR 252.227-7013 and as described in FAR 12.212. Any use, modification, reproduction, release, performance, display or disclosure of the SOFTWARE PRODUCT and any accompanying documentation by the United States Government shall be governed solely by the terms of this Agreement and shall be prohibited except to the extent expressly permitted by the terms of this Agreement.

7. **LIMITED WARRANTY.** Gateway warrants that the media on which the SOFTWARE PRODUCT is distributed is free from defects in materials and workmanship for a period of ninety (90) days from your receipt thereof. Your exclusive remedy in the event of any breach of the foregoing warranty shall be, at Gateway's sole option, either (a) a refund of the amount you paid for the SOFTWARE PRODUCT or (b) repair or replacement of such media, provided that you return the defective media to Gateway within ninety (90) days of your receipt thereof. The foregoing warranty shall be void if any defect in the media is a result of accident, abuse or misapplication. Any replacement media will be warranted as set forth above for the remainder of the original warranty period or thirty (30) days from your receipt of such replacement media, whichever is longer. EXCEPT AS EXPRESSLY SET FORTH HEREIN, GATEWAY, ITS SUPPLIERS OR LICENSORS HEREBY DISCLAIMS ALL WARRANTIES, EXPRESS, IMPLIED AND STATUTORY, IN CONNECTION WITH THE SOFTWARE PRODUCT AND ANY ACCOMPANYING DOCUMENTATION, INCLUDING WITHOUT LIMITATION THE IMPLIED WARRANTIES OF MERCHANTABILITY, NON-INFRINGEMENT OF THIRD-PARTY RIGHTS, AND FITNESS FOR A PARTICULAR PURPOSE.

8. **LIMITATION OF LIABILITY.** IN NO EVENT WILL GATEWAY, ITS SUPPLIERS OR LICENSORS, BE LIABLE FOR ANY INDIRECT, SPECIAL, INCIDENTAL, COVER OR CONSEQUENTIAL DAMAGES ARISING OUT OF THE USE OF OR INABILITY TO USE THE SOFTWARE PRODUCT, USER DOCUMENTATION OR RELATED TECHNICAL SUPPORT, INCLUDING WITHOUT LIMITATION, DAMAGES OR COSTS RELATING TO THE LOSS OF PROFITS, BUSINESS, GOODWILL, DATA OR COMPUTER PROGRAMS, EVEN IF ADVISED OF THE POSSIBILITY OF SUCH DAMAGES. IN NO EVENT WILL GATEWAY, ITS SUPPLIERS' OR LICENSORS' LIABILITY EXCEED THE AMOUNT PAID BY YOU FOR THE SOFTWARE PRODUCT. BECAUSE SOME JURISDICTIONS DO NOT ALLOW THE EXCLUSION OR LIMITATION OF LIABILITY FOR CONSEQUENTIAL OR INCIDENTAL DAMAGES, THE ABOVE LIMITATION MAY NOT APPLY TO YOU.

9. **Miscellaneous.** This Agreement is governed by the laws of the United States and the State of South Dakota, without reference to conflicts of law principles. The application of the United Nations Convention on Contracts for the International Sale of Goods is expressly excluded. This Agreement sets forth all rights for the user of the SOFTWARE PRODUCT and is the entire agreement between the parties. This Agreement supersedes any other communications with respect to the SOFTWARE PRODUCT and any associated documentation. This Agreement may not be modified except by a written addendum issued by a duly authorized representative of Gateway. No provision hereof shall be deemed waived unless such waiver shall be in writing and signed by Gateway or a duly authorized representative of Gateway. If any provision of this Agreement is held invalid, the remainder of this Agreement shall continue in full force and effect. The parties confirm that it is their wish that this Agreement has been written in the English language only.

"Rev.3 9/24/98".

Mission

To help everybody unlock the power of their computer to achieve their fullest personal, professional and lifestyle potential.

Deep inside one of America's leading computer companies you'll find a group of very smart, very dedicated people who have nothing to do with manufacturing computers.

With fresh insights and breakthrough techniques, the Survive & Thrive team is transforming the way we acquire technology skills. And putting a human face on the digital revolution. Yours.

Online Learning Subscription

Flexible and affordable, Online Learning gives unlimited access, anytime, anywhere. With one click, you get cutting-edge curriculum, message boards & online community.

Learning for your lifestyle

- Discover Digital Music and Photography
- Brush up your software skills
- Power your productivity

Start anytime - learn anywhere

www.LearnwithGateway.com

Learning Library

Delivering the benefits of classroom learning experience without the classroom, Gateway's Learning Library provides a step-by-step approach using powerful CD-ROMs to allow you to learn at your own pace, on your own schedule.

Offers include the following Learning Libraries:

- Microsoft Office XP Professional (Also in Spanish!)
- Microsoft Works Suite

Classroom Learning

Come to a local Gateway® store classroom to enjoy the face-to-face learning experience and state-of-the-art facilities.

Courses include:

- Get Started with Your PC
- Use and Care for Your PC
- Create and Share Digital Photos
- Use Your PC to Explore Digital Music
- Communicate and Connect to the Internet
- Capture, Create and Share Digital Movies

Call, click or come in!

For More Information about this and other Gateway Solutions, Services, and Special Offers visit us online at www.gateway.com/home, phone us at 800-Gateway or come in to a store near you!

We are located in most major metropolitan cities throughout the United States!

Topics

Look for these and other exciting topics from Gateway that will allow you to further explore the digital lifestyle and take advantage of the power of your PC.

- Windows® XP
- Digital Music
- Quicken®
- Microsoft® Word
- Digital Photography
- America Online®
- Microsoft Excel
- Digital Video
- Internet
- Microsoft PowerPoint®
- Microsoft Money
- Home Networking
- PC Security